Genet, Lacan and the ontology of incompletion

ALSO AVAILABLE FROM BLOOMSBURY

Lacan: A Genealogy, Miguel de Beistegui
Critical Theory Between Klein and Lacan: A Dialogue, Mari Ruti and Amy Allen
Lacan Contra Foucault: Subjectivity, Sex, and Politics,
ed. Nadia Bou Ali and Rohit Goel

Genet, Lacan and the ontology of incompletion

James Penney

BLOOMSBURY ACADEMIC
LONDON • NEW YORK • OXFORD • NEW DELHI • SYDNEY

BLOOMSBURY ACADEMIC
Bloomsbury Publishing Plc
50 Bedford Square, London, WC1B 3DP, UK
1385 Broadway, New York, NY 10018, USA
29 Earlsfort Terrace, Dublin 2, Ireland

BLOOMSBURY, BLOOMSBURY ACADEMIC and the Diana logo are trademarks of
Bloomsbury Publishing Plc

First published in Great Britain 2023
This paperback edition published in 2024

Copyright © James Penney, 2023

James Penney has asserted his right under the Copyright, Designs and Patents Act, 1988, to be identified as Author of this work.

For legal purposes the Acknowledgements on p. vii constitute an extension of this copyright page.

Series design by Charlotte Daniels
Cover image: May 29, 1968 – *Die Wände* (The Walls) by Jean Genet, Berliner Theatertreffen. Pictured: A scene with Ilse Anton as Leila "the ugliest woman in the world". (© Keystone Press / Alamy Stock Photo)

All rights reserved. No part of this publication may be reproduced or transmitted in any form or by any means, electronic or mechanical, including photocopying, recording, or any information storage or retrieval system, without prior permission in writing from the publishers.

Bloomsbury Publishing Plc does not have any control over, or responsibility for, any third-party websites referred to or in this book. All internet addresses given in this book were correct at the time of going to press. The author and publisher regret any inconvenience caused if addresses have changed or sites have ceased to exist, but can accept no responsibility for any such changes.

A catalogue record for this book is available from the British Library.

A catalog record for this book is available from the Library of Congress.

Library of Congress Control Number: 2022948728

ISBN: HB: 978-1-3503-0050-7
PB: 978-1-3503-0054-5
ePDF: 978-1-3503-0051-4
eBook: 978-1-3503-0052-1

Typeset by Integra Software Services Pvt. Ltd.

To find out more about our authors and books visit www.bloomsbury.com and sign up for our newsletters.

Contents

Acknowledgements vii

Introduction: Acts of poetry, acts of interpretation 1
    The nothing and the abyss 1
    Poetry and logic 7
    Ontology, femininity, orientation 10
    Jouissance, undeconstructed 15
    Genet now 18

1 Logic and fantasy: Freud on Moses 21
    Moses: Michelangelo's and Freud's 21
    Scrolls and whorls 24
    The psychoanalytic act 30
    The emancipation of interpretation 37

2 Towards feminine being: *Our Lady of the Flowers* 45
    Out from under Sartre 45
    Saint Divine 50
    Feminine sexuation against gender theory 59
    Seeing through the phallus 65

3 The phallus unveiled: *The Balcony* 73
    A gigantic phallus 73
    The image in history 78
    An image of castration 83
    The power of the dildo 87
    From revolutionary to populist hero 92

Contents

4 Residue of modernity, wound of being: Genet on art 97
    Science, or Cartesian hysteria 99
    The essence of *ousia* 106
    Stranger on a train 110
    Solitude and the non-relation 116
    The wound of being 119
    Towards sublimation 122

5 Postcoloniality meets indeterminate negation: *The Screens* 127
    An ontology of defecation 127
    Jouissance after the revolution 131
    Hysteria's sublation 134
    Nomadic negativity 144
    The image that refuses to form 151

6 The image of absence: *Prisoner of Love* 157
    Missing cards, absent ancestors 158
    A supernumerary orange 163
    Maronite enjoyments 168
    Ethical commemoration 169
    The eclipse of femininity 174
    Being and melancholy 181

Notes 188
Bibliography 211
Index 215

Acknowledgements

An earlier version of Chapter 1 was published by Taylor & Francis as '"That Despotic Finger": Traces of the Act in Freud's "The Moses of Michelangelo"', *Parallax* 22.4 (2016): 438–57, https://www.tandfonline.com/.

An earlier version of Chapter 4 was published by Edinburgh University Press as 'The Phallus Unveiled: Lacan, Badiou and the Comedic Moment in Genet's *The Balcony*', *Paragraph* 42.2 (July 2019): 170–87.

Introduction: Acts of poetry, acts of interpretation

The nothing and the abyss

In the opening lines of his final work *Prisoner of Love*, Jean Genet conjures the image of a piece of paper covered in his own handwriting as he voices scepticism about the possibility of capturing historical reality in prose. 'Originally blank', he writes, the page is now 'covered from top to bottom in miniscule black signs', which make it 'legible' to any reader with the requisite linguistic competence.[1] Immediately, however, Genet takes his distance from this impression of legibility, attributing the judgement to some anonymous and untrustworthy opinion and drawing attention instead to the feeling of nausea triggered by the white spaces around and between the ink marks. Modern incarnation of ancient clay or parchment and precursor to today's ubiquitous pixelated screen, the page has its own peculiar, empty presence, one which has 'perhaps a stronger reality than the signs that defigure' it.[2] Pithy, to be sure, this historicization of writing technology manages nonetheless to capture the mutual implication of sign and medium, figure and ground, sense and nonsense. But the blank page, as Genet here presents it, is not the positive, material substrate – the stuff, you could say – on which signs take form. Rather, it is an object, or perhaps a quasi-object, more elusive and paradoxical: a faultline or rift, a rupture in continuity, that pulls the rug out from under any philosophical pretension to a neutral and consistent zero-level of being.

For Genet as for psychoanalyst Jacques Lacan, representations emerge in conjunction with the creation of a negativity into which they threaten to collapse, losing in the process their power to generate symbolic worlds of more or less coherent meaning. The coincidence or simultaneity of the positive act of creation and the negative opening of a void is crucial here. Out of the primeval, and certainly mythological, pre-ontological nihility, a second-order nothing manifests in a way that tethers matter to its shadow, to its own oblivion. This uncanny redoubling of negativity, the emergence of the void out from a (conceptually prior) nothingness, both attributes to the nothing a strangely positive quality and renders precarious even the void itself. In a more intuitive (but also abstract) material sense, chalk sticks to slate; ink absorbs into paper; pixels differentiate by colour, by reflected light. There is nothing in the substances themselves with the power either to separate off what comes to signify from what is merely stuff or else to distinguish the boundary that separates code from noise. For human perception, however, things are decidedly different. For us, subjects of the unconscious, the signifier splits off, lifts away from its background, be it the blank space of a page or screen, or else the noise or silence of the aural environment. As words and images become phenomenologically distinct from that against which they appear, we are reminded that whatever cognitive sense we decide to attribute to them, they retain a quality of precarity and incompleteness that threatens to have them collapse back into the ground from which they emerged. The human world is a world of social signs whose construction has been botched, interrupted; and from this world the promise of some more authentic or reliable reality enigmatically recedes.

Though both thinkers produced an ever-shifting and sometimes severely autocritical body of work, Genet and Lacan share one unwavering conviction, one that rightly merits the epithet ontological: the discursive representations that make up the world of appearances are inherently enigmatic not only on the level of their problematic link to sense and meaning, but also, and more fundamentally, as regards the robustness and reliability of their existence, of their very being's power of self-actualization. The play of signifiers balances precariously on the edge of an absence, never properly managing to conceal it. But the hermeneutic or semiological incompleteness of sense in fact functions to dissimulate a more troubling and scandalous ontological void. Words and images, on the very level of their semantic ambiguity, are at once the direct manifestation of, and the necessarily failed attempt to conceal, the underlying inconsistency of being. It is not merely signification that remains irremediably unconsummated, unfulfilled; reality itself is disfigured by a misfire, as if prematurely removed from the ontological oven, disappointingly underbaked. Like Lacan's psychoanalytic act of interpretation, Genet's poetic image functions to expose these fissures in being for which fantasy normally compensates, altering in the process the collective relation to our symptomatically repressed experiences of enjoyment.

Genet's body of work is a rigorous and unprecedented inquiry into the nature of the construction and collapse of signification against this backdrop of ontological unfulfilment. The early novels struggle with the complicity of criminality and transgression with the dominant social order, painfully advancing towards an understanding of betrayal as a gesture of subjective subtraction that manages to evade and subvert that complicity. The plays and writings of the 1950s turn to a celebration of the void which, in Genet's view, forms the background of the world of appearances both within the theatre and without. During this period, Genet probes the connection between eroticism and ideology, speculating about a modality of desire that moves beyond the goal of mystifying and dissimulating the void. Finally, the complexly engaged writings and activism of the 1960s and 1970s – leading up to the long-delayed completion of his masterwork *Prisoner of Love* before his death in 1986 – negotiate the vagaries of partisanship's relations to ethics, politics and poetics. This last work, the culmination of a life of impassioned and sometimes desperate creativity, finally suggests an ethics of poetic creation that strives in a utopian fashion to reconcile the irreconcilable, more specifically to conciliate the image with its own undoing; to suture the signifier, without remainder, to the void.

In *Prisoner of Love*, Genet sets his thoughts about the inconsistency of discourse and the incompletion of being against the backdrop of his personal experience of political fellow-travellership with the Palestinian resistance and the Black Panthers in the United States during the 1970s. In the broader context of Genet's lifework as a whole, however, these thoughts acquire a special importance, conveying something essential about its deepest preoccupations. In spite of his growing and genuine concern during his lifetime for oppositional social movements and what we might loosely call politics, Genet remains nonetheless a resolutely, albeit idiosyncratically, philosophical or theoretical artist-thinker, one who always situates the specific instances of historical experience within broader meditations on representation, desire and being in general. The opening passage of *Prisoner* distils the distinctive and inherent onto-semiology of Genet's creative lifework. This work rests on the deep conviction that the world of discourse-appearance can only gain whatever modicum of consistency it can muster by virtue of the nothingness against which it is invariably cast. Even more consequentially, however, this nothingness occludes a more fundamental abyss, harbinger of an unmitigated ontological disaster.

As any casual reader will readily acknowledge, however, Genet's imaginative world is anything but the abstractly conceptual meditation that this formulation of its fundamental convictions might misleadingly suggest. Indeed, the work could not be more attuned to the manifold ways in which the negative space between signs has always-already been fleshed out by fantasy, which imbues them with the seductive promise of signification. The production of the promise of sense, of ideological meaning, can only work against the backdrop of its inherent incompleteness: revelation is apocalypse, the literal end of the world. In sympathy with psychoanalysis, for Genet this potentiality of signification, this lure that meaning holds before us as a means of eliciting our desire, is grounded in repression: the absence or subtraction of a representation from the field of possible appearances and its replacement by alternative forms capable of providing the illusion of a potential fullness. As this book will explore in myriad ways, this is indeed the quintessential insight that Genet's lifework strives to articulate: art holds the power to disrupt the social hermeneutic, the very terms by which transpersonal experience comes to signify, by including within the field of representation an image that holds the power to disrupt the anticipation of consistency lent to the social field by fantasy. Wilfully and painfully constructed images, in other words, can expose an excessive, dissimulated libidinal charge that knocks the ground out from beneath a field of meaning, exposing a peculiarly assertive nothingness that inheres within each of its constitutive terms, and barring these terms from achieving any semblance of unity, of wholeness. This disruption is what Genet calls poetry and what I will call the poetic act.

All the key motifs in Genet – from the miracle and betrayal to saintliness and evil – gravitate around the fundamental problem of how artistic creations can work to subvert dominant forces of meaning-generation by giving symbolic form to the disavowed libidinal forces that bind us to them, thereby exposing an underlying inconsistency of being. One of the most notorious examples is surely the figure of the sexy Nazi from *Funeral Rites*, which has given rise to myriad claims in favour of a Genetian antisemitism[3] and which has caused even as sympathetically bold a reader as Leo Bersani to take his qualified distance.[4] In his early work, Genet grasps intuitively, while falling short of explicitly recognizing, that the exorcism of the libido's complicity in oppression requires the open acknowledgement of the erotic power inherent in the idealized images that lend fuel to its insidious seductions.[5] In short, the explicit admission that the Nazis could be disarmingly attractive efficiently short-circuits the normally unacknowledged enjoyment that undergirds the standard pious condemnations of fascist aesthetics, even once we acknowledge that Genet's recourse to erotic images of Nazis serves in part to complicate any clear-cut distinction between subversion and celebration. Moreover, this short-circuit displaces the more intuitive early reading influentially promulgated by Georges Bataille (via Sartre) according to which Genet's work, through its will-to-abjection and provocative embrace of 'evil', would effect a thoroughgoing reversal of normative social values.[6] Surely it is no revelation to claim that fantasies of racial purity or reclaimed national glory demonstrate how there is no idealization without an attendant repression. This repression is the condition of possibility of the erotic in both intimate and social spheres, a prerequisite for the construction of any concretely livable psychosocial reality.

Here we come upon the second facet of the profound and under-recognized sympatico of Genet's work with the psychoanalytic project. Though both aim at the disclosure of repressed libidinal contents, this disclosure is counterintuitively anti-erotic, or saintly in Genet's own terms. When Freud corrected the course of psychoanalytic practice at the nineteenth century's close by wedding technique exclusively to speech, the scandal of a practice designed to give open expression to human sexuality should have been attenuated – it was not, of course – by the objections of its first patients, the hysterics, who were not exactly known for a penchant for the louche. These consummately bourgeois young ladies would insist that the notorious Freud, in comparison to his chortling and sneering rivals, was beyond reproach. The respectability of a method that knowingly seeks to disinter what appears to be a buried sexual life turns out to be not so paradoxical a notion, however. Sexuality thrives on allusion, circumlocution, double entendre; stating things directly in precise clinical terms is a surefire way to purge an intimate moment of its erotic charm. In ordinary language sex is neither fully present in nor entirely absent from the utterance; its inherently problematic being is undecidable in any given segment of speech. This is surely the dirty secret of the opposition to sex education in public school systems around the world. Sex immediately loses its allure – it becomes absurd, disgusting, even improbable – when presented coldly in its unadorned biological reality, stripped of its cloak of erotic obfuscation.

This also explains why it is so ill-conceived to connect psychoanalysis to the long tradition of confessional practices outlined by Foucault in *The History of Sexuality*'s over-influential first volume. If the Christian institution of the confession functioned to compel 'everyone to transform their sexuality into a perpetual discourse',[7] then psychoanalysis revealed the fruitlessness of the effort by insisting on the disjunction that irremediably separates sex from speech. It follows from this that discourse is not *incited* in the psychoanalytic clinic. Indeed, words progressively exterminate unconscious enjoyment, which thrives not in a wildly productive search for truth in knowledge or discourse but rather in the repressive force of silence. For the patient in analysis, the telling of an ostensibly erotic dream becomes a shameful burden. Anyone who has tried to engage in the activity known as free association knows how misleadingly it is named: it is neither liberatingly unrestrained nor likely to happen without the exercise of effort. In short, there is nothing 'free' in free association. Analysis in this sense is the antithesis of idle erotic daydreaming: it forces us to put those daydreams into words, a process that immediately transforms them into embarrassing secrets that should never be shared. This is surely also a main lesson of a novel like *Our Lady of the Flowers*: the limitlessly expansive sensuous narcissism of the narrator's textually foregrounded literary-creative daydreaming, which Sartre in *Saint Genet* transforms into the linchpin of his excessively masterful reading, is suddenly transformed, at pivotal moments in the text, into a harrowing encounter with a deathly absence of meaning, a disorientating inconsistency in being.

Poetry and logic

Sex's unavailability to full disclosure in discourse is closely linked to a conceptual keystone of this book: the poetic act. The expression is designed to tie Genet's particular understanding of the power of words to the Lacanian doctrine of the act of interpretation, which is similarly premised on the notion that signifiers can instigate transformation, in the clinic and out, by exposing both semantic and ontological incompletion. The first term of my expression is of course extraordinarily old and complicated; we will not delve into its history in any sustained or systematic way. A few elementary etymological observations may prove salutary, however. By 'poetic' I mean in part to evoke the properly Platonic sense of the creation, the bringing into being, of an object or form that did not previously exist. In Socrates's presentation of Diotima's teaching in *The Symposium*, however, *poiesis* engages in the ascent towards the contemplation of a beauty imagined as supremely intellectual and entirely self-contained: 'absolute, pure, unmixed, not cluttered up with human flesh and colours and a great mass of mortal rubbish', in the Mantinean stranger's own recounted words.[8]

Genet's idea of poetry could not be more different. Indeed, he would likely have endorsed Lacan's reading of Plato's dialogue, which finds Diotima's doctrine quite ridiculous in the philosopher's own judgement and speculates suggestively about a subversive Platonic irony.[9] Indeed, for Lacan, Plato may have wished to invite his reader to consider Diotima's discourse in a spirit of derision. From this perspective, the Platonic tradition offers an auspicious approach to the poetic, especially in comparison to Aristotle's elucubrations in the *Poetics*, which famously ties poetry not to creation but to representation (*mimesis*), the medium by which tragedy brings about the pleasure of catharsis.[10] Genet's poetic image and Lacan's analytic act have nothing whatsoever to do with either imitation or nature because they both emerge ex nihilo, out of an act of pure creation resulting from a suspension of both natural causality and the dominant hermeneutic logics of social discourses.

Not only does the poetic act manifest out of nothing, but it is also just an appearance, a mere artifice. There is nothing natural about the act, 'natural' here assuming some fully pre-constituted physical or material reality. But neither is the act properly historical-discursive in the later Foucaultian sense, since it occurs in the place where the wheels of productive determination of not only nature, but also the knowledge-power matrix get stuck. This book aims to show that the poetico-analytic act, in a manner of speaking, performs the sublime Diotimean ascendancy in reverse. It circumscribes the void behind the beautiful or erotic image, and then it indexes this void's secret complicity with both dissimulated enjoyment and the possibility of ontological catastrophe. These effects are accomplished through the creation of new signs that interrupt the ordinary construction of the potentiality of meaning, but without instantiating a new regime of signification. Note, however, that these novel representations do not allow us to descend back down to some anti-Diotimean, thoroughly unaesthetic or non-redemptive level of a pure libidinal drive, one with the power to exempt itself from the requirements of repression and idealization. Rather, poetry makes us realize that the very distinction between the beautiful and its deathly, obscene support simply no longer obtains, at least for an ineffable, though not entirely unknowable, moment in time.

The idea that the poetic act coincides with a certain failure of determination or production is intimately linked to the second word in my expression of concern in its relation to psychoanalysis, and more specifically to Lacan. Chapter 1 undertakes a detailed reading of Lacan's teaching on the subject of the act from the perspective of his interest in the history of the discourses of logic; the reader looking for material on Genet's writing will be required to wait for, or else jump to, Chapter 2.[11] To be sure, there would seem to be nothing more removed from modern ideas about poetic language, or even from the oeuvre of a self-consciously provocative writer like Genet, than the philosophical subfield of logic. To grasp the seemingly unlikely connection, we need to know something about why the discipline attracted Lacan, whose early interests in surrealism and paranoia seem similarly foreign to the rigour and austerity of logic discourse. In short, for Lacan, the critical study of classical and postclassical logic is the best way to understand how human symbolic systems – so-called ordinary language, but especially the more specialized and abstract languages of logic and mathematics – eventually break down before an impasse, aproria, contradiction or inconsistency, always requiring the supplement of a further operation that either runs afoul of the founding axioms according to which the system is constructed or else requires illicit transcendence to a second, higher level of inferential power. In short, logic for Lacan performs an increasingly rigorous, if largely unwitting, demonstration of the in-built incompletion of our symbolic systems, that is to say the non-existence of what he called the universe of discourse.

Far from taking logic discourse on its own terms, however, Lacan *interprets* it in his precise psychoanalytic sense, singling out its neurotic (and illogical) recourse to tools capable of creating semblances of consistency and linking this recourse to the indigenous Freudian concepts of repression and fantasy. To the extent that poetry (in Genet's sense) and classical logic can be said to be fundamentally at odds, Lacan comes down firmly on the side of poetry, whose resemblance to what psychoanalysis calls interpretation is quite uncanny. In Lacan's view, the history of logic is in large measure (though not without significant complications) the history of its failure to conceive of its inability to reconcile thought with itself, to create fully unified and consistent systems of inference. Still, we find in Lacan's work no categorical rejection of the legitimacy of the practice of logical thought, whose intellectual rigour the psychoanalyst wished explicitly to import in modified form into his own praxis. Indeed, the impasses of logic only emerge in consequence of the strictest application of its rules; there is no queue-jumping, no proceeding directly to the aporia without having first grappled with the stringency of the logical exercise itself.

More rigorously put, Freud's conceptualization of the unconscious forces logic discourse to grapple with the impossibility of creating a fully coherent programme of rational inference without resorting to what Lacan calls metalanguage: a sign or set of signs that would hold a power of reference over all the others. This master or phallic signifier may be necessary in a psychosocial sense, but it is also illegitimate, an imposture as viewed from the perspective of reason. For Lacan, the psychoanalytic act draws our attention to the consequences in repression of this sign's function as a marker for both a signifying absence or inconsistency and a disruptive excess of bodily jouissance; an incompletion of discursive meaning, that is, as well as an imbalance in enjoyment. Analogously, for Genet, the poetic image effects both the subversion of a social field's most intensively sanctified signs and symbols and the disclosure of their implication in histories of social violence and exclusion.

Ontology, femininity, orientation

Now Genet was famously what we used to call, with less self-conscious apprehension about seeming hopelessly behind the times, gay. Any approach to his oeuvre is therefore forced to decide what exactly to make of the relation, if there is one, between his homosexuality and his creative work. Jean-Paul Sartre set the stage with retrospectively obtuse inauspiciousness, soldering the object choice (a now-quaint phrase) of *Saint Genet*'s literary subject to an aggressively voluntarist mythology of self-creation.[12] Here, with more sobriety and realism, though possibly as much controversy, I aim to connect Genet's doctrine of the poetic act not to homosexuality per se, but rather to a properly psychoanalytic, and currently decidedly unfashionable, understanding of sexual difference. One of this book's fundamental assumptions is that there is something inherently, *ontologically* feminine in the way Genet goes about questioning the phallic attributes of the structuring signposts of social meaning. In fact, I will argue that the very premise that allows Genet in his work to connect that social meaning to the problem of the phallus is already feminine in the precise psychoanalytic sense.

This argument will make no sense at all, however, unless we take care to separate out this idea of the feminine, or more precisely a specifically feminine modality of being, from the more familiar notion of gender viewed as a socially constructed performance or script. By the same gesture, my approach categorically distinguishes this idea of feminine being from the justly maligned historical norms of femininity that have aimed to keep (not only) women in their traditionally circumscribed place. I concur with the later Lacan, along with uncommonly insightful readers like Joan Copjec and Alenka Zupančič,[13] that psychoanalysis since Freud has struggled to theorize femininity as one of two varieties of (failed or contorted) being rather than as a set of attributes, manifestations or expressions of some determinate feminine identity. The essence of feminine sexuation is in fact its lack of an essence. The same cannot be said of its masculine counterpart, however, even if masculinity as psychoanalysis understands it only manifests as the failure to incarnate its exceptional identity. Sexual difference for psychoanalysis is a question not of qualities, of attributing this or that predicate to this or that (or that ...) sex, but rather of the very nature of the space or medium, ultimately the ontological medium, in which those qualities take form.

Genet's work acknowledges that any field of representation that makes up a world must be phallically grounded; any system of signification requires at least one sign or image imbued with special status and libidinal investment in reference to which that system is organized. What is specifically feminine about Genet's ontology is its open disclosure of the radical contingency of that ground, its ordinariness or even banality. In other words, if any object whatever is potentially capable of assuming the phallic function, then there is no end to the appearances that can be described as feminine in the world of feminine being, including those appearances conventionally qualified, including by gender theory, as masculine. If it makes sense to describe Genet's creative universe as feminine in this way, then what makes it gay or queer is merely the fact of his biological sex. This strikes me as a more accurate and consequential way of assessing what is sexually specific about Genet's work than the approach that would tie its significance in this domain to particular representations on the level of content, as one would do in a more intuitive way by linking an idea of the gayness of the novel *Our Lady of the Flowers*, for example, to the seminal character of Divine.[14]

By extension, my alternative framework also features the consequence of de-specifying Michael Lucey's recent and notable approach to Genet's *Querelle*. In a virtuosic 'metapragmatic' commentary of a passage from that novel featuring the eponymous character's questioning of the meaning of French slang terms related to homosexuality, Lucey skilfully exposes the disjunction between sexual discourse and sexual experience. In Lucey's view, this disjunction is specific to a particular set of subjects to whom he refers as 'sexual misfits'.[15] These subjects sport identities that are associated with, but irreducible to, the category 'queer', and they struggle to reconcile their biographical experience of the sexual with the explanatory possibilities offered by existing social categories. From the perspective of psychoanalysis, however, the disjunction that Lucey associates with a particular experience of socially marginalized sexuality is simply a generic attribute of sex as such, one that does not vary along with the various lexicons available to us in our (inevitably failed) attempts to render this experience in the terms of public discourse.

My reference to a possible ontology that would be shared by Genet and psychoanalysis calls out for contextualization against the by now well-documented resurgence of ontological inquiry in contemporary philosophy. This book is not explicitly written for readers or practitioners of either object-oriented ontology or the variously associated new realisms, speculative or otherwise, and indeed does not set for itself the task of engaging with these discourses in any semblance of detail. Nevertheless, we can take the occasion to signal in a very elementary way my properly critical and dialectical perspective with reference to the seminal work of Quentin Meillassoux and leave it to the concerned readers to assess this book's argument against the competing ontological developments in contemporary thought. In my view, object-oriented ontology merely shifts the historicist, late-Foucaultian project to abolish the category of the subject construed as a metaphysical construction of the knowledge–power nexus from the realm of semiology-epistemology (albeit an aggressively, if ill-advisedly politicized version of these) to the realm of being. Both discourses feature the same ultimate desire to overcome the abyssal conundrum of subjectivity.

Generally speaking, the new ontologies posit themselves as capable of gaining access to a neo-premodern, post-human (or perhaps *a*human) and mathematically hyper-rational objectivity characterized by its autonomy with respect to the idiosyncratically species-centric vagaries of sensual-perceptual receptivity. For Meillassoux, the cardinal sin of post-Cartesian or post-Kantian modernity is correlationism, namely 'the idea according to which we only ever have access to the correlation between thinking and being, and never to either term considered apart from the other'.[16] Consciousness for phenomenology and language for the analytic tradition are the media in which the inter-implication of thinking and being, subject and object dominates over either of the related terms. In my estimation, the psychoanalytic rejoinder to Meillassoux's object-orientedness is oblique in that it sidesteps the scope of his objections. For if psychoanalysis remains firmly in the Cartesian and Kantian philosophical orbits in its insistence on both the sovereignty of the subject of methodological doubt and the irreducibility of subjectivity's transcendental constitution, it does not properly speaking rest on the gesture of correlating thinking and being, at least in the sense Meillassoux associates with the post-Kantian critical tradition. *Ou je ne pense pas ou je ne suis pas*, Lacan repeats over and over again in his *Logic of Fantasy* seminar: I am either not thinking or not being (not existing).[17] The Lacanian refrain may indeed relate thought and being in a generic sense, but it does so *disjunctively*, grounding the relation between the two terms in a non-relation. Thinking and being for psychoanalysis are both non-simultaneous and non-contiguous. Not only are they incapable of occurring together, but they operate in distinct, albeit complexly interrelated, 'spaces': either on the level of the signifier (discourse) or in the libidinal body (jouissance).

Not only are thinking and being only disjunctively 'correlated' for psychoanalysis, but Lacan, in his reading of modern science, insists on the discursive nature of mathematical language. And crucially, all discourse for psychoanalysis is finally inconsistent, aporetic, disoriented by a properly immanent negativity. For Meillassoux in contrast, certain (if not all) properties of an object can be expressed mathematically, and this mathematical expression captures the being of these properties in themselves, irrespective of any transcendental constitution of this object by a subject of consciousness or language. Alenka Zupančič has remarked insightfully on the oddity of the absence of sustained interrogation of mathematical language in Meillassoux's work, especially considering how it privileges mathematics as the royal road to knowledge of the being of the 'great outdoors' that remains absolute, entirely autonomous vis-à-vis the vagaries of human subjectivity.[18] This leads me to a second objection to object-oriented ontology. This one complements Lacan's move to redefine the terms of correlationism as disjunctive rather than rejecting outright, as does Meillassoux, the critical modesty with which it casts the Kantian *Ding-an-sich* (Thing-in-itself) as out of philosophical bounds. From the Lacanian point of view, to the extent that mathematical language as a modality of discourse can deliver certain properties of the object without subjective mediation, these properties are necessarily inconsistent, and whatever knowledge of being they can offer bears witness to what I have been describing as this being's necessary incompletion.

Two further psychoanalytic rejoinders can be added on to the premise of possible access to a modality of objective being cleansed of the deformations of subjectivity. First, objectivation – more precisely, the intellectual impetus to reduce subjective apprehension to nothing, the very meditative premise of Cartesian method – delivers not being as such, but rather its point of convolution, its non-identity with itself. Instead of disclosing the truth of being, absolute subjective reduction produces rather truth's impossibility, its perforation or infection by an ineffable quantum of non-being that estranges being from itself. And second, this same objectivation, while producing truth as impossible, also brings forth its opposite: subjectivity in its purest form. This is demonstrated in a quite straightforward way in Freud's writing. The wilful suspension of judgement, the disciplined withholding of moral concerns, the detached endeavour to record only the patient's own associations, all finally offer evidence of what Lacan calls the fundamental fantasy: the peculiar, idiosyncratic libidinal bias by which the subject, who cannot as it were 'handle the truth', always fails to see only what is really there, only what would be present in their absence. Though mathematization for Lacan, here in quasi-agreement with Meillassoux, can attenuate the transferential dynamics of subjectivity by obliterating the obfuscation of meaning (or its promise), mathematical discourse finally runs up against the same *real*, the same internal or immanent limit, that impedes subjectivity as expressed in so-called ordinary language.

Jouissance, undeconstructed

There is of course no lack of existing scholarship on Genet, and we can now turn very selectively towards the most consequential of the historical approaches as they relate to this book's specific concerns. Previously mentioned, Sartre's monumental *Saint Genet* set the tone prematurely early, challenging the literary author it subjected to crypto-psychoanalytic existentialist scrutiny to keep up with the breathless pace of sweeping commentary and requiring the young writer to attempt to break out of the strictures of precocious canonicity as well. Perhaps no other major figure in the history of literature has been accorded the decidedly mixed blessing of virtually instant notoriety and prestige. Within the French context, most mid- to late-twentieth-century literary and philosophical intellectuals worth their self-measured salt have felt obliged to engage with Genet, from Georges Bataille to Lacan and Jacques Derrida, from Hélène Cixous (with Catherine Clément) to Alain Badiou. Moreover, Genet has been famous and dead long enough to have survived numerous waves of literary-critical and theoretical fashion: existentialism, deconstruction, postmodernism, queer theory and most recently a generally quite reactionary revival of archival, literary-historical and socio-biographical criticism in France.[19] The world is not lacking in critical commentary on Genet, much of it insightful, suggestive, of considerable enduring value. One might then legitimately wonder: What could there possibly be left to say?

This book will not conform to the standard and usually quite boring scholarly convention by which previous critical approaches are found wanting. However, it does engage consequentially, if very selectively, with the best work on Genet, both historical and contemporary, that treads on the terrain of my quite circumscribed concerns. I would perhaps be remiss, however, were I not to sketch out, even if in necessarily inadequate fashion, a perspective on Derrida's forbidding coupling of Genet with Hegel in *Glas*, surely the most monumental of the philosophical engagements with Genet since the publication of Sartre's magnum opus in 1952. The typographically distinctive excursus on Ferdinand de Saussure, one of the two founders of what became known as semiotics, can serve to illustrate how this book's approach to Genet's texts differs from Derrida's. Notoriously dense for some to the point of near total inscrutability, *Glas*'s right-hand column singles out for virtuosic deconstructive analysis a variety of signal words and phonemes present in Genet's oeuvre prior to the publication of *Prisoner of Love*. As one would expect, Derrida performs a thoroughgoing and erudite reading of their etymological and historical resonances, as well as their multiple associations within the context of Genet's own textual world.

Equally unsurprisingly, *Glas*'s gloss of Saussure performs a deconstruction of the inaugural semiotician's fundamental distinction between the symbol and the signifier, the latter 'motivated' – holding a morphological or logical connection to its ideational partner the signified – and the latter famously arbitrary, bereft of any link of these types. Just as he scrutinizes with support from Genet's literary work the premise of the proper name to the point that it is deprived of all propriety, becoming indistinct from all its fellow improper substantives, Derrida shows meticulously how Saussure's well-known examples of signifiers that are at least in part motivated, namely onomatopoeia and the exclamation, cannot decisively be purified of arbitrariness: 'there is no authentic onomatopoeia,' he declares.[20] The method is classically deconstructionist: the foundational categorial distinctions that buttress a claim to systematicity in conception or signification are shown to be faulty, inherently contaminated by their binary counterparts. The end result of the process is the assertion of a kind of absolute difference that remains irreducible to the difference between the structuring binary terms under scrutiny.

The parallel with the psychoanalytic outlook is significant. To the arguable extent that deconstructionist method can be held to imply an ontology, this ontology rests on the post-classical premise of a negativity that disallows any claim to consistency, totality or completion. For deconstruction as for psychoanalysis, the category of being is inherently problematic, neither dependably foundational, in the sense of providing the solid ground necessary for the elaboration of a consistent and determinate epistemology, ethics or aesthetics, for example, nor amenable to vitalist or productivist accounts of limitless becoming, Deleuzian or otherwise. If being for deconstruction can only fail to achieve identity with itself, however, this failure is not, as it is in psychoanalysis, placed into relation with jouissance, with the experience of the body, and therefore with the ethical imperative of responsibility vis-à-vis this experience, the imperative of analysis as such. From the Lacanian perspective, deconstruction takes account only of one side of the paradoxical incompletion of being. If its method magisterially exposes the lack of the signifier that could bring order to the signifying system so as to render it as a totality, it remains blind to the surfeit in bodily intensity with which this lack is always accompanied in the subject of the unconscious.

My insistence on this excess of embodiment might account for the curious generality of *Glas*'s Genet reading, more precisely for the reader's uncertainty as to what Derrida's awesome analytic apparatus and seemingly limitless etymological knowledge bring to our understanding of Genet's literary creativity properly speaking, especially on the level of its subjective specificity. For clarification, we might compare Derrida's engagement to the course of an analysis. Though it surely provides a peerless demonstration of the signifying associations lying latent in Genet's literary discourse, we are left to wonder if these associations have as much to do with lexicographer Émile Littré's 1873 masterwork *Dictionnaire de la langue française* as with the peculiarities of the Genetian unconscious. Even if we were to grant that etymological history is in some impersonal but significant way present in a subject's discourse, particularly one as well-read as Genet's, it remains the case that Derrida's analysis discovers no psychic structure, no fundamental fantasy in the text, in other words the place in Genet's oeuvre where the signifier becomes non-arbitrary, motivated by the demands of jouissance. What is perhaps novel in my approach to Genet's body of work is the premise that progressively his text *undertakes this work for itself*, effectively performing its own analysis as it struggles towards the impossible aim of subjecting even its last remnant of enjoyment to merciless, at times outright masochistic, scrutiny.[21]

Genet now

I have thus far staked out a theoretical claim about an under-appreciated simpatico between Genet and psychoanalysis, and Lacan in particular, not only on the topics of poetry, interpretation and the act, but most especially on the 'deeper' ontological convictions that inform them. On a more intuitively political level, however, Genet's work retains an undeniable contemporary relevance that calls out for re-examination and re-engagement at this specific moment in time. Genet's writing was eventually informed by, and intervened in, the discourses of numerous historical struggles and events, all of which have renewed significance and urgency today: from the attack on the pre-Stonewall cultural stigmatization of homosexuality to the movements of liberation from the legacies of European colonialism; from the dissident post-Marxist anti-racism of the Black Panthers during the US civil rights era to the inaugural uprisings of the Palestinians against the ravages of both political Zionism and anti-Nasserite Arab neofeudalism. It is perhaps simply a manifestation of Genet's always laser-sharp sociopolitical prescience that none of these struggles has achieved a state even remotely resembling resolution today.

Indeed, the struggles with which Genet chose to engage have proven to be among the most intractable of our early twenty-first century. Even the startling victories of the past decades for the legitimization of stigmatized sexualities have run up against a seemingly unsurpassable geopolitical limit. Men, women and others continue to be murdered in too many locales for deviance from rigid gender conventions or the allowable repertoire of sexual practices. The unfinished era of right-wing populism accelerated by Donald Trump's electoral victory unleashed a new wave of racial violence against African Americans, as well as Black and Indigenous people outside the United States, performed by state-sanctioned agents of law enforcement. Despite the 'Third-Worldization' of the most disadvantaged pockets of the post-industrial North in the age of a neoliberal austerity now back on the ascendant after a brief Covid-era hiatus, the former colonies of Africa and the Arab world in particular continue to suffer scandalous levels of underdevelopment in result of the neocolonial policies enforced by multilateral trade agreements and world financial institutions.

Moreover, the good old-fashioned colonial practices of Israel come more and more to resemble South African Apartheid as illegal settler colonies continue to be constructed in the West Bank, an alarming ethnic cleansing project goes on unabated in East Jerusalem and an insidiously racist Jewish nationalism takes hold of Israeli political discourse. Amid mounting international condemnation of Israeli policy in the occupied territories, the rising tide of Euro-American Islamophobia in tandem with frequent eruptions of Arab and Muslim antisemitism[22] buttress the moral blackmail implicit in the now-vulnerable post-Holocaust victim narrative that has served until now to rationalize Israeli exceptionalism to international law. There is no doubt that if he were alive today, Genet would be deeply and critically engaged with Black Lives Matter (surely too precious and delicate, at least on the level of its underwhelming moniker[23]) as well as the Boycott, Divestment, Sanctions movement (noble, but perhaps of questionable practical efficacy from his mature point of view).

For a thinker as invested as Genet in the power of the negative in all its disparate forms, however, this last comment about his would-be engagement with the issues of the day cannot be taken as the final word. To put into practice an ontological reading of Genet is to acknowledge that its logic moves beyond the expression of support for any specific, positive cause, however crucial this support surely must be. Though advocacy for the oppressed and marginalized is without question urgent and necessary, the truly political act lies not in the expression of the demand (for rights, equality or justice, for example), but rather in the open acknowledgement of the absence that haunts that expression, depriving it of any reliable ground, of any final addressee capable of honouring or instituting it. The social finally should not be conceived as an ensemble of relations between and amongst a multitude of established differences. Rather, it resembles what Genet calls solitude: the weirdly plastic or liquid identity of all individuals disjunctively united by their non-relation to themselves and to one another; that is, by the impossibility of achieving an identity with identity in a reality where being is never properly ironed out, never fully formed. The ontology of incompletion is what makes possible the creation of the poetic image and the intervention of the interpretative act. Both forms of impersonal agency introduce new signifiers into the order of representation, undoing that semblance of order and exposing thereby the insuperable fault-line, the disorienting twist, that untethers being from its own ontological fabric.

1

Logic and fantasy: Freud on Moses

Moses: Michelangelo's and Freud's

Evidently, Freud had a thing for Moses. In *Moses and Monotheism*, the founder of psychoanalysis famously pulls the rug out from under the exodus myth of the Judeo-Christian tradition by positing an Egyptian origin for the eponymous Old Testament hero, all the while affirming the indelibility of his attachment, however critical or distanced, to the Judaic tradition or, less problematically, to a sense of his own Jewishness.[1]

Less famously, in the earlier essay 'The Moses of Michelangelo' Freud engages in a spellbinding and obsessively detailed reading of the famous statue in Rome's San Pietro in Vincoli Basilica, the intensity of his identification with the stern patriarch becoming more patent with every paragraph. As Freud guides his reader through a number of initially perplexing inconsistencies in the accounts of what various interpreters have actually seen among the statue's features, we gain a vivid sense of the dramatic scriptural context surrounding the moment captured and immortalized in its form: Moses has come down from Mount Sinai with the tablets of Judaic law which God has just bequeathed him; he has sat himself down in the ambiguous and awkward posture with which a long list of distinguished commentators has struggled to come to terms.

Despite their wildly divergent interpretations, virtually all commentators agree on one key point: the conflicted orientation of Moses's body – the gaze directs his head in a rightward direction while the rest of his body shifts slightly towards the viewer's left – can be explained with reference to the biblical episode of the Golden Calf. By all accounts, Moses has just been startled by the loud carousing of his tribe's intemperate idolaters, engaged in the violation of the new Mosaic law by prostrating themselves before a false, pagan god. On the statue, Moses has pivoted his head and shoulders in their direction to shoot them his famously transfixing, scornful and also deeply disappointed look.

Readers already familiar with his difficult relations with certain members of the nascent psychoanalytic movement of the early twentieth century hardly require the speculations offered in editor James Strachey's discreet footnote[2] to intuit that Freud saw himself reflected in the reprobation Michelangelo arrestingly captures on Moses's face. Only too aware of the difficulty of propagating a doctrine that recognizes the inevitability of resistance to its insights, Freud with increasing intransigence came down hard on both the culturalizing (Carl Jung) and biologizing (Alfred Adler, and later Karen Horney) deviations of the revisionists. Quite simply, Freud would have no truck with those who, like the worshippers of Aaron's Golden Calf, bow down before false idols, in this case by attributing specious and misleading cultural or biological meanings to an unconscious whose deep implications with an alternatively defined human sexuality he would unswervingly defend to the end.

But Freud also makes clear that his feelings of kinship move well beyond the mere acknowledgement of Moses's insistence on the difficult truth of a new law, however suggestively this law's immediate unpopularity anticipated the hostility of the reaction to Freud's psychoanalytic discoveries. In short, 'The Moses of Michelangelo' reveals that what Freud found so moving in the statue is how it makes visible the singular difficulty of the task God entrusts with the Jewish patriarch. In short, Michelangelo's Moses *suffers*: desperately, he wants to rage against his own people, as indeed he does in the subsequent narrative moments of Exodus as he orders the faithful Levites to slaughter Aaron's pagan infidels. In the end, the figure with whom Freud identifies is not the heroic leader who triumphantly secures for the tribes of Israel a new covenant with God. Instead, in seeing himself in Moses, Freud apprehends a flawed, conflicted and even reluctant militant burdened with the thankless task of overcoming his own passionate resistance to the unsettling implications of the very doctrine for the propagation of which he is responsible.

The formidable rigour Freud brings to his analysis of the statue is in this sense a function of his desire for an inspirational model of perseverance which he could enlist to his advantage in the struggle with both his uncomprehending followers and a growing but ambivalent public. As I will explore further later on, Freud is led by his desire to imply in his interpretation of the statue an alternative narrative development that deviates quite dramatically from the scriptural source. This is to say that the Moses of Freud's 'The Moses of Michelangelo' essay is most emphatically not the biblical one. More importantly for my specific purposes, however, the interpretative intricacy on display in Freud's reading clears fertile ground for the theoretical cultivation in visual and aesthetic terms of what Lacan in a starkly different way develops in his work under the rubric of the psychoanalytic act, the act that closely parallels the poetic act that I will go on to explore in Genet's literary work in subsequent chapters. What is an act? How do we define an act that would be properly psychoanalytic in nature? And how does this act help us to understand Genet's sense of the poetic image's subversive agency? As a first step in addressing these questions, I develop in what follows a speculative link between a specific aspect of Freud's analysis of the Moses statue's aesthetic form and Lacan's enlistment of logic discourse in his theory of the psychoanalytic act of interpretation.

Sceptics will immediately note that the strictly verbal medium of orthodox clinical psychoanalysis seems to exclude what we commonsensically attribute to acts, namely that they are characterized by motion of a properly physical kind. But there is indeed a clinical analogue of the act in this last sense, and its implications require us to rethink what we usually understand by the term. The relevant analogue is indeed what Freud in his essay calls interpretation. With this term, Freud names the method by which he uncovers what he calls, quaintly from today's perspective, 'the meaning and content of what is represented'[3] in Michelangelo's statue. But how precisely does psychoanalytic interpretation instantiate the act? And how does Freud's reading of the sculpture not only exemplify the act of psychoanalytic interpretation, but also identify what we can precisely call the product, or better the *creation*, of the act?

Scrolls and whorls

In a postscript written thirteen years after his essay's original publication, Freud is eager to enlist in his argument's support information contained in an article sent to him by his friend and biographer Ernest Jones. In the article, a certain H. P. Mitchell describes two small twelfth-century bronzes in the Ashmolean Museum of Oxford attributed to the early medieval metalworker Nicholas of Verdun. One of the two statuettes, Freud argues, directly prefigures the Michelangelo artwork. Not only does it represent a seated male elder in a flowing robe supporting with one hand the Tablets of the Law. Also, it features the key figural detail given pride of place in Freud's reading: the peculiarly muscular gripping 'as in a vice'[4] of a strand of beard. Freud implies that Michelangelo must have been aware of the earlier figure, hinting that there could be other lost works of statuary depicting Moses in a similar posture lost, as it were, in the sands of time.

Certainly, Freud intends his elucidation of the beard detail's significance to explain the dramatically contrasting descriptions in the critical literature of this element of Michelangelo's statue. Over the centuries, interpreters had returned to one central, vexing question: What exactly is Moses doing to his beard with the fingers and, we presume, thumb of his right hand? If the tablets are so crucially important to Moses (if not so much to his people), as surely they must be given their properly divine origin, then how do we account for their casual positioning in the statue's composition, balanced precariously on one of their corners? To be sure, the tablets are supported only by the edge of Moses's right hand, the same hand that appears preoccupied by the strands of beard so sensuously rendered on the artwork.

Freud takes inspiration in his own reading from the interpretative method practised by a late-nineteenth-century Italian physician named Giovanni Morelli. Working under the alias of a Russian art connoisseur, Morelli called into question the authorship of significant artworks of the period and reattributed them to the artists who, he argued, were their true creators.[5] Drawing attention to the parallel with analytic practice, Freud describes the aspect of Morelli's method that aims to divert 'attention from the general impressions and main features of the picture' and instead 'lay stress on the significance of minor details, of things like the drawing of the fingernails' or 'the lobe of an ear'.[6] Morelli's art-historical and Freud's analytic methods hold in common the attention they insist on fixing, against the looker's (or listener's) spontaneous inclinations, on those elements that are rarely noticed – what Freud suggestively calls the 'refuse', offered in English in the original, or the 'rubbish-heap (*Abhub*) of our observations'.[7] It is as if the act of looking produced a residue or excess that can find no place within the figure's representational logic. Like discarded trash, this figural supplement is left unseen by the observer. Or more precisely, it is seen but left unnoticed, un(re)marked, unacknowledged. Or yet again, it is hidden from view by more pleasing representations unconsciously projected onto the artwork in the beholder's mind.

By contrast, Freud insists on seeing *and* remarking every detail of the sculpture, in particular the incongruous or innocuous elements our attention tends blithely to pass over. Equally importantly, he strives to notice only what is actually present among the artwork's elements, wilfully holding in check perception's tendency to see things that are not really there. Freud makes two main observations in his corrective interpretation of Michelangelo's statue. First, the unusual arrangement of beard and fingers only makes contextual sense if we assume that Moses's index finger is pressed 'deeply' against the hair in a way that suggests an expenditure of force alien to so casual an action as the 'playing'[8] suggested by other interpreters. Second, the strands of hair pressed against Moses's body by 'that despotic finger'[9] of his right hand originate from the left side of his body, the viewer's right.

Some crucial specification: just as Moses's body seems pulled in a direction opposite to the pivoting motion of his head, the hair strands of concern are directed against the orientation of the rest of the beard. Precisely, the pressure exerted by that single index finger of the right hand quite literally *causes* the formation of the complexly composed interlacing curls over Moses's tunic. In a text already dense with detail, Freud's description of these features of the statue is especially remarkable in the intensity and evocativeness of its language. The description forms the linchpin of the essay in that it distils what it has to say, to some extent unwittingly, about the essence of the act. While Freud may be correct to identify this element of Michelangelo's composition as the statue's most 'unusual',[10] my argument will focus instead on how Freud's articulation bodies forth a theory of the psychoanalytic act as an act of interpretation. Here is the key passage of Freud's analysis:

> What has received the most unusual treatment is the thick mass of hair on the inside of (the strand of hair on Moses's left side)… It is not suffered to follow the turn of the head to the left; it is forced to roll over loosely and form part of a kind of *scroll* (*aufrollenden Bogen*) which lies across and over the strands on the inner right side of the beard. This is because it is held fast by the pressure of the right index finger … Thus, the main mass of the beard is thrown to the right of the figure, whereas the head is sharply turned to the left. At the place where the right index finger is pressed in, a kind of *whorl* (*Wirbel*; vortex) of hairs is formed; strands of hair coming from the left lie over strands coming from the right, both caught in by that despotic finger.[11]

Freud goes on to argue that the movement of Moses's body prior to the moment captured in the statue can be deduced retrospectively from these details. Also, these same details furnish an explanation for the oddly precarious positioning of the precious tablets which, according to Freud, are in fact resting upside-down. Essentially, Freud argues that upon seeing the superstitious frolicking of his tribesmen and women, Moses turns his head in their direction and lifts his foot with the intention of standing up. As he does this, he makes an effort to suppress his rage by plunging his right hand into his beard 'as though to turn his violence against his own body', in Freud's suggestive turn of phrase.[12] In turn, this action causes the tablets to loosen from his grip, risking to fall and shatter to pieces on the ground, as indeed they do in the biblical narrative. Michelangelo's statue fixes on the precise instant when Moses has begun to move his right hand back to the right side of his body (our left) to prevent the tablets from falling. Sensibly, Freud suggests that the various and otherwise incomprehensible errors of vision that mar the descriptions of so many art critics who have studied the statue are in fact the result of unconscious retrospective visual constructions of the moments immediately prior to the one immortalized in marble. In other words, Freud proposes that our perception, of its own volition as it were, provides the visual faculty with a kind of explanation for the statue's perplexing composition, effectively setting the statue in motion by completing backwards in time the full action of which it can display only the final part. Of course, these explanations are buttressed by the interpreters' knowledge of the exodus story, which effectively blinds them to the details of the statue that hint at the possibility of alternative, unrealized narrative developments.

No doubt some will wonder about the plausibility of Freud's bold analysis of the statue and his criticisms of previous interpretative efforts. I find the analysis compelling and the observations sharp. But the plausibility question is quite tangential to my central concern, which relates less to the problem of what the content of the artwork represents than to its form, both in itself and on the level of Freud's description of it. More precisely, I am interested in how the statue's form figures Moses's act; that is, how Michelangelo materially renders the consequences of what Freud perceives to be Moses's masochistic suppression of his angry passion, condensed into the form of that 'despotic' finger, sign of the exercise of a stubborn sovereign will.

Even though he presents his concerns as primarily involved in problems of representation or content, Freud too is deeply interested not simply in the statue's formal details, but more consequentially in how these details manifest what we might call an aesthetic rendition of the ethics of perseverance: how persevering through the consequences of an act can be embodied in artistic form. The ensuing analysis will zoom in on how the interpretation's details construct a kind of visual allegory of Freud's refusal to 'give way on his desire', to quote Lacan's supreme ethical maxim; or, in terms more specific to Freud's psychoanalytic act, to remain faithful to the disquieting truth of his discovery and theorization of the unconscious. In so doing I will try to say something about the act in general with respect to its consequences and the traces it leaves behind.

In sum, Freud's reading of the statue suggests a notion of the act as an event that renders on the level of appearances what psychoanalysis tries to describe with its thematic of the subject's splitting. For Lacanians, this splitting is the result of our alienation in the structure of language, or more technically by the signifier. The headache-inducing minutiae of Freud's analysis of the statue's indexation of the movements of the various parts of Moses's body, and especially of the convoluted dynamic morphology of his beard's tufts of hair, wind up highlighting one pivotal observation: the artwork's surface is rife with evidence of a tension between two opposing vectors of force, namely the rage directed at the waywardness of Moses's iconophilic tribespeople and ... well, what exactly? How are we to describe the energy, which Freud explicitly qualifies as masochistic, on which Moses draws in his effort to subdue his roiling anger? And crucially, how does this agency disclose the essential properties of the act?

To introduce the turn to Lacan, we can note as a preliminary move the most obvious difference in quality between the two objects towards which these opposing forces are directed. The Golden Calf is an image, one we can qualify as phallic in the precise sense that, to the difference of the phallic signifier, it is attributed with the potential power to body forth the lack of lack: self-relating being for which nothing is forbidden, incomplete or impossible; an imaginary plenitude, as it were, secured through a miraculous healing of the wound inflicted by the signifier's puncturing torsion of being. By contrast, the tablets express the Law through the medium of language, understood here as a sequence of articulated signifiers, by outlining the set of prohibitions imposed upon the Jewish subject: the well-known series of *thou shalt not*s. By naming the forbidden forms of enjoyment, the Old Testament commandments introduce the lack that causes and sustains desire. With prohibition, that is, the subject becomes free to daydream about – and crucially, to idealize – the forms of enjoyment or jouissance to which they are barred access.

To bring more context and precision to this still vague intuition of the act's embroilment with the signifier, we can take an instructive, if perhaps unfamiliar or surprising, detour through elements of Lacan's still under-explored theory of the act.[13] Initially, this detour might seem improperly motivated, since the discourses to which Lacan has recourse to develop this theory, namely mathematics and especially logic, are precisely defined by the exclusion of the very perceptual or visual considerations – intuition, in this precise sense – of concern to Freud in his essay on Michelangelo's statue. To justify the interconnection between the visual and the formal-linguistic, however, we need only recall how Freud compares the dreamwork to a 'picture-puzzle'[14] or rebus, which can only be decoded by making precisely such a connection between the image or icon and the properly linguistic signifiers with which it can enter into relation.

More exactly, the unconscious arranges images in a way that takes account of a specific variety of relation that exists between the signifiers with which they are problematically associated. By the time we reach the conclusion of this excursus on Lacan, we should be in a position to grasp the connection between the image of the 'despotic finger' that Freud sees on Moses's right hand and a special kind of signifier at work in the act of psychoanalytic interpretation. This connection will serve in turn to bring some unexpected illumination to Genet's idea of the poetic act. To reiterate the immediate premise: a direct analogy can be drawn between, first, the interpretative signifier uttered by the analyst, which can momentarily overcome the defenses of the patient's ego by precipitating an encounter with the real of desire; and, second, Michelangelo's rendering in marble of that finger on Moses's hand, the one Freud memorably describes as despotic.

Within the spatial-aesthetic organization of the statue, this finger quite literally indexes what we might call in a Lacanian manner the *extimacy*, or 'intimate exteriority',[15] of its own form: the point at which it appears to subvert itself as a geometrical volume by refusing to close itself off completely from its outside, in fact incorporating this outside within itself in a way that calls into question the very distinction between what lies within and what remains without. In the end, this is the invaluable, if semi-implicit, point Freud makes in his essay: on Michelangelo's statue, Moses conspicuously *points* to the capacity of the artist to include within an aesthetic form an indication of this same form's self-undoing. Analogously, the properly trained analyst possesses the skill required to make use of an element of the patient's own discourse in order to gesture towards that which this discourse is designed precisely to conceal.

Like Moses's finger, the unintentional slips and spontaneous utterances of the patient direct attention to a current in their discourse concealed by its very conspicuousness. This current harbours a privileged relation to unconscious desire. When we look or listen in an attentive but unfocused way, we might see that both Michelangelo's artwork and the analysand's speech in fact draw our attention to their respective failures to defend themselves against discontinuity and incompletion, be it the whorl in Moses's hair on the statue or the patient's peculiar slip of the tongue. In this sense, the performance of the interpretative act of both art critic and analyst requires us to resist the strong temptation to restore integrity, familiarity, coherence and regularity; to compensate, that is, for what we spontaneously perceive *without remarking* as deficiencies or deviations of logic or form.

The psychoanalytic act

Despite his frequent insistence that the concepts developed in his teaching are addressed first and foremost to analytic practitioners, Lacan routinely peppers his discussion of the psychoanalytic act with comments more general in nature. Considered together, these comments sketch the outlines of something like a theory of the act as such. Indeed, it is as if Lacan were suggesting that we can take the capacity of the speaking human subject to act as someone else's analyst – a premise, by the way, which it was Lacan's life's work to defend and precisely describe – as a sort of proof of the possibility of the performance of acts in the so-called real, that is to say social, world.

The analyst's capacity to nurture a clinical encounter that provides the patient with an opportunity to draw consequences from the momentary overcoming of the ego's force of resistance bears a close but complex relation to the power of the generic subject socially to exercise their 'agency', to use that Anglo-American cultural-theoretical term reactivated in the 1980s and 90s in an attempt to wiggle out of the melancholic determinisms of a structuralism altogether more fixed, and therefore more vulgar, than Lacan's. What the psychoanalytic and generic acts hold in common is simply the impossibility of finding a prior empirically or discursively defined cause for which the act itself, in any of its forms, might be construed as the effect. This means that whatever the act may be, it breaks with the patterns of determination, the laws of causality, that define the status quo, be it that of the symptom – the suffering that appears to stand between us and the life to which we aspire – or that of a given social formation, whose dominant discourses eventually fail to silence the voice of the dissident and to suppress the affect of the discontented.

By now, numerous (not only, but perhaps especially) Anglophone Lacan readers culturally and intellectually ill-equipped to deal with these elements of his teaching have found themselves exasperated with, and uncomprehending of, Lacan's increasingly significant recourse to the discourses of logic and mathematics (and in particular mathematical or mathematized logic) in his numerous, protracted and certainly experimental attempts to formalize psychoanalytic praxis. Seemingly preposterously, the recourse to logic nevertheless informs the fundamentals of his doctrine of the act. Inconveniently, the dominant forms of today's literary-cultural academic training prepare us badly for the novelty and significance of one of Lacan's most fundamental intellectual wagers: an encounter such as the misleadingly named analytic dialogue, which takes so-called ordinary language as the medium for its task of precipitating the manifestation of evidence of an unconscious subject, can paradoxically benefit from discourses whose very historical aim has been to *eliminate* all traces of this subject from articulated thought. Since Aristotle's *Organon*, the strain of the philosophical tradition that for our elementary purposes we can simply call logic has taken on the mission of giving form to the very possibilities for valid inference in thought. Logic seeks after the rules for true or correct cognition, one could also legitimately say, rules that function autonomously vis-à-vis the subject who thinks.

Of utmost interest to Lacan is the endeavour of logicians through the centuries to compose these sets of rules for right thinking above and beyond any consideration of whether or not thought's manifold assertions can be said to be factually true or false. This remains the case even if these same logicians show great interest in how the true and the false can be inferred on the level of what they call the proposition. By aiming to create worlds of thought in which the true and the false can be determined with certainty and without exception, however, the problems of meaning and reference fall entirely out of the picture. While mathematicians and logicians can argue endlessly with one another about how their formal systems succeed or fail in fulfilling the classical, by now in some measure abandoned, ambition of seamless, absolute consistency, none of them will be able to tell you, Lacan asserts echoing Bertrand Russell, what it all means; that is, how the search for systematic clarity with respect to the true and the false holds consequences for anything of a more concrete nature beyond the signifying limits of the formal system itself.[16]

For my purposes here, one of the most illuminating premises of Lacan's argument about the significance of logic for psychoanalysis foregrounds the importance of the philosophy of René Descartes, a marginal figure in most Anglo-American accounts of the tradition. In Lacan's view, Descartes's early modern philosophy inaugurates the empty, universal subject of science while at the same time making a move with unprecedented consequences for logic.[17] In Descartes's method, Lacan asserts, thought about thought comes to jettison entirely the category of being, at least insofar as this being is held to retain a modicum of independence vis-à-vis the activity of thinking. The illustrious Cartesian cogito – I think, therefore I am – succinctly distils this desire to situate thinking and being on the same logical level, or more precisely to posit being as nothing other than the effect or consequence of thought.

Historically, this question of being had echoed ambiguously through the logic-related elements of the work of both Aristotle and Plato, and then much later conspicuously re-emerged in Lacan's lifetime in the work of twentieth-century phenomenologists such as Husserl, in Sartrean existentialism, and finally in the philosophy of Heidegger. By evacuating being through a self-imposed gesture of limitation to what can be articulated strictly on the level of thought, the logical project as emblematized by the Cartesian gesture radically calls into question for Lacan what he calls the Other. In this context, this 'big' Other is the 'locus of speech'[18] to which, through the transference, power is granted to validate, or indeed reject, a truth claim viewed to be embedded in the very expression of thought in speech. More rigorously: speech (or *discourse* in the exact sense of language linked to its capacity for verbal expression), in contradistinction to what Lacan calls *writing* (*écriture*: the formal, non-'ordinary' languages of logic and mathematics), carries within itself an implicit, structural – non-psychological, that is – plea for validation or falsification by virtue merely of the utterance itself.

Consider this banal example from academic life. I used to have a colleague who would compulsively add the interrogative expression 'yes?' to the end of his assertions to the arguable point of calling into question their very status *as* assertions. 'Virginia Woolf introduced a new perspective on gender to English fiction, *yes*?' he might have said, or perhaps asked. From the Lacanian perspective, we should resist the psychologizing temptation to qualify this recourse to the question as a betrayal of a lack of confidence in one's opinions. This would be the preferred interpretation: the professorial tic simply marks out, draws attention to, how any enunciated assertion implicitly addresses another anonymous party: Lacan's Other, that is. The big Other's judgement 'yes, that is true' or 'no, that is false' is always anticipated, but also always eventually fails to manifest in a way that evacuates all doubt from the equation. Anyone's claim to know the validity of the assertion can immediately be called into question by someone else, which is indeed what makes both necessary and impossible this opaque function of the Other in its incapacity definitively to sanction any statement's validity.

This emphasis on the idea that doubt cannot be eradicated from the articulation of thought in language is surely one of the ways in which Lacan's theory of the subject remains decidedly Cartesian. It is also what Lacan means to say by his suggestion that the operation of the function of the proposition in logic discourse *creates* the dimension of truth. Crucial to specify, however, is that this truth does not correspond to a sense of certainty that might lend itself to verification, empirical or otherwise. Rather, truth emerges as the objective or structural possibility of a judgement that would establish, once and for all, the truth or falsity of the utterance, of the proposition. The problem, of course, is that this decisive or final judgement is forever clouded in ambiguity; it can neither be eliminated from the function of speech nor made communicably transparent. In discourse, truth emerges only in partial form as an objective enigma, which no one, not even our cherished Other, possesses the required knowledge to solve.

Lacan further probes the implications of logic discourse for truth by considering the status of science at the very beginnings of Western thought. This element of Lacan's discussion sheds helpful light on the recourse to formal languages – 'writing' in his own idiom – considered as a strategy with which it is possible to move beyond the transferential supposition of knowledge embedded in the structure of ordinary language. Exploring the origins of the concept of science in antiquity, Lacan argues that the conundrum of the Other was already a central epistemological concern for Plato. Science in this context (or scientific knowledge) is not understood in the modern sense as empirical or natural science, nor more specifically as the experimental method on which these depend, but rather as the pure science of thought: *epistêmê* to the Greeks; the science or logic of the signifier, in Lacanian vocabulary. Science here corresponds to language viewed as form in the basic way we have been considering it thus far under the rubric of logic.

In his commentary of the historical theory of science, Lacan singles out one of the fundamental Platonic questions, which in his view lies at the foundation of the logical enterprise: 'What (scientific) knowledge constructs', did anyone 'know it before' its construction?[19] Platonic dialogues such as *Meno* or *Phaedo* famously explore this problem via the notion of recollection. The question was thus already an acute one for Plato, whose Socrates famously argues that the non-sensuous ideas (or forms) of which the mind can gain knowledge were known to a person's immortal soul and then forgotten at the moment of their birth. For Plato, the premise that knowledge is acquired from remembrances of notions whose existence predates one's own embodied consciousness was at minimum worthy of serious philosophical consideration.

Lacan asserts that the history of modern logic provides a clear rebuttal to the Socratic argument, which may or may not have been Plato's own. This is the most radical lesson logic can teach psychoanalysis: knowledge (or thought – these two complicated terms are roughly interchangeable for my purposes here) is not a mimetic reflection of some natural or historical real. Rather, knowledge is the product of a creative act that founds an order of truth structured by language in the broadest sense, which here spans the distinction mentioned earlier between discourse and writing. Most significantly, this order of truth indexes knowledge's internal limit. That is, language does not impose a limit that prevents us from knowing a truth outside of language, as even the less vulgar postmodernist discourses often wind up contending against their best intentions. Language is not a more or less coherent referential system that fails to refer adequately to a reality outside itself. Instead, language is itself dysfunctional: the problematic elaboration of increasingly sophisticated formal systems in logical thought demonstrates for Lacan that language's inconsistency stems first and foremost from its own internal malfunctioning before its capacity to signify or represent is even brought into consideration.

For these reasons, logic offers to Lacan a potential solution to the problem of transference, which he famously evokes through his notion of the *sujet supposé savoir*, or subject supposed to know. The solution remains 'potential' because, as we will see later on, logic discourse must necessarily fail to eliminate all traces of what Lacan calls the subject from its articulations. Nevertheless, the best way to minimize subjectivity's ineradicable dependence on the unconscious assumption that something or somebody, somewhere, possesses knowledge in a sanctionable and fully verifiable form is the path of logico-mathematical formalization. In other words, the logical project derives its psychoanalytic significance from its attempt, however inconsistently realized, to 'exclude as such', as Lacan puts it, 'the subject supposed to know'.[20] Take care to note, however, that Lacan can only say this because he has assumed that all possible articulated constructions of thought in the formal languages of logic and mathematics are acts of pure creation, as opposed to reflections or representations of something other than themselves. In consequence, these creations cannot previously have been known by anyone or anything, be it Freud, some Sufi mystic, Hegel, an 'authentic' indigenous culture, nature, or even and especially, God.

Logic discourse holds the advantage over ordinary language in that it harbours the power more rigorously to question the relation of thought to truth. Strange things begin to happen, however, when logic attempts to eradicate or resolve the problem of truth by trying to make truth appear – complete, consistent, verifiable – from within the forms of thought themselves. Hubristically, classical logic strives to create fully elaborated systems of inference in which truth can be ascertained entirely and unambiguously within the system, leaving no unsavoury residue of undecidability. Despite his clear admiration for the standard of formal rigour upheld by logic's best practitioners, Lacan asserts unequivocally that the logical and psychoanalytic vocations ultimately diverge.

This remains the case even once we acknowledge that Lacan drew significant inspiration from such roughly contemporary phenomena as the axiomatic set theory that charged the revolutionary but uncomfortably paradox-producing work of Georg Cantor (and to some extent Bertrand Russell as well) with the crime of naivety.[21] We can add that Lacan's enlistment of logic in his teaching is in implicit conversation with developments in post-classical logic that have recently been labelled 'paraconsistent' in the work of Graham Priest, for example.[22] Of central interest to Lacan in all of the modern logical and mathematical discourses with which he engages is the way in which they inevitably encounter difficulty as they strive to create fully self-contained thought systems in which all possible contradiction and inconsistency have been successfully ironed out.

In this specific sense, we can consider this aspect of Lacan's discourse a brand of (critical) logical argument that affirms the irreducible but unthinkable insistence of the unconscious subject's *being* by indexing the repeated failure of logic discourse to eliminate its possibility from the traces of thought. According to Lacan, as the discourse of logic mathematizes itself by abstracting from ordinary language in more and more complex ways, it unwittingly discovers increasingly precise conceptualizations of the subject of the unconscious as a stubborn lack that prevents the system from achieving seamless consistency. This subject appears only indirectly in these discourses as such a fault or inconsistency, in the very non-existence of a sign within the system thanks to which full coherence could be achieved. Schematically, the only means available to the logician to compensate for this systemic insufficiency is a decision or axiom that cannot be deduced from within the strict terms of the system itself. In Lacan's own idiom, logic requires the illicit introduction of metalanguage – second-order formalizations, that is, that hold a power of specification over the first – in order problematically to realize the elusive ideal of seamless consistency.

In ordinary (i.e. non-logicized) social discourses, the subject of the unconscious is occluded thanks to the illusion of consistency afforded by the symptom's repression and the precarious formation of the ego, with its supporting series of symbolic identifications. With the bundling of enjoyment in the symptom and its banishment to the unconscious, the social world begins to appear to the 'normal' neurotic subject in a meaningful, if troublingly distant or inaccessible, way. We pay a price, however, because the symptom causes us to experience the excessive enjoyment – the jouissance that repression works to corporealize – in the form of suffering, of pain. By contrast, in the more rigorous formal systems of *écriture*, this same subject of the unconscious appears for Lacan in the paradoxical form of an internally problematic lack of closure; that is, in the absence of a signifier or letter that would smooth out the system's functioning from within the defined limits of the system itself. The grammatical excess of enjoyment in speech (*discours*) is echoed for Lacan by the logical lack of the signifier of consistency or completion in formal writing (*écriture*). Both the excess and the lack index the insuperability of the same properly inarticulable subject of the unconscious.

In (simplified) technical terms, Lacan's teaching on logic aims to draw a precise analogy between, first, the second-order axiom or decision that logicians must add to their formal systems in an attempt to achieve an acceptable level of consistency and, second, the function of the unconscious fundamental fantasy in psychoanalysis. Both the axiom and the fantasy provide the subject with what Lacan calls a signification. This signification anchors the system of representation, logical or psychical, allowing it to achieve an imperfect level of referential and internal functionality, but only on condition that it is repressed, in other words subtracted from that same system of representation. Psychoanalysis parts ways with the logical enterprise, most dramatically in logic's classical forms, in its disciplined insistence on *interpreting* the signification encoded in the symptom. The act of interpretation is designed to draw the subject's attention to the signs – plainly audible or visible on the surface of its speech and actions – of a traumatic and ineradicable lack/excess of meaning. In his doctrine of the act, Lacan identifies a kind of insoluble, but also inaccessible and unscrutinized, logical inconsistency lying at the centre of our socio-symbolic world.

The emancipation of interpretation

This last point provides an opportunity to return to Freud's discussion of the Michelangelo statue with a view to clarify the speculative link between my two main strands of argument. In the first section I argued that what attracts Freud to Moses has something to do with the masochistic expenditure of effort, the exercise of self-inhibition or self-discipline, that might have allowed the patriarch to divert his attention away from the wanton idolaters and hold in check his angry passion, in so doing regaining his grip on the Tablets of the Law, thereby stopping them smashing to bits on the ground.

At that point I refrained from rehearsing what in today's ideological climate is no doubt the more intuitive way of considering Moses's act. Indeed, the dissenting questions ring out from the cultural atmosphere: Rather than figure a heroic gesture of perseverance, does Michelangelo's statue not give form to a conservative desire to repress the human capacity for pleasurable and celebratory community? Does it not do this by subjugating this capacity under blind obedience to a monotheistic divinity whose law sets the terms for an authoritarian order, one that grants control of society to one or many self-appointed religious elites? The Mosaic identification of the sometimes uncomfortably bourgeois Freud could be tainted to some degree by such regressive sentiments; certainly there is evidence of these scattered widely across his work. But a better interpretation is available. The question hinges on the significance we grant to the tablets and more specifically to Freud's implicit view of the law they set down, as it were, in stone. In my view, the tablets for Freud do not finally stand for the gauzily reactionary ideal of a law-abiding society in which the dominant values are the maintenance of social order and the buttressing of conventional morality, whatever the cost in neurotic suffering – and worse – might be.

What, after all, is 'the law' in Lacan's Freudian psychoanalysis? It is certainly not the system of laws that upholds bourgeois property relations, forbids public nudity or institutes a heterosexual matrix for desire, for instance. First and foremost, it is the law of castration, the law that subjects us to the signifier by marking the psyche with evidence that our efforts to position ourselves as the object that will satisfy the Other's desire will always eventually prove futile. But specialist knowledge is hardly required to know that 'the law' is also the law of free association, which in the present context we can conceive as a kind of exercise in logicization. Both exercises – the logical and the free associative – have the ultimate effect of transforming the Other to whom or to which we address our speech. In free association the Other ceases to function as the guarantor of our unconscious signification, as a sort of underwriter for our symptom's repression. Instead, it begins to assume its more opaque and mysterious incarnation as Lacan's 'locus of speech', whose truth can only ever be partially disclosed. *This* law is an especially apposite figure for the law Freud sees Moses struggling with himself to defend in Michelangelo's statue. As I tried to show earlier, this law has effects that leave conspicuous and interpretable traces on the statue's aesthetic form.

These traces finally set themselves apart from what Freud says his rival interpreters see in the Moses statue: a spatial animation that retrospectively affords its form an explanatory narrative arc culminating in its actual figural composition. Rather, the traces are the direct result of the pressure exerted by Moses's 'despotic' finger, which creates what Freud calls a vortex or 'whorl': the central, somewhat enigmatic, term of his description. Derived from a late middle-English word for the pulley or flywheel of a spindle, the word evokes a spiral, coil or verticil. Taken together, these objects and shapes suggest a circular motion around a vertical axis that both ascends or descends and also moves closer to, or further away from, the axis. The motion creates a central void one can imagine partially occupied by the spindle of a spinning wheel, for example. The visual analogue of this void is plainly visible on the statue. And Freud argues that the whorl of concern entertains a logical relation to Moses's finger as the effect of the causal force this finger exerts on the strands of his beard.

By introducing discontinuity and incompletion into the statue's spatial organization – a spiral-shaped rupture on its surface, that is – Freud's whorl has an effect we can describe in terms opposite to those used in the retrospective constructions misleadingly featured in the rival accounts. Instead of providing a scripturally supported narrative rationale for the current composition of the statue, the scroll-like shape imposes rather a break in, an interruption of, the narrative. This interruption marks the possibility of future happenings that cannot be foreknown, that do not follow logically from what has gone before. In other words, the vortex in Moses's beard marks the point where the story undoes itself. When we imagine the strands of beard beginning to coalesce into a new form, we anticipate that it might require a different narrative in order to become meaningful, in order to make contextual sense.

The clear implication of Freud's interpretation of the statue's immediate narrative background, however, is that the tablets would have been lost if Moses had allowed himself to harangue his tribesmen and women for their mindless worship of the idol, likely only exacerbating the force of what Judith Butler might call their 'passionate attachment to subjection'.[23] Of course, this is exactly what happens in the biblical narrative, as Moses commands the slaughter of the members of his idolatrous tribe. But surely the remarkable discrepancy between Freud's view of Moses's self-inhibition and the immediate development of the exodus story is precisely the point. Though he failed to do so, Moses *could have* held himself in check, as Michelangelo's work for Freud suggests, remaining faithful in the act to both spirit and letter of the law. Instead, like Freud's primal father, Moses becomes a figure of power who violates the law, exempting himself from its jurisdictional purchase while at the same time imposing it hypocritically on everyone else. Through his acting out, the scriptural Moses positions himself as an exception to the law of castration. His disastrously murderous rage functions unconsciously as a demand for recognition from the Other that he is not, like everyone else, subjected to the lack that the signifier carves out of the fibre of every speaking mammal's very being.

In the psychoanalytic act of interpretation, Lacan argues, the subject appears in an evanescent way as identical with the signifier. Rather than signify a subject for another signifier, as signifiers normally do, the interpretative signifier manages for once to refer to itself, thereby succeeding, if only for a fleeting moment, in collapsing the subject into the signifier; in signifying the subject, as Jean-Paul Sartre might say, in and for itself. Among other things, this implies that in the psychoanalytic context the act *is* a signifier. In other words, the psychoanalytic act has a properly symbolic function, or more accurately a symbolic *dys*function, in the precise sense that it has the effect of de-totalizing or de-unifying what is conventionally and too simplistically understood to be a symbolic order.

Lacan also makes clear that the psychoanalytic act is not a sexual act in the ordinary sense of the term. Though the act discloses, makes tangible, a repressed sexuality – the form of enjoyment with which the subject fails to come to terms – it does so counter-intuitively by impeding the sexual act's performance, by placing the act in this different sense behind the wall of an inviolable taboo: in the analytic chamber the impossible injunction to say everything goes hand in hand with the cardinal rule to do nothing. The act of interpretation interprets the transference. This means that the analyst's utterance is designed to sublimate what is properly sexual in the patient's relation to the Other by distilling this sexuality into a signifier whose function is to unsettle the signification of the repressed fantasy around which, unbeknownst to them, the patient's world is constructed. An effective interpretation will reveal to the subject the unsettling truth that, as Lacan says, the Other, here viewed as a consistent and trustworthy order of signifiers, does not exist. The Other only appears to us as a consistent entity holding the power to validate our being so long as the signification constructed by our fundamental fantasy remains unsignified, uninterpreted. This is the sense in which psychoanalytic interpretation performs a function effectively opposite to the construction of meaning.

Of course, the ego is the force that resists the disclosure of the sexuality repressed in the unconscious fantasy around which we construct our reassuring and manageable, if necessarily fragile, personal worlds. I have claimed that the strategy psychoanalysis enlists to overcome this egoic force is the technique of free association. It is difficult to resist the temptation to compare the resistance we put up in the clinic to the task of uttering each and every thought without heed to sense or meaning (or propriety) with the similar resistance most of us experience when faced with the challenge of reading a forbidding logic textbook, or even for that matter trying to read Lacan. But I have also proposed that Lacan does not argue that logic discourse already says everything psychoanalysis wants to say. Indeed, it is not the case that modern logicians advance from the premise of the impossibility of creating a fully consistent formal language from which all undecidable, inconsistent or contradictory propositions have been eradicated (not a position shared by all logicians, mind you) to the non-logical and properly Freudian conclusion that the reason for this is because as properly sexed subjects we can only pass through the trauma of castration with the help of a fantasy. The repression of this fantasy, and more specifically of the signifier with which it is enmeshed, replaces what appears to us consciously as the disruptive non-sense of enjoyment with a reassuring meaning. This meaning grants us a place in the world that we can apprehend comfortably, as it were, from the outside.

This is perhaps the last word on Lacan's engagement with logic: like the subject who conjures a fantasy to compensate for their inability to submit themselves fully to the slippery and unreliable terms of language, the logician coins his axiom or makes his decision in an attempt to introduce rules into his system that will finally achieve a modicum of consistency, or even paraconsistency; to iron out the intellectual wrinkles that the application of the strictest logical rigour will always produce. In his Moses essay, Freud interprets the transferential fantasy of the other Michelangelo commentators by introducing a gap in the seamless, affect-heavy logic of the biblical narrative according to which the tribe's pagan ideology functions as the cause of Moses's murderous passion. For Freud, Moses's despotic finger is the aesthetic index of an application of will that disrupts the momentum of the narrative referenced by the statue. In Freud's reading, the vortex Michelangelo creates in his sculpture has the effect of opening the biblical story up to alternative, unforeseeable developments; also, it retrospectively casts the gleam of contingency on the cornerstones of a narrative long since hardened into the resistant forms of a sacred cultural tradition.

Analogously, Lacan's logicized psychoanalysis founds a discipline, a rigour that enables the analyst to isolate certain signifiers in what the patient says in the view of disclosing how unconscious fantasy functions to cover over the ineradicable aporia of discourse as speech, potentially reorganizing our very experience of being in the world. The excursus through logic, and more specifically through its medium of *écriture*, has the benefit of reminding us that the traces of this fantasy are legible on the surface; that the texts of culture have a way of indexing irregularities and inconsistencies that wrench them out of their own narrative contexts. Required to identify these privileged points is the self-discipline of the analyst's peculiar kind of sustained, unfocused and non-selective attention.

At an early-twenty-first-century moment when our full integration into the circuits of production and exchange is promoted by the lure of a decidedly eroticized and idealized enjoyment, the seeming austerity of a logicized psychoanalysis presents itself as both authentically subversive and, frankly, a bit of a relief. Perhaps we should not be surprised then when, like Freud's Moses (as opposed to the biblical one), we check our worldly passions once in a while to grapple with the logic of the signifier and, as a result, we find our world shifting a little and ourselves unexpectedly transformed.

The rest of this book brings this variety of attention to our engagement with a selection of Genet's texts in the view of exploring this affinity between the analytic act's negative power to undermine meaning and the poetic act's analogous capacity to create images that undo themselves, introducing death into the most venerated and sacrosanct forms of life. Just as Lacan reads logic discourse for the way its rigorous interrogation of the forms of knowledge points inevitably to the contorted incompletion of being that is the subject of the unconscious, Genet subjects the world of appearances to unrelenting scrutiny, uncovering its lack of foundation by disinterring the unacknowledged libido that provides any given world with a false sense of unity and fullness. Both the Lacanian analysand and the Genetian literary subject take aim at an impossible subjective reconciliation with irreconcilability, where the insistence of the negative takes on an oddly affirmative cast, and where the infinite disunity of the phenomenal world becomes a mere reflection of the incompletion of being itself.

2

Towards feminine being: Our Lady of the Flowers

Out from under Sartre

It may hardly be groundbreaking to begin a reading of a classic, over-interpreted text like Genet's *Our Lady of the Flowers* with a dig at Sartre. Though the reproaches of the various generations of Genet critics are in large measure justifiable,[1] Sartre's approach to the text features numerous laudable insights nevertheless. These include two that I will develop extensively in this chapter. The first is Sartre's idea that the novel amounts to a 'detoxication' that sees the author turn away from asocial reverie and towards 'the outside world'.[2] The second is his intuition about the specifically 'feminine desires'[3] that offer themselves to be read in the novel. Overwhelmingly, however, the frame through which Sartre apprehends Genet's first work lends it a weighty and unjustified atmosphere of sadism, hopelessness and resentment, as has often been noted.[4] For Sartre, Genet indulges in *Our Lady of the Flowers* his fantasy of demiurgical and often sadistic masturbatory creativity, conjuring a tightly unified and retractile fictional space that bends to no law other than that of the author's own megalomaniacal desire.

The inauspiciousness of Sartre's outlook should be glaringly apparent to both psychoanalytic critics and Genet specialists alike. Not only does the premise of a desire that would be 'Genet's own' violate the fundamental Freudian thesis concerning desire's inherent alterity. Also, the Sartrean reading is remarkably oblivious to the mountain of textual evidence attesting to the wilful, indeed stubborn poetic practice through which Genet endeavours in fact to overcome the force of the repression that conditions his libidinous literary daydreaming. Moreover, the effort required to perform Genet's poetic miracles is diametrically opposed to the kind of intentional transcendence that informs the existentialist project and thanks to which, according to both Sartre and Simone de Beauvoir, an individual can heroically overcome the constraints of their situational circumstances. Indeed, Genet's acts of poetry perform a radical centrifugal self-estrangement that violently separates the subject from its own intuitions of self. As this chapter will explore in myriad ways, they mercilessly expose what Lacan called the barred Other, and ultimately the inconsistency and incompletion of being itself.

Sartre is however correct to discern in *Our Lady of the Flowers* a tendency toward a dynamic of idealization, even if he remains oblivious to the dominant, opposing force with which Genet consistently associates his idea of poetry. For Sartre, the Platonic element of what he calls Genet's 'essentialism' manifests in the way Divine, the novel's seminal drag queen sex worker, perceives Darling, the object of his romantic love, as 'the symbol … of an idea that remains in heaven'.[5] For its part, the Aristotelian aspect of the same essentialism consists in Genet's purported belief that 'naming changes being'.[6] For 'us', by which Sartre presumably means mid-twentieth-century existentialist philosophers, literary metaphor normally projects onto an imaginary or figurative realm. In the phrase 'His head is a singing copse,' for example (which Sartre lifts from Genet's novel), a distance remains in the modern rational mind between the head and the copse. For Sartre, however, Genet's 'exile from our bourgeois, industrial democracy', together with his extensive experience of incarceration, thrust him 'into a grim feudal system'.[7] In Genet's medievalist imaginary, then, the verb 'to be' performs a veritable transformation, even a transubstantiation, that causes the head quite literally to become a copse. Further, when Genet writes that 'Gabriel is a soldier', he means not only that Gabriel is a military man, but also that he somehow incarnates the full panoply of cultural associations connected to the concept of organized battle. In Sartre's words, this Gabriel would 'share suddenly and magically in the virtues, mysteries, and legendary history of a huge, multicolored beast'.[8] For Sartre, Genet's world is not only one in which earthly objects reflect an unchanging transcendental reality. More than this, it is a place where you can trust that the signifier will directly link up with a special kind of signified: a common, unified world of historically consolidated cultural connotations.

Of course, Sartre does not pull his analysis out of thin air. His insights are gleaned from carefully selected textual evidence, even if some of it never made it to conventional publication.[9] Nevertheless, Sartre's reading demonstrates a remarkable numbness to the novel's vitality, which moves in a direction markedly contrary to the points summarized above. On the question of the function and power of language, for example, consider the passage on the depressive period Divine suffers as a result of her jealousy of Our Lady, the stylish young pimp who eventually commits one of the novel's two climactic murders. In the midst of the episode's depiction, the text flashes back to Culafroy's alienated childhood, Culafroy being the provincial boy Divine used to be before her eventual move to the capital and what some would now call her transition. In a dense and elusive passage, Genet evokes the hallucinatory Renaissance – not medieval, note – world to which Culafroy escapes as he strolls by night through the garden behind his house, ingesting leaves of hallucinogenic aconite. Back in the textual present, the prose evokes how a certain word – 'a mere trifle'[10] – which in normal circumstances would leave Divine unshaken and unmoved, suddenly acquires in her state of melancholy the power to shame, or even to humiliate her.

With some justification, we might assume as readers that Genet's intention in this passage is to make a Sartrean point about the 'power of words', which here would be deemed capable of immediately indexing a field of meaning, in this instance one with the capacity to inflict a psychological wound. A complication arises, however, when the narrative voice connects this efficacy of language to neither its faculty of reference nor its power to injure, but rather to its opacity to meaning, its semiotic emptiness. For Divine, words take on 'the magic of boxes empty of everything that is not mystery'; when these boxes 'open up, their meanings escape in leaps and bounds that assault and leave us panting'.[11] Sartre's philosophy is ill-equipped to register this negativity of language, its propensity to divest itself of signification. Speech and language assail us not by legislating unwanted meanings, but rather by withholding sense, by failing to provide a final or definitive reference. Indeed, Genet's passage demonstrates how Culafroy – but Culafroy is of course a surrogate for Genet the author or narrative voice; to be sure, the text slips briefly into the first person precisely at the key moment we are about to discern[12] – fashions his phantasmagorical *quattrocento* world, populated by such figures as 'The Borgias, Astrologers, Pornographers, Princes, Abbesses, and Condottieri', precisely as a refuge from ordinary reality's endless parade of stale and empty signs. The 'logic and element of reassurance', the 'continuity' of these signs escape Culafroy; they offer only new and endless questions that vex him 'word by word'.[13]

Sartre would have Genet designing a fictional cosmos in which disparate elements of reality condense through the action of language into unified and richly meaningful ontological essences. After the aconite's effects have presumably subsided and Culafroy is returned to his mother's garden's prosaic vegetables, his historical imaginings are shorn of their signifying order, deprived of any 'episode from history or a novel' that might organize 'the dream mass' into an achieved narrative or signification. The technical botanical vocabulary leeching off the foliage – '*Datura fastuosa, Datura stramonium*, Belladonna' – are merely a 'few magic words': opaque signifiers that 'thicken the darkness'[14] rather than give form to scientific knowledge. Left forlorn in the night, Culafroy finds none of the engaging reality effect to which his Renaissance world aspired but could only haltingly achieve. The jumble of signs in the garden's dark and damp is the symptom of a reality that, stripped of daydream's romantic trappings, lacks the magical aura that could lift Divine, reminiscing about her childhood alone in a Montmartre attic, out of her depressive funk.

But perhaps the greatest drawback of Sartre's reading of *Our Lady of the Flowers* consists in its inability to appreciate how the novel takes account of its own genesis precisely as an instance of the practice of expansive but semantically subtractive image-making that it not only explores as a subject or theme, but also begins to define as a concept. Here lies an opportunity to explore the affinity of Genet's account of his own writing with the anti-narrative impetus of psychoanalytic method, which I explored in Chapter One through Freud's reading of Michelangelo's Moses statue. The practice of free association must eventually butt against the aporia of nonsense. As the following comparison should make patent, each of its pair of constitutive terms invalidates Sartre's egregious premise that the novel is a magisterial exercise in regressive, ego-based self-creation. Near the end of the novel, between Our Lady's trial and the final scenes describing Divine's death, Genet (or his narrative persona) writes about rereading himself. He sets the act of composing loosely autobiographical fiction against the desire to see his own childhood reflected back to him in the faces of the young boys he sees in the visitor's room of the prison, which stands as both biographical and textual scene of literary composition. An initial observation appears to ratify Sartre's view of a resounding literary narcissism. 'In each child I see, I try to find the child I was,'[15] Genet writes, connecting the emotion he feels to an identification not with the young boy himself, but rather with the sexually enticing man he will soon become.

A dramatic shift occurs just when the boy smiles, however, and the moment breaks decisively with the vignette's identificatory logic. By this point in the novel, Genet has spilled considerable ink portraying his/Culafroy's childhood as one blighted by social alienation and unrequited love. But: 'When the child laughed, I crumbled, so to speak, before my very eyes,' Genet attests.[16] The boy's smile becomes an emblem for the incorporation into his writing of the renunciation of the high-tragic self-dramatization through which he filters out material incommensurate with the heightened atmosphere of melodrama his prose would otherwise seek to cultivate. The resulting 'poems' allow Genet to 'free (him)self' from the compulsion to edit out of his text its 'elements of mischievousness, levity, and prankishness', only to replace them with 'properly tragic ones' that would evoke – note the histrionic capitals – 'Fear, Despair' and 'unhappy Love'.[17] Not unlike the patient in analysis, Genet becomes aware that underneath the image of the childhood of suffering he wishes to transmit to his reader/Other lies a 'second' drama, one that 'destroys' and 'falsifies' the original narrative. Remarkable here is how the distinction Genet draws between the two versions of his (character's) past is not based on their divergent contents, as if the act of poetry consisted merely in the substitution of one set of themes for another. Instead, the form itself changes or, more precisely perhaps, the form becomes de-formed. In smiling, the child with whom Genet had identified 'tears to bits the memory of a harmonious (though painful) life', forcing him to see himself 'becoming another',[18] someone other, that is, than the character he originally set out to sculpt in literary form.

Lacking somewhat in detail and rigour, this thin passage succeeds nevertheless in setting Genet on a course that will see him, over the ensuing decades, lend further refinement to a concept of poetic practice that invalidates the Sartrean reading in two fundamental and interrelated ways. First, by force of subjective will, through the overcoming of a *soi-disant* natural resistance, the Genetian poem opens itself up to what Freud called 'another scene'.[19] That is, it works to overcome the temptation to create an image of self intended to please the reader by providing them with a character with whom they can spontaneously identify. But further, on a more conceptual level, the poetic act incorporates negativity into the image, compromising its consistency and powers of unification. In the process, it also effectively de-realizes reality by exposing the image's difference from itself. In this sense, Genet's poetic act goes much further than is suggested by Didier Éribon's noble but simplistic claim that it merely transforms 'the pariahs of the world' into heroes by 'moving from shadow to light, shame to pride'.[20] For Genet, the act of poetry involves the production of an image that breaks itself up, jettisoning the harmonious unity we lend to reality through heedless romanticization, through our spontaneous idealizing reverie.

Saint Divine

It would be difficult to argue against the idea that the iconic character of Divine is the most memorable example of the poetic image in *Our Lady of the Flowers*. The passages leading up to her unspeakable crime – an act of manslaughter committed against a young child – offer key insights into Genet's struggle to formulate at this early juncture of his lifework a concept of the poetic image informed by a variety of negativity beyond mere opposition. These same passages also engage with another central Genetian motif, that of saintliness, which plays a key role in Genet's development of his idea of poetry. This notion, specifically with respect to its application to Divine, captures the contradiction at the heart of Genet's early meditations on its nature. Does Divine's saintliness consist in her acquiescence to, or rather her struggle against, the properly divine desire to sanctify her? In psychoanalytic terms, Genet's question asks after the most ethical way of confronting the problem of the Other, which here takes on the guise of a powerful and confounding demand. A close consideration of the novel's depiction of Divine's struggle with God's demand that she allow herself to be beatified will demonstrate how, at the earliest stages of his thought, Genet sets the act of poetry against the difficult dynamics of subjectivity at the turbulent meeting point of maternal jouissance and the primary, or phallic, signifier.

To set the stage, however, it will prove helpful first to return to the questions previously posed about the nature of Divine's saintliness. Perplexingly, the textual evidence points in both, seemingly contradictory, directions at once. At the outset of the passage, Genet offers his reader a generic definition: Divine's saintliness consists in 'her vision of God and, higher still, her union with Him'.[21] The divinity's spatial proximity and perceptual availability to the prospective saint are thus at the core of Genet's conception. The union of concern, however, does not 'occur without difficulty (pain) on both sides',[22] Genet specifies. Union is placed in dialectical tension with separation, the former now explicitly qualified as a source of displeasure and implicitly as the seat of ambivalence. This is where the apparent inconsistency comes to light. On the one hand, the prospect of Divine's sanctification requires her to 'give up a stable, familiar, and comfortable situation for too wondrous a glory'.[23] This implies that her earthliness or prosaic being is a state of equilibrium or rest from which rapprochement with God requires a wrenching expenditure of effort. Already, however, the presence of the adverb 'too' in Genet's phrasing hints at Divine's struggle *against* God's will to beatify her. And as it turns out, this is where the weight of the passage eventually comes down.

Indeed, it is in connection not with her acquiescence, but rather with her resistance, to God's overpowering call that we encounter Divine's curious 'gestures'. This is the key Genetian notion with which the author develops the theme of poetry's embroilment with images, understood here as appearances unmoored from any solid or reliable grounding in being. The gestures, which consist of a variety of poses 'as astounding as those of certain Japanese acrobats',[24] embody – literally – Divine's frenetic endeavour to shield herself from the magnetic power of God's will to bring her to Him. 'She made some gestures of frightful despair', Genet writes, 'other gestures of hesitation, of timid attempts to find the right way, to cling to earth and not rise to heaven'.[25] Invoked to 'keep her on earth' and 'replant her firmly in matter', these gestures are a hyperactive practice of corporealization through which Divine invents new and 'barbaric' bodily forms. Further, they transform her into a 'mad tragic actress' who, after countless intense performances, finds herself 'unable to re-enter her own personality'.[26] Divine's tussle with God is at the same time a contest with herself, a kind of harried embrace of self-alienation. The promise of divine union – impossible to ignore the acid irony of Divine's name here – now takes on the sheen of psychical death, the only alternative available being a mad arrogation of multiple personalities that enacts only the destitution of personhood and identity.

One sympathetic way of gauging Divine's corporeal contortions from the psychoanalytic perspective is to describe them as a kind of anti-hysteria. Whereas the hysteric engages in provocative acts as a means of inciting the appearance of the Father and the solemn utterance of his Law, here Divine would aim rather at His incapacitation, her wild actions designed to give physical form to God's self-division, to His estrangement from Himself. However theoretically exciting, this prospect falls short on a number of counts when the novel's broader context is taken into consideration. First, the will-to-sanctify that emanates from the divine Other wields an overwhelming gravitational force. Immediate and visceral, its presence remains unarticulated in the forms of language. Moreover, as we have already had occasion to remark, Divine's gestural response to the divine will is intensively embodied and, as such, at an equally distant remove from the signifier's logic. Second, Culafroy's childhood world in *Our Lady of the Flowers* is preponderantly maternal. On this count, the most telling narrative detail is the mention of the suicide of the father who, during the boy's early childhood, leapt 'into the green moat of the local castle'.[27] As is typical in Genet's literary world, the father's place is attenuated or absent, and even the paternal name belongs to the maternal line. Instead of a Lacanian Name-of-the-Father, more precisely, we have rather a Name-of-the-Mother's-father, the M deliberately capitalized in lieu of the F. The Genetian subject's castration is neither failed nor compromised, or at least no more significantly failed that that of any other neurotic subject. Instead, its effectivity is drawn from the mother's father's name, from where it acquires its properly feminine quality.

Obsessed with the baroque ornateness of Catholic paraphernalia, Culafroy is also left defenceless against the seductive prestige of nobility. One day coming upon an old volume on French history, he opens to a page with a turned-down corner and sees a reference to a certain Jean de Picquigny, late-medieval governor of Artois, who was involved in an attempt to rescue the imprisoned King of Navarre. Picquigny is his mother's maiden name, we are informed, and Ernestine shares her son's obsession with the upper classes, taking pride in the presumed nobility of her *nom de jeune fille*. Indeed, we are led to believe that it was she who marked off the page featuring the Picquigny reference. Not coincidentally, later in the novel we learn from court testimony that the identity of Our Lady's father is as unknown to himself as it is to the civil record. Here begins a long series of Genetian textual worlds in which the paternal figure is marginal, even if, as is the case here, the father's name does manage to make its presence felt, albeit in connection with the mother's genealogical line.

Viewed through an analytic lens, Divine's showdown with God's will counts as evidence for the difficulty of negotiating the Other's presence when the paternal signifier thanks to which the subject creates distance for itself from maternal jouissance is not absent per se, but rather confined to the mother's orbit, proximate to the force of her demand. Genet's narrator makes clear that Divine would rather die than succumb to what he describes, quite literally, as a sort of holy suction, God here figuring as a giant, insatiable and distinctively maternal, vacuum appliance that only the most extreme acts of self-defence could repel. For Divine, there are only two options: a 'saintly', properly perverse self-instrumentalization aiming at the transformation of the God-mother's mysterious desire into a stern but obeyable command to enjoy; or else the raving recourse to the gesture, by which Divine seems fated to an exhausting life of athletic, frenetically embodied performances. This is indeed the second possible sympathetic psychoanalytic reading, in my view the more convincing of the two: Divine's gestures aim not at fending off hysterical desire, but rather at circumventing the structure of perversion. At any rate, Divine fails in her efforts: 'Finally, one day, when she wasn't expecting it … God took her and made her a saint'.[28] And now Divine finds herself confronted with two fresh, but hardly more auspicious, options: suicide or a variety of acting out, the former surely merely another version of the latter.

Here is where the reader comes upon the novel's pivotal moment when Divine removes the wire netting across her ninth-floor balcony, knowing that her neighbour's two-year-old girl will soon scamper there to consider the view, only to fall off into the void to her ghastly, premature death. The novel's readers will know that this is indeed what transpires, with the result that, in the wake of her dreadful act, Divine's 'goodness' is now 'dead'.[29] Certain that her crime is 'inexpiable', her person irredeemable, Divine decides henceforth to harden herself and 'be bad', becoming 'indifferent' to the world and slowly 'dying'.[30] Remarkably, this is the text's penultimate account of Divine before the final flashbacks to her childhood and the scenes at her wake that bring the novel to its conclusion. Indeed, *Our Lady of the Flowers* seems unhappy with Divine's decision, disappointed by her inability to persevere with her defensive gestures. 'She wanted to kill herself', we read, 'to kill my kindness',[31] the first-person pronoun signalling the diegetic author's sense of distance from the development of his own literary creation.

Indeed, the jarring intrusion of the first person in the form of the possessive article reintroduces the matter, foregrounded repeatedly in the novel, of the relation between authorial creativity and narrative events. It is as if Genet, invalidating once again Sartre's main thesis, wished to limit his own imaginative power by inserting into the text a disjunction between his own desire and the destiny of his central character. Genet's narrative voice implicitly places itself on God's side, waiting expectantly for Divine's acceptance of her beatification, only to see her refuse his authorial generosity, committing instead the vilest of crimes. As readers, however, we cannot but wonder why there could not have been a third option for Divine, an alternative to the implacably binary dilemma of either self-immolation in divine-maternal jouissance or the dismal embrace of unspeakable evil. How, then, are we to account for the text's strange, self-sabotaging recourse to this melodramatic, high-tragic narrative outcome, the very same tragic sensibility it wants, on another level, unreservedly to condemn?

The answer lies perhaps in what I have already claimed with respect to Divine's experience of God's demand, namely the fact that it is so visceral in nature, carrying none of the opacity or ambiguity that comes along with linguistic articulation, with discourse or speech. The Other's unmediated, claustrophobic proximity also determines the highly corporealized nature of Divine's gestural response. Here it becomes essential to recall the distinction between Genet's authorial voice and the character of Divine. The novel – or more precisely, the act of its composition as reflexively featured in the narrative discourse itself, indexed here by Genet's inclusion of the possessive 'my' – is effectively the act of sublimation by which the former separates off from the latter precisely through the creative medium of literature.[32] If I were more concerned with Genet's biographical life than with his text, I might even wish to claim that the act of composing the novel in conditions of incarceration is the means by which Genet the biographical person works out, in a fashion parallel to the psychoanalytic process, his own problematic psychical proximity to maternal jouissance. This would take place through the literary reinforcement of the (here 'maternalized') paternal signifier, now strong enough to break through its encrustation of enjoyment.

Returning to firmer literary-critical ground, Divine's failure to resist the pull of God's will is a paradoxical gesture of mourning thanks to which Genet can abandon the binary, and in this sense unified, moral universe of good and evil in which Divine apprehends her options for action, choosing instead what becomes the definitive Genetian world, the one that comes to define his lifework. In this world, appearances are not only cut off from any stable grounding in being. Further, they are rendered precarious by the void around which they are required to circulate, and which prevents them from achieving even a modicum of consistency, indeed of reaching any state of accomplished realization.

This is the interpretative light in which the final, otherwise confusingly unmotivated passages of *Our Lady of the Flowers* should be read. In the midst of recounting Ernestine's visit to Paris to witness the death of her now-daughter, the narrator brusquely intervenes in the first person to recount his experience of 'revelation' in a Yugoslav prison, the diaphanous transition between the two seemingly unrelated textual circumstances being Ernestine's revelatory vision of 'God gulping down an egg' at the hour of Divine's death.[33] The narrative voice recounts an experience of incarceration in the company of a group of Romani (the now-pejorative 'gypsies' [*tziganes*] in the text) 'who had organized a school for pickpockets' inside the prison.[34] To demonstrate their prowess, students take turns delicately removing and replacing objects from the pockets of a sleeping prisoner. When his turn comes, Genet's nerves get the better of him and he faints. Regaining consciousness, he finds himself squatting in a corner of the cell with his fellow inmates opposite pointing and laughing, one of them 'scratch(ing) his hair and, as if he had pulled out a louse, mak(ing) a show of eating it'.[35] Reassuring the reader that the object in his hair was most certainly a flake of dandruff rather than a louse, the narrator launches into a complex meditation that sees him understand, 'for a fraction of a second', what he calls 'the essence' of the prison cell, itself posited as a 'prison of the world'.[36]

The evanescent insight couples the experience of a loss of consciousness and the ensuing exile 'to the confines of the obscene'[37] with the activities of the Romani men, more specifically 'the role they were *playing*' by honing their pickpocketing skills. Trickery and subterfuge, ludic performativity, the 'supernatural' emergence of the empty space left behind by the stolen object, 'detachment from the human', the idea of obscenity (literally 'the off-scene of the world'[38]): collectively, these motifs spell out the narrator's discovery of a kind of ontological fault line that deforms and separates reality from itself, with the consequence that consciousness is beset by negativity and the world becomes haunted by an inherent, indwelling otherness at once itself and not. The ontological significance of the passage becomes less of a literary-critical flight of fancy as the narrator explicitly qualifies this 'role' played by his cellmates as situated 'at the origin of the world', indeed as being this origin ('this role *was* the origin of the world'[39]). In the beginning, as it were, there was what amounts to an act of ontological pickpocketing by which a piece of being was absconded. This act of subterfuge hollows out a void, depriving being of both fullness and consistency. Crucial to specify here is how the making-incomplete of being occurs not only without our knowledge, but also without the knowledge of being itself.

Genet's novel brings an additional crucial nuance to this observation, however. While being may go on in blissful ignorance of the fault line that divides it from itself, the human subject for its part is capable, 'thanks to a kind of extraordinary lucidity', of apprehending, however fleetingly, how 'the world dwindle(s) (*se réduisit*)', as Genet puts it, 'and its mystery too'.[40] Though the poetic practice by means of which this lucidity may be accessed is fundamentally a question for Genet of subjective will, the novel also suggests that an experience of social marginalization – figured in my upcoming example as homophobia – can function as an effective catalyst.

The narrator compares the 'supernatural' sensation of 'detachment' occasioned by the world's decomposition to his encounter with a warrant officer in a Parisian prison who, forced 'to write a report on (the narrator's) sexual practices', finds himself unable to utter the word 'homosexual', indeed even to touch the word printed on the documents on the desk in front of him. Because the signifier indexing his sexual identity is repressed in the discourse of the Law's representative, the narrator is granted privileged access to the abject zone of ontological incompletion, gaining in the process a liberating, if also harrowing, apprehension of what Lacan calls the barred Other, that is the symbolic 'order' revealed as inconsistent, disordered. We can also make a more general point here about Genet's early fascination with the Parisian demimonde depicted in *Our Lady of the Flowers*. Yes, this is indeed the sort of locale in which the author lived his early years of nomadic vagabondage, and so there is some truth in the notion that he is writing, as they say, what he knows. But the seedy lanes and louche joints of wartime Montmartre also figure the point of convolution in Paris's otherwise unmarred bourgeois ontology, haunting its monuments to cultural identity and imperial power, and subverting its claims to respectability from within.

We left Divine defeated by her uniformly binary, imaginary world of good and evil. In its final pages, however, *Our Lady of the Flowers* offers, in its idiosyncratically imagistic way, a glimpse at the inherent or immanent negativity that Genet will further develop and complexify in his future work. Divine comes to the realization on her deathbed 'that death had always been present in life'.[41] Her observation could be dismissed as hackneyed were it not immediately followed by this extravagant, quintessentially Genetian, image: death's

> symbolic face had been hidden by a kind of mustache which adjusted its ghastly reality to current taste – that Frankish mustache which, once soldierly, now falling from the scissors, made it look as sheepish as a castrato, for its face at once grew gentle and delicate, pale, with a tiny chin and rounded forehead, like the face of a female saint on Romanesque stained glass or a Byzantine empress, a face we are accustomed to seeing capped with a veiled hennin.[42]

Unhelpfully, Bernard Frechtman's otherwise-laudable translation obscures the identity of the antecedent of the pronoun 'it', which in the original French refers plainly to the soldier, present as a noun there only to become a mere adjective in the unfortunate English rendering. This is to say more simply that the original conveys a clear image of transformation by which a distinctively butch, Teutonically moustachioed military man is in no uncertain terms feminized, softened, de-phallicized and also importantly veiled under a hennin, an early Renaissance headdress in the shape of a towering cone. Here we find an early, important association – only to gain in strength as Genet's oeuvre progresses – of the practice of poetic image-making with femininity, and more specifically with the feminization of a man. In this, Genet anticipates Lacan's insight about how the image of virility is in fact a manifestation of femininity on the level of its embrace of the inconsistent multiplicity of appearances released from their grounding in a false construal of coherent, fully present being. To fully confront the fault in being and gain the experience of reality's 'dwindling', one must sever the obfuscating link between masculine identity and the premise of an exception to castration, which in the present context we can view as an exception to the rule that every appearance is required to weigh its ontological anchor.

Feminine sexuation against gender theory

This reference to the specifically feminine character of Genet's ontology will benefit from a survey of Lacan's groundbreaking work on sexual difference and will serve to support future discussions of that topic in this book. After 1968, Lacan's teaching turns with renewed focus to this question, and more specifically to the controversial topic – both within psychoanalysis and without – of feminine sexuality. Lacan's innovation consists in his application of the rigour of logical formalization, explored in the previous chapter, to what has no doubt proven to be the most original, challenging and consequential element in all of Freudian theory. Lacan bases his theory of sexual difference on the insight that there is a direct correspondence between those premodern and prescientific cosmologies that place man at the centre of a coherent and fully formed universe and the resistance to the properly Freudian contention that there is an inherent discontinuity, a radical disjunction, between the sexes that renders them inherently non-complementary. In short, the myth of the unified cosmos is a displacement of the illusion that man and woman combine to form a unique whole. Lacan further insists that sexuation – the determination of a subject's being as either masculine or feminine – is ordained by the subject's relation to the signifier rather than by some innate anatomical, biophysiological, genetic or evolutionary predisposition.

On the manifest level at least, Freud's writing had characterized the castration and Oedipus complexes – the psychic structures responsible in his view for situating human sexuality in the field of culture – as reflections of a statically conceived nuclear kinship structure characteristic of bourgeois European modernity. By contrast, Lacan takes these same structures to refer instead to the split in the subject occasioned by the ambivalence with which they accept the transcendental determinants of sexuate being. The bourgeois family matrix around which sexual difference operates in the Freudian texts becomes, in the later Lacan, two asymmetrical pairs of logical expressions that qualify a fundamental, abstractly conceived 'phallic function'. This function stands for the invincible castrative condition of subjectivity for the speaking animal; the inseparability of acculturation, in other words, from an unconscious experience of radical loss.

More cleanly than Freud, Lacan comes to sever the father's symbolic function from both the real of genetically defined paternity and the imaginary ideals of masculinity that this or that culture associates with fatherhood. Notoriously for many, Freud had connected the representation of the interdiction marking the masculine subject's accession to language with the penis, more specifically with the prospect of its loss; further, he qualified a particular response to the feminine variety of castration in terms of envy for that same male organ. With his widely misconstrued concept of the phallus, Lacan rather emphasizes the abstract symbolic function of a privileged signifier in the unconscious that stands in for the loss of the subject's position as the privileged object of the mother's love, the loss that catalyses desire properly speaking. In this light, the phallus is the signifier chosen by the unconscious to account for the fact that there is no final signifier (for maternal desire), no means of forming a series of signifiers into a self-enclosed chain that would stabilize the process of signification once and for all. Lacan allows that the phallic image gains its privileged status by virtue of the way the erect male organ figures a possibility for fertilization and conception. Though in this sense only there exists a contingent imaginary link between them, the phallus is finally irreducible to the penis.

By the early 1970s, Lacan had reformulated his phallus concept in complex logical terms as the function by which the normative neurotic subject – masculine or feminine, there is no other – struggles to come to terms with the real of sexual difference; with the uncomfortable fact, that is, that *il n'y a pas de rapport sexuel* (there is no sexual rapport or relation), as he famously claims.[43] Despite the existence of two different (psychical rather than biological) sexes, there is only one signifier available to represent both. This means that there is no one-to-one, symmetrical relation between the elements of masculinity and femininity. Symbolically, the only way to represent the real of sexual difference is by marking the presence or absence of an imaginary phallus, with the proviso that in the symbolic order even presence becomes indissociable from lack. (The Freudian boy's penis functions psychically as an object that can be removed; for Lacan, the phallic subject paradoxically lacks lack.) The corollary is that feminine being is determined by the absence of an alternative signifier to the phallus to represent the difference of femininity. In this precise sense, femininity is characterized by difference as such: not a difference *from* phallic sexuality, but rather an inherent difference within. In consequence, femininity manifests as a certain groundless proliferation of representation or appearance; a disordering through infinitization, as it were, of the (phallic) symbolic order. From the Lacanian perspective, any reactive or compensatory project in the vein of Luce Irigaray's, for example, to create a distinctively feminine signifier for the unconscious is a misleading and ultimately doomed example of feminist ideology, which can only impede the psychoanalytic effort properly to theorize sexual difference.[44]

Articulated through an unconventional application of predicate logic, Lacan's somewhat-notorious formulas of sexuation represent his attempt to bring formal rigour to Freud's efforts to distinguish what he called the girl's version of castration from the boy's. With Lacan's formulas, sexual difference becomes a pure question of enunciation, more specifically of the two possible ways in which spoken or written language, and the knowledge to which this language gives form, can only fail to render the real of sex, which as such does not avail itself of the signifier. Clinically, the only legitimate criterion for judging how any particular subject unconsciously places themselves with respect to sexual difference is what this subject says in speech. In this light, the analyst is obliged to abstract completely from what contemporary theory would no doubt call the patient's gender identity or gender performance, cleanly distinguishing between its gender identifications and the real of its unconscious sex. All of our efforts to symbolize sexual difference through the mechanism of gender norms or any other means always fail. For Lacanians, gender identity, no matter how normative, fluid or non-binary, can only be a symptomatic manifestation of the non-existence of the sexual relation, and as such it must always be subjected to properly analytic interpretation.

In his formulas for sexual difference, Lacan writes two symbolic expressions for each sex. Each expression is composed of a quantifier (universal $\forall$ or existential $\exists$) and a predicate (the phallic function per se Φx, designating the speaking mammal's castrated condition), and each of these is either affirmed or negated. The first logical moment of masculine sexuation posits an exception to the phallic function, which is then immediately followed by an assertion of the function's lack of exception. In short, Lacan interprets the Freudian boy's Oedipus complex as implying the existence of an exception to the rule of castration and his castration complex as an antithetical affirmation of the universality of castration. As per convention in predicate logic, the negation that distinguishes the masculine Oedipus complex ('there is a subject who is not subject to the phallic function') works on the predicate, in other words on the phallic function itself. The logic at work involves a contradiction, and it is based on an Aristotelian, intuitively convincing, totalized field of possibility for masculine being in which the castration of all subjects is grounded in that castration's singular, constitutive exception. In brief, all masculine subjects can be assembled together in a group by virtue of what they all, in common, lack: the unimpeded sexual access to *all women* enjoyed by Freud's mythical primal father, who remains in this sense ineradicably present in the masculine unconscious. Put differently, the masculine subject's acceptance of castration must be accompanied by the presence of a contradictory belief at the level of the unconscious, which is simply another way of stating that masculine subjectivity is always and by definition minimally fetishistic.

Things become logically less conventional as we move to the girl's, or rather the feminine subject's, formulas. On this side of sexual difference, both logical expressions feature a novel negation not of the phallic function itself, but rather of the quantifier that specifies it. Freud argued for the subjective priority of the castration complex for the girl; unlike the boy, she sees that she is castrated 'in a flash', as he summarily wrote.[45] Lacan expresses this always-already feature of feminine castration via a double negation, first of the existential quantifier ('there is no subject') and then of the predicate ('who is not subject to the phallic function').

From the perspective of predicate logic, however, Lacan's more consequential innovation comes in the expression he writes to capture the feminine version of the Oedipus complex. While Freud had controversially linked the girl's castration with penis envy and the desire for a baby, Lacan chooses instead to connect feminine sexuation with a certain tradition of mystical writing and a form of ecstatic being separated from knowledge, which he places in dialogue with Heidegger's notion of *ek-sistence*.[46] By negating the universal quantifier ('*not-all* subjects are ...'), Lacan forces open the classical universe of discourse that comprises the intellectual cosmos of traditional predicate logic. With his novel motif of the *pas-toute*, he insists that feminine being, in addition to its involvement in a sexuality that can only ever be phallic, participates in an alterity that, though certainly not *non-phallic* and in this sense complementary to masculinity, immanently de-totalizes phallic sexuality. If the logic of masculinity is one of contradiction, femininity introduces indeterminacy and undecidability to the phalllic law, in so doing disjoining a distinctively feminine quantum of jouissance from all possible forms of knowledge, since there is no knowledge that is not phalllic in Lacan's psychoanalytic view.

In this light we can better appreciate the reason why, when Lacan asseverates provocatively that feminine subjects, in speaking or writing of their distinctive jouissance, 'don't know what they're saying',[47] he is far from issuing another in a long line of stupid claims about women's inherent deficiency with respect to the workings of reason. What he is doing instead is insisting on the unknowable *ek-sistence* of an enjoyment essential to feminine being that questions, without however violating, the terms of the phallic law. As sympathetic feminist commentators have often repeated,[48] Lacan's deliberately inconsistent logic of femininity does not banish its subjects from the symbolic order, relegating them to some secondary status before speech or thought. Rather, by inhabiting this order so fully as to challenge its consistency, and therefore its very status as an order, feminine being exposes masculine phallic sexuality to its inherent contingency and inadequacy. At the same time, however, femininity proves incapable of offering an alternative to the phallic regime, which differentially and unconditionally underwrites both forms of sexuation.

In sum, femininity is caught between the assertion that phallic knowledge is incomplete and the impossibility of offering an alternative knowledge that would be distinctively other-than-phallic. For all its seeming logical exoticism, Lacan's formalization of sexual difference elegantly conveys how the desire for a less elusive and knowable feminine essence is ultimately a construction of a properly masculine fantasy. Indeed, this misogynistic construction is one of the psychical mechanisms by which the masculine subject can displace his libidinal investment in Freud's primal father, that subject who enjoys unlimited sexual access to *all women*, onto a singular and fetishistic fantasy-figure of Woman as such – an *all-Woman*, if you will. Though this is not a term that Lacan himself used, it is a possible translation of a phrase used by Genet in *Our Lady of the Flowers*, as we will soon discover below.

Lacan's insistence on theorizing femininity as an alterity within the phallic order rather than as an entirely distinct non-phallic sexuality casts suggestive light on the familiar theme of gender performance first introduced by Judith Butler in the 1990s and still a dominant feature of gender and feminist discourses today.[49] As psychoanalyst Joan Riviere argued almost a century ago, femininity for psychoanalysis is always and only a masquerade, a performance for which there is no script, no original, no foundation, no term of reference.[50] Behind the infinity of possible appearances of femininity there lies no reality, no truth other than the absence of feminine identity – the lack, to be precise, of either a phallus or else some feminine alternative. Where gender theory attributes this lack of ground to gender generically conceived, however, psychoanalysis insists on seeing sexual difference: gender performativity is an attribute of a specifically feminine variety of being-in-the-world. The novel, unfamiliar corollary, of course, is that masculinity is not performative. This implies in turn that the performance of masculinity – take the iconic Tom of Finland imagery from gay culture as an example – is from the psychoanalytic perspective a specifically feminine phenomenon. The glamorous (or faded, in the case of Divine) drag queen and the macho leather man, strictly opposed to one another when viewed through the lens of both gender identity and identity-subverting gender theory, are for psychoanalysis precisely equivalent manifestations of the baseless and scattered multiplicity of feminine being.

Seeing through the phallus

Divine is again the key figure through which Genet introduces into his writing the distinctively feminine ontology that will go on to structure his literary world in its entirety. A pivotal passage of *Our Lady of the Flowers* signals the moment when Culafroy abandons the infantile, and potentially perverse, position vis-à-vis the Other to embrace the essential groundlessness of feminine being. Not coincidentally, the narrator explicitly associates this variety of sexuate subjectivity with a shift from heterosexual to homosexual desire. The scene is set in Montmartre's famous rue Lepic. Divine is following behind Seck Gorgui and Notre Dame after a night of revelry; she is jealous of the couple's newfound love and beset by melancholy at her exclusion. When Gorgui allows her to climb into the taxi before him, Divine is surprised, since 'a pimp never effaces himself before a woman'.[51]

The reader then witnesses Divine's extended meditation, replete with retrograde ideas of gender, on the difference between the sexes. Though she feels herself to be a woman, Divine must draw from her biological masculinity in situations requiring thought or action. Thought is indeed 'an act' according to Divine, and 'in order to act, you have to discard frivolity and set your idea on a solid base'. And because she views the image of solidity as indissociable from 'virility', Divine can only live out her femininity 'through her submission to the imperious male'. Thus, in her own mind, Divine finally is 'not a woman'.[52] Far from representing a gesture of gentlemanly masculinity, then, Gorgui's act of granting Divine first entry into the taxi not only compromises her picture of him as an ideal embodiment of the male sex, but also limits her capacity to experience her own being as a woman.

Divine's reactionary relegation of femininity to a realm beyond thought and action is a clear manifestation of the patriarchal mindset that Simone de Beauvoir would mercilessly skewer in *The Second Sex* just a few years after the publication of Genet's novel. In this light, gender theory *à la* Divine is a spectacularly inauspicious departure point for a discussion of Genet's enlistment of a certain idea of femininity for his practice of poetic image-making. Importantly, however, the ensuing passage sheds critical retrospective light on Divine's ideas, and it provides an opportunity to link more rigorously Genet's discourse of the feminine with the psychoanalytic theory of sexual difference. In fact, Divine's false notion of femininity corresponds exactly to what Lacan called *La femme*, the one who does not exist. Even more importantly, Genet's text sketches out how this version of femininity – a properly hysterical response to a neurotic masculine fantasy of Woman as determinate essence or unified totality – can be transformed into the feminine modality of being that informs his doctrine of the poetic act.

The crucial passage begins with the scene suddenly shifting from that taxi at the bottom of rue Lepic to another sudden flashback to Divine's childhood as Culafroy. As we have just considered, Divine cannot fully consider herself a woman due to her non-conformity with the qualities of gender she associates with the female sex. We learn the identity of the exemplar of authentic femininity against which Divine judges herself deficient through the narrator's relation of Culafroy's early heterosexual attachment to a village girl named Solange, in whom he found – in a phrase that resonates contrarily when set against Lacan's *pas-toute* – 'all of woman (*toute la femme*)'.[53] The boy's love for Solange blossoms during stifling summer afternoons spent in conversation in the shade of a viburnum, their thoughts and feelings flowing seamlessly between them. This idyllic intimacy is complicated, however, by the presence of the Grotto Rock, a granite outcrop saturated in phobic local folklore to which the young couple makes terrified pilgrimages and whose phallic attributes are almost comedically highlighted in the text. Adding to the borderline mock-tragic tone, the narrator adds a 'gathering storm' to the scene when, one summer evening, the children approach the monolith, which advances towards them 'like a prow through a sea of golden crops with glints of blue'.[54] The atmosphere is thickly, excessively romantic, marked by fir trees that evoke 'the charm of winter nights … gypsy musicians and vendors of postcards'; Culafroy even expects to find amid their swaying branches 'a miraculous virgin … made of colored plaster'.[55]

The dark and stormy night reaches its melodramatic apogee with Solange's sombre prognostication that, within a year's time, a man will commit suicide by throwing himself off the rock. Possessed by her fanciful imaginings, Solange weaves a 'complicated and cunning' 'Japanese drama' around the prospective event, adding the curiously picturesque detail that the suicide will be 'a pig dealer returning from the fair'.[56] While Solange's queer narrative at first only heightens the young couple's pious reverence for the outcropping's occult powers, Culafroy begins to doubt his paramour's clairvoyance as the deadline begins to approach. And when it finally passes, he discovers their relationship entirely transformed:

> At once (Culafroy) realized that (Solange) belonged to a world different from his. She was no longer a part of him. She had won her independence; this little girl was now like those works that have long since dropped away from their author: no longer being directly flesh of his flesh, they no longer benefit from his maternal tenderness. Solange had become like one of those chilled excrements which Culafroy used to deposit at the foot of the garden wall among the currant bushes. When they were still warm, he took a tender delight in their odor, but he spurned them with indifference – at times with horror – when they had too long since ceased to be part of himself.[57]

Culafroy is barely recognizable to himself; all the charm of his connection with Solange has been lost forever. For her part, Solange is emancipated from Culafroy's incorporative, 'maternal' presence, her excremental abjection the proof that she will never be part of him again. Genet's narrator makes clear that the source of Culafroy's newfound disgust is the revelation that the Other can be duplicitous, unreliable; that fellow creatures 'can play at not being what they are',[58] just as he does himself. No longer capable of considering himself 'an exceptional creature', Culafroy's amorous attention shifts from Solange to Alberto, the village hoodlum, who now represents to him 'all the marvelousness of the external'.[59] What had been a hermetic intimacy separate from, and invisible to, village life becomes a more socialized desire inscribed within the tension between respectability and ostracism, law and transgression.

In psychoanalytic terms, Culafroy's discovery of Solange's limitations triggers a renewed experience of castration. No doubt the repugnance he now feels for the girl is a projection of the revulsion he feels for the object he has now himself become for the Other's desire. The failure of Solange's prediction reveals an inconsistency or gap in discourse that subverts Culafroy's pretensions to exceptionality, to being at one with the Other. The realization of the exception's illegitimacy, the decisive split between being and acting (i.e. 'playing at not being what you are'), alongside the expropriative casting off of the phallus to the realm of 'the external', together lend to the boy's castration its distinctively feminine quality. Indeed, the association with femininity is explicitly present in the text itself: through these occurrences, we read, Culafroy suddenly discovers 'one of the facets of feminine glitter'.[60] Moreover, and not unrelatedly, the narrator assures us that after Culafroy's involvement with Solange comes to its conclusion, Divine will never have 'any other experience with a woman'.[61] Now psychically aligned with the gap between discourse and the real revealed by the failure of Solange's strange prediction, Culafroy/Divine will struggle from now on with the challenge posed by feminine being: Will she embrace the groundless proliferation of inconsistent appearances through which the essence of femininity becomes identical to its lack of an essence? Or alternatively, will she succumb to the temptation of hysteria or perversion, aiming either to incarnate femininity's secret in the figure of the impossible Woman, or acquiesce passively to the divine demand for saintly adherence to His omnipotent will?

We can return to the scene of Divine's deathbed for clues that point in the former alternative's less inauspicious direction. In the novel's final flashback, we are transported back in time to the funeral of Culafroy's old cousin Adeline. The passage is narrated as a kind of mock-epic journey that sees the young boy conquer his fear of death by weaving his way through the crowd of mourners towards the room where lies the old woman's corpse. The episode reads as an encounter, and attempt to reconcile, with the ontological fault-line signified by death. Setting out into the crowd already 'more dead than alive', he is met with a concatenation of souls and 'shades' which, rising 'up from the beginnings of the world', form 'an immense, a numerous cortege'.[62] The atmosphere is quintessential early Genet: theatrical images of religious faith become luxuriant evocations of artifice. Indeed, Culafroy advances towards Adeline's corpse as he would the sugared almonds his mother brings back from a baptism or wedding; the nuts are 'a sacred food, a symbol of purity' to be regarded as if they were 'white wax orange blossoms … under a glass globe'.[63]

As is routinely observed, Genet's prose revels in the aesthetic seductions of the trappings of faith to the point where the elements of ceremony and ritual are entirely cut off from any semblance of authentic religious feeling or even of a convincing lifeworld. All that remains is the void, conjoined uncannily with the 'truth' mutely embodied by Adeline's corpse. As we saw at the conclusion of the previous chapter, the putative consistency of being is subverted by a strange quasi-object that brings together excess and lack. 'Death creates a vacuum otherwise and better than an air pump', the narrator tells us, and at Culafroy's approach the inanimate body is revealed to be 'fecundated' with a kind of supernumerary 'reality'[64] that de-realizes everything around it.

Being having been revealed as discontinuous, discourse is shown to be as well. The world of culture giving meaning to reality turns out to be a sham. When Culafroy touches Adeline's face, he is invaded 'by a disorderly troop of memories of readings and stories he had heard'.[65] The example provided is drawn from the story of Bernadette Soubirous, the Pyrénées teenager whose visions of the Virgin Mary in the mid-nineteenth century led to the commemorative construction of the notoriously gaudy Sanctuary of Our Lady of Lourdes. Though, at the hour of Bernadette's death, the room was 'full of the scent of invisible violets', Culafroy fails to smell beside his cousin's body 'the odor that is said to be the odor of sanctity'. The moment turns out to be portentous, 'the starting point of the thread that was to lead Culafroy-Divine, in accordance with a superlatively devised fatality, to death'.[66] The narrator sets Culafroy's moment of disillusionment within 'remote, misty, opaque ages, when he belonged to the people of the gods, exactly like the primitives, who have not yet been unswaddled of their urine-scented wrappings'.[67] Having seen the senseless lump of his cousin's dead body, however, Culafroy has to exit the fullness of this antediluvian world. Now he possesses the 'knowledge' that will lead him on the path of 'the exactly poetic vision of the world'. This vision features a foundational absence that deprives reality of its haptic solidity. Here the 'joyous rebound' triggered by contact with empirical objects exists no longer; the boy's 'blindly scrutinizing little finger' happens upon 'emptiness' instead. Moreover, doors open of their own accord to reveal only 'nothing'.[68]

It is a measure of Genet's precocious maturity as an artist-thinker that, instead of delivering some ultimate reconciliation with the paradoxical excess-absence of death, Culafroy's fateful encounter with his cousin's body forces him rather to dig up a compensatory memory with unmistakably phallic features. To be sure, these final pages of *Our Lady of the Flowers* evoke an experience akin to Lacan's notion of subjective destitution which, during a period in the latter stages of his teaching, heralds the moment in analysis when the patient must withstand the collapse of their universe of meaning and confront the ego-shattering unconscious fantasy that unwittingly structures their world. As Lacan in the final stages began increasingly to emphasize, however, this moment of evanescent and traumatic unworlding is unsustainable; to regain a viable psychic life, the subject must return to the structure that sustains desire by keeping the fantasy in its more or less manageable state of repression. The clinical wager, however, is that this can take place in a way that grants both a newfound awareness of the fantasy's obfuscatory world-mending function and a weakened disinclination to 'traverse' the fantasy, to use Lacan's term, in other words to follow the logic of desire to its shattering conclusion.

This is indeed how we should read the novel's presentation of the post-traumatic 'Memory' (note the capitalization) that comes to Culafroy's 'rescue' at his moment of desperation beside his cousin's corpse:

> As a man who, through some unexpected privilege, has caught a glimpse of the very heart of the mysteries, quickly looks away so as to regain his footing on earth, so the terror-stricken Culafroy flung himself, burying his head, into the warm, enveloping memory of Alberto's trousers, where he thought to find, to his relief, comforting broods of titmice.[69]

Having reached this ultimate point not of illusory disillusionment, but rather of disillusioned illusion, there is nothing left for the novel to do than to return to the narrative first person, to 'Genet' writing in prison the night before the fateful hearing that may or may not condemn him to a long prison sentence. Culafroy's 'glimpse at the very heart of the mysteries' has had a similarly liberating effect on the author, who writes: 'I no longer belong to the prison. Broken is the fraternity that bound me to the men of the tomb. Perhaps I shall live'.[70] This evocation of broken fraternity bears witness to the sublimation of enjoyment by which the narrator gains independence from the illicit compacts that subject the prisoners to the insidious power dynamics of life under incarceration.

Relatedly, the loosening of the ties that bind the narrator to the defensive and phobic currents of what we call life provides a newfound creative impetus that will enable him to 'refashion new lives for Darling, Divine, Our Lady and Gabriel'.[71] *Our Lady of the Flowers* leaves us with a memorable image lifted from a letter addressed to Divine, written from prison by Darling, his first Parisian love. Like no other in the novel, it condenses what is most essential to the Genetian poetic image, namely its seductive but nonetheless revelatory juxtaposition of desiring aspiration and abyssal absence, at once concealing and revealing the fundamental incompletion of being. At the end of his letter, Darling asks its addressee to identify the shape made out by a dotted line drawn just under the valediction. Probably, you will not need to have read the novel to have guessed what this shape is designed to figure. Sure enough, the narrator informs us that 'the dotted line that Darling refers to is the outline of his prick'.[72] It will not be an exercise in over-interpretation to draw attention, in this final remark, to the fact that Darling's sketch is an outline. In agreement with psychoanalysis, Genet would intend this detail to suggest that if the fantasy that protects us from being overwhelmed by the incompletion of being is ineradicable, it may still be possible, through acts of sublimation literary and otherwise, to learn to see through it.

3

The phallus unveiled: The Balcony

A gigantic phallus

At a pivotal but underappreciated moment of the final scene of Genet's canonical play *The Balcony*, the Chief of Police, long suffering from the absence of his likeness from the erotic set-pieces performed in the eponymous brothel, announces with trepidation that he has been advised to appear within its confines 'in the form of a gigantic phallus, a prick (*chibre*) of great stature'.[1] When the Judge, one of three classical figures of authority who have long since benefitted from representation in the brothel, expresses scepticism about the feasibility of such a costume, the Queen's envoy responds reassuringly: new techniques in the rubber industry have made its production eminently possible, he explains; only the Church's potential objections cast doubt on the chief's otherwise-entirely plausible notion. As is evident even from this cursory overview, the moment is comical, farcical even, and it brings to mind Lacan's association of the phallus's role in sexuality with comedy's foregrounding of appearances – or what Genet calls 'seeming (*paraître*)'[2] – a topic that any casual reader of the play will immediately recognize as central to its concerns.

On the level of the action, however, the ridiculous phallic image seems to have little consequence. Though subsequent goings-on have no evident causal link to it, the chief's strange idea has the benefit of suggesting, insightfully if unintentionally, that the exposure or unveiling of the phallus in the visible world is always a comedic moment, one that activates a potential energy, a subversive momentum, that can trigger transformation if it is not immediately contained.³ If the choice to conjure the image of a police chief dressed as a giant phallus provokes laughter, however, Genet's play as a whole cannot be described as a simple comedy. Indeed, it foregrounds and scrutinizes the peculiar solemnity characteristic of the resistance to that impetus towards change. The uneasy, equivocal tone of *The Balcony* is stretched provocatively across comedy and (mock or ironic) high seriousness. In the scene concerned, the momentary hilarity of the phallus episode gives way to the concluding ceremonial earnestness with which Roger, erstwhile Hero of the revolution, makes his sacrifice and enters the mausoleum, icon of the old social order's decisive and disappointing restoration.

This chapter explores how the image of *The Balcony*'s Chief of Police dressed as a giant phallus is the misconstrued key to its optimal interpretation. Drawing on, but also moving beyond, the invaluable readings of philosopher Alain Badiou and Jacques Lacan in their respective seminars, I suggest that the image of the costume condenses the play's extraordinarily insightful, and still eminently relevant, examination of the functioning of ideology in the visible world: the link between the realm of appearances and the failure of social change. In other words, *The Balcony* is a play about the upholding of the political status quo framed as the failure to acknowledge ontological incompletion.⁴ The figure of the phallus costume is the poetic act through which Genet's play exposes the non-occurrence of the social transformation that might have taken place; it destabilizes the political restoration with which the play concludes by kicking away the ground of (false) ontological consistency on which it rests. Further, in a more properly historical sense, the play allegorizes ideology's workings at a late modern historical juncture when spontaneous identification with, and allegiance to, traditional authority figures is no longer possible. To be sure, it anticipates with uncanny prescience the political culture of today's liberal democracies in crisis, where increasingly large constituencies of citizens demand leaders who appear as economically aspirational versions of their own selves: persons who look and behave exactly as we would if only we were exempt from the limitations that stand between us and the fantasmatic happiness to which we aspire.

The contemporary moment has only further demonstrated the value of Genet's insight. As the *paraître* of traditional forms of leadership – embodied in the play by Bishop (church), Judge (judiciary) and General (military) – begins to appear ridiculous, the people turn to false rebels, alternative figures whose political purchase is grounded contrarily on impudence, in other words on the rejection of the very authority they must also claim hypocritically in order to realize their reactionary political agendas. *The Balcony*'s eminently psychoanalytic insight is that social power, in a world of speaking subjects alienated in and by language, is inherently, internally split. Because power's official symbolic embodiment is haunted by a disturbing stain of jouissance that compromises its popular legitimacy, the citizen becomes vulnerable to the fantasy of an exceptional, masterful, masculine[5] figure – Aristotelian prime mover, originary One or Freudian primal father – who can denounce the image as false from an impossible position seemingly outside the realm of appearances, and therefore immune to the social world's inescapable imperative of 'imagization'.

In this light, when Genet claims in his amusingly bitchy performance note that his play effects 'a glorification of the Image and the Reflection',[6] he is not pledging allegiance to the register of human experience that Lacan calls the imaginary. We should understand this last term in the play's context to evoke an idealized, humanistic vision of the classical liberal political virtues of 'the People', 'Freedom' and 'Revolution',[7] listed by Genet in his prefatory *avertissement* and alerting us to what we should not expect to discover in his theatre. In the mid-1950s, a full decade before his temporarily definitive abandonment of literature in favour of more directly political forms of writing and activism, Genet is already all too aware of the tendency of a certain type of political art – Zhdanovian socialist realism, but also probably the aesthetic of existentialist authenticity, are no doubt in the crosshairs – to function as wish fulfilment. Applied to the political aesthetic of the play, the Freudian term evokes the unconscious instrumentalization of theatrical representation as a surrogate for the kind of praxis that requires a disorienting immersion in the real of social antagonisms. That is, the theatre for Genet must not imagine utopian futures as a substitute for a risky plunge into the depths of political contradiction where action and knowledge can only be dangerously, but potentially creatively, non-simultaneous.

The political art for which *The Balcony* offers itself as an alternative unwittingly dissuades the risk of ambiguity inherent in genuine political engagement. Counter-intuitive though it may seem, Genet's self-professed glorification of the image exposes the tenuousness with which the world of appearances – the only world to which we have perceptual access – holds together, thereby coaxing us to act, or else to fall back on a defensive embrace of (an imaginary grasp of) the status quo. The intensification through stagework of reality's dependence on images is the play's way of exposing a structural instability, a precarious 'cantilevered (*en porte-à-faux*)'[8] quality always on the verge of giving way. As we watch or read *The Balcony*, we sense with increasing acuity that the absences and interstices inherent in the socio-symbolic fabric of culture, reflections of the inherent inconsistency of being, threaten to cause this fabric's unravelling. To our discomfort and even to our shame, we are shown – after the event as it were – that the advent of something new and unforeseen might indeed have been possible all along.

Confined within the walls of Madame Irma's brothel, Genet's mise en scène endlessly multiplies the surfaces of the phenomenal world, which begin to reflect only the void that haunts all possible meaning and representation. Mirrors cover multiple surfaces, the border between the brothel's inside and outside is made ambiguous, and characters muse repeatedly about the impossibility of distinguishing reality from illusion. As if to compensate for all this ambiguity, for the difficulty of finding an authentic way of being amid all these reflections, Madame Irma strives to assert her command over the field of vision by peering through a panoptic seeing machine. Also, near the end of the play, trendy young photographers work to rehabilitate the prestige of the (presumably assassinated) three authority figures by capturing their identities in appealing poses assumed by brothel clients. Displaying the artificiality of the visible in these ways, *The Balcony* incites a desire to see through to a truer reality. But the only possible response to the visible world's inducement of ontological vertigo is the desperate production of yet more images in a doomed attempt to penetrate through all the layers of reflection to secure a tangible sense of our collective humanity's elusive being.

In spite of this, however, it would be a mistake to fall back on the assumption that the general atmosphere of 'equivocality (*équivoque*)'[9] that Genet aims to create in his work is merely a function of some quality of undecidability inherent in the familiar, classical binaries of reality and appearance or truth and illusion, for example.[10] My approach to *The Balcony* is based instead on an alternative assumption about what I have been calling Genet's ontology. The standard Kantian philosophical problem of modernity concerning whether a given object of experience is the 'thing-in-itself' or merely its perceptual construction is undercut by a more primordial, indeed transcendental negativity that has the effect of making the one equivalent to, substitutable for, the other. The *Ding-an-sich*, in its very inaccessibility, becomes the sign of every possible object's difference not from its presumed original 'in reality', but rather from itself. In Genet's theatrical world, in other words, objects become their own reflections, divided within themselves by a hiatus in the continuity of their being. There are indeed only images in Genet's theatre. More unsettling, however, is the fact that these images are also at the same time not themselves, being at a remove from their own essence or identity. The only accessible modality of being is (an) appearance, yet this appearance is also non-identical with itself. *The Balcony*'s dizzying display of *le paraître* serves only ambivalently to dissimulate – paradoxically to expose, that is, through dissimulation – the abyss in being that prevents any representation, indeed any possible (ontic) existence, from cohering even to itself.

Genet's postclassical rendering of the comedic form applies this insight about 'identity in non-identity' (or alternatively 'the identity of identity and difference'[11]) as related to the world of appearances to the very operation of power. The play splits power's agency between its symbolic representation in the three authority figures and the Chief of Police, who personifies its concrete or executive purchase. In its opening scenes, *The Balcony* theatricalizes the perverse act of theatricalization by means of which the brothel clients, in costumed erotic set-pieces, strive to remediate authority's failure at a moment when its representatives no longer elicit spontaneous identification. Later, at its pivotal comedic moment, the play unleashes an impetus for social change that is then immediately and conspicuously contained. If comedy, as Lacan argues, 'enjoys (*jouit de*) a relation to an effect fundamentally linked to the signifying order, namely the apparition of the signifier called the phallus',[12] then this apparition, this coming-to-visibility, requires a return to the phallus's prior function as a signifier-image thanks to which it re-eroticizes the world in the resumption of its role as the veil that incites desire. As we will discover, however, whether or not concrete political consequences can be made to ensue from the phallus's momentary and disruptive unveiling is another question altogether.

The image in history

An inquiry into Badiou's suggestive and avowedly Lacanian reading will set the stage for my own consideration of the political implications of the moment of phallic unveiling in Genet's play. According to Badiou, *The Balcony* delves into the dynamic relation between a regime of dominant images and the passage of time at a historical moment marked by social instability and the equivocal possibility of political transformation. Importantly, Badiou reminds us that Lacan undertook the commentary of (the original 1956 edition of) *The Balcony* in his 1957–8 seminar at a dramatic early moment of the bloody Algerian war of independence. In fact, Lacan began his reading a mere two weeks prior to the fateful Algiers coup d'état that would eventually restore General de Gaulle, still at the time a staunch supporter of French Algeria, to power. Philosophically speaking, for Badiou the most significant characteristics of the historical present are its ambiguity and obscurity, its vexing unavailability to thought. The contemporary world's lack of transparent tacit significance makes 'the now' depend on after-the-fact reconstructions that grant it retrospective meaning. Only retroactively does history acquire its contingent significance; in turn, and perhaps less obviously, this meaning is subject to future re-sedimentations of sense, during which our understanding of the past can be radically transformed.

Badiou suggests that Genet's interest in the image bears down on precisely this problem of the present's opacity, and the resulting need for a repertoire of visual symbols with which to organize collective experience in time. The inherent ambiguity of history is pinned down in the process of its rendering as a coherent narrative buttressed by an ensemble of privileged images. This dominant regime of the visible is supported by specific idealized emblems that organize, and effectively police, our understanding of the past by preventing dissident counter-histories from coming to light. As Badiou goes on to develop, these images are by nature politically conservative because their function is ideological in the most classical sense: they dissimulate the inherent antagonisms that tear apart the social world, class conflict of course being the particular antagonism privileged in the Marxian critical tradition to which Badiou in his work professes a complicatedly critical brand of fidelity.

But what role could the phallus have to play in the evolution of hegemonic interpretations of collective historical experience? Badiou takes Lacan's reference to the phallus to designate in this context the image of power; more precisely, the particular image of power that serves to organize social relations at a given historical juncture. The comedic effect produced by the phallus under specific conditions makes visible the mechanism of naked power stripped of the decorative and discursive accessories that lend legitimacy and inspire the desire to obey. This for Badiou is what lies at the root of the Chief of Police's ambition to become one of the characters in the brothel: he envies the erotic power that their ceremonial auras wield, even if the scenarios in which the clients engage are made necessary by their tarnished social legitimacy. Badiou adds that the play's patent interest in the putting-on and taking-off of the personages' ceremonial garb has an aggressive, contemptuous edge; the exposure it effects makes power a target for laughter and derision. In this sense, the comedic moment occurs in result of the revelation that underneath the symbols of power lies a generic human being as isolated, vulnerable and inherently powerless as any other.

It thus becomes clear that when Badiou defines the comedic as 'the signifying foundation of power itself, the foundation in the present of the derision of its demonstration (*monstration*),'[13] he does so with implicit recourse to a properly psychoanalytic conception of power. Power's necessary articulation in language, like any other human utterance, is alienated in the signifier. This means that it depends without condition on a medium composed only of differences, as Ferdinand de Saussure famously argued, deprived of any purely positive or independent term. In consequence, power is inherently split from itself. That is, the solemnity of its manifest display is haunted by the spectre of a potentially ridiculous and laughter-inducing enjoyment, which it will always eventually fail to conceal. In this sense, every display of power is on one level an imposture in its attempt to camouflage the evidence of its fundamental impotence.

We can take the ponderous solemnity of patriotic military ceremonials as an indubitably Genetian example. Is the atmosphere of high seriousness not designed to stifle the outbreak of hysterical laughter, which would of course instantly lend an aura of pretension and stupidity to proceedings? A second example: the exercise of authority in its traditional patriarchal form is only effective when it is evoked or named, rather than embodied directly. When a real, present father or male authority figure attempts to lay down the law in his own name, his vituperations are bound to seem desperate, excessive, impotent. Surely Freud revealed only what is latently obvious when he pointed out in the Wolf Man case history that the threat of castration, and by extension the father's power to punish, was in fact issued by a woman: his nurse Nanya, quite clearly a psychical proxy for the mother.[14]

Badiou's reading highlights how the police chief's particular modality of power is effective but invisible; he is at once the foundation on which the social order rests and absent from that same order on the level of its official symbolic representation. On the one hand, Genet draws attention to the political alliance between the chief and Madame Irma, revealing how their former sexual passion has transformed into a strategic and self-interested political alliance. *The Balcony* makes clear that the viability of the brothel, the erotic logic that regulates its panoply of images, depends directly on the protection provided by the Chief of Police. On the other hand, however, though he is granted ease of access to the brothel, the chief is not *of* it; he does not properly speaking belong within its confines. The proof lies in the fact that none of its clients wants to play the role of Chief of Police with Madame Irma's girls. Badiou teases out of these key features of Genet's play the insight that the chief is the invisible (in the sense of unrepresented, unmaterialized) support for the dominant regime of visibility portrayed in the play. The chief goes without an emblem so that the system of emblems, the order of appearances, can complete itself as a consistent whole, gaining in the process a convincing semblance of reality and furnishing steady ground for the normal, day-to-day functioning of the social world.

Readers familiar with Lacan's concept will already have remarked this key character's affinity with the phallus. Indeed, it comes as no surprise when Badiou enlists the support of Lacan's reading when he declares without circumlocution, 'the Chief of Police, he's the phallus'.[15] For Badiou, the phallus is a representation that upholds power's repertoire of images without itself being an image, without belonging to that repertoire: the 'power of images does not have an image'.[16] This is how Badiou interprets Lacan's famous contention that the phallus is first and foremost a sound image as opposed to a putatively unified and self-sustaining visual image. As a signifier, the phallus indexes its own abscondment, its unavailability to the sense of sight; it is the marking in the visible world of the possibility of another, as-yet-unseen but nonetheless pivotal, visual possibility. The catch, however, is that the very existence of this alternative, ultimate image paradoxically depends on its non-appearance in that same visible world.

The crucial political consequence for Badiou is that 'there is a moment when we come upon the real of power as an unrepresented real'.[17] As regards *The Balcony*, this implies that Genet's police chief character is meant to embody, in contrast to Bishop, Judge and General, the effectively functioning power behind power's official and ceremonial appearances. Though the president of the United States is 'the leader of the free world', we could say by analogy, it is really the murky and unelected authorities in the Pentagon, FBI and CIA who pull the strings of American policy, foreign and domestic. Because to a considerable degree these off-stage authorities remain unidentifiable or invisible, they are left free to work without accountability, their spokespeople merely the outwards signs of a power that is always exercised elsewhere, or so we imagine, away from public view at the level of the so-called deep state.

Though his analysis insightfully identifies the chief as the embodiment of naked power in the play, Badiou's commentary remains curiously insensitive to the properly comedic aspects of the phallus costume image. Indeed, I am not entirely convinced that Genet intends this image to convey the obscure, surreptitious power dissimulated by a social formation's dominant ideological symbols. The play's logic rather suggests that Genet wants the costume to evoke the obscene sexual enjoyment that precisely subverts these symbols' ideological efficiency. The former interpretation of the phallus's significance speaks to the ambiguity in Badiou's reading as to whether what he terms naked power is meant to suggest a quasi-paranoid, late-period Foucaultian construal of the deep state's insidiously effective biopolitical purchase, or rather the more properly psychoanalytic notion of the impotent truth of power's every articulation in linguistic form.

Details from *The Balcony* can be put forward to explain why Badiou's reading winds up prioritizing the former over the (in my view more politically significant) latter understanding. As I have already mentioned, the chief voices the idea for the costume against the backdrop of a photo shoot during which brothel clients pose before the cameras as the traditional authority figures. They are preparing to be paraded before the public in an attempt to revive their fading legitimacy and consolidate the popular insurrection's repression. Meanwhile, the Queen, whose ceremonial role has now been taken on by Madame Irma, speaks of the construction of a mausoleum beneath the brothel to be dedicated to the Hero, a function she clearly intends to be filled by her ally, the Chief of Police. The scene's allegorical logic proposes that as the revolution is stifled, the population demands the restoration of the old dignitaries' collective aura. In *The Balcony*, this is accomplished in a thoroughly modern way: a fashion shoot for the restoration. Significantly, the makeover is undertaken in the public relations- and celebrity culture-friendly manner that has expanded dramatically in the economically liberalizing half-century since Genet wrote his play. In other words, the glamour-creating magic of media is enlisted to revive the allure of outmoded regalia such as mitre, cope or lace.

For Badiou, the police chief's mention of his phallus costume serves merely as a metaphor for Genet's putative thesis about power's lack of representation in an image. His reading interprets the costume simply as one among many details of the play's concluding depiction of the return of the status quo of social relations, which is accomplished through the renewal and reinforcement of the complicity between power's symbolic representation and its genuinely effective off-stage operation. For Badiou, *The Balcony* scrutinizes the visible world's defensive response to the threat of change with no purpose other than to communicate a resigned sense of inevitability. Cynically, Genet's play would suggest that the subversive, socially invisible forces of insurrection will inevitably become complicit with the regime of hegemonic political emblems that it originally set out to attack. In this view, the play's final word is that the parade of images in history obeys a Nietzschean logic of eternal return according to which 'there will be nothing new'. In writing his play Genet would 'crave nothing more fervently' than that the same 'succession and sequence' of appearances repeat itself indefinitely.[18] Nihilistically, *The Balcony* would dramatize the complicit temporality of false eternity by means of which the incessantly repeated reincarnation of the obfuscatory image of power guarantees the concrete impossibility of the emancipatory event.[19]

An image of castration

Despite its professed desire to stay close to Lacan's, Badiou's reading of *The Balcony* struggles in my view to communicate the profound ambiguity of the psychoanalyst's intervention. For Lacan, the play does not in fact end on a note of resigned or nihilistic conservatism, as Badiou avers. Rather, its political implications remain unclear in Lacan's commentary, to some extent – though not entirely, as I will finally argue – in the spirit of the play itself.

Instead of the police chief's absurd phallic attire, Lacan selects for his interpretation's keystone former rebel Roger's impersonation of this same character at the moment of his climactic sacrifice at the replica mausoleum. Yet another example of identity-shifting or role-playing in the play, the event makes abundantly clear that the Chief of Police has finally become an icon in the brothel thanks not to one of its regular clients, but rather to the now-defeated popular insurgent. At the play's conclusion, the restored social order has been monumentalized in the form of the mausoleum's mirror-filled architecture. Earlier, Roger had been involved in discussions with comrades about enlisting Chantal, one of the brothel girls, as the revolution's sacred image, to be emblazoned on banners and flags as a means of edifying the ranks and embodying the nobility of the insurrectionary cause. By the end of the play, however, we have learned that Roger has simply used Chantal's connection to the brothel to insinuate himself into its confines and assume his role as the vicarious instrument of the police chief's status quo-rescuing final deed.

As one might expect him to do, Lacan seizes upon another startling detail of *The Balcony*'s conclusion, the one that has proven more successful than the phallus costume in capturing the attention of commentators. Shockingly, and seemingly out of nowhere, Roger, now dressed as the Chief of Police, castrates himself, clearing the way for the latter's redemptive inclusion in the brothel's iconography. Despite our bewilderment at this violent turn of events, we know intuitively that the outcome would have proven impossible to secure had Roger been outfitted in the comedic phallus costume instead. This is indeed the play's key scene for Lacan. It draws our disoriented attention to the link between castration, that is the subject's experience of loss consequent to its forced entry into the order of the signifier, and alienation, or the sense that as subjects we have no recourse but to submit to the psychical splitting that ensues. For Lacan, we recall, the subject's capacity to assume a position within the social order must necessarily be marked by loss.

But how does Lacan interpret the theatrical violence of Roger's self-immolation? In his status as a vaguely leftist rebel figure fighting against authority to create a more fully human world, Roger can only make his mark by in essence losing that (false) humanity. More precisely, Roger must accept the power of language, indeed of representation in general, to frustrate the desire, or more properly the demand, for a dis-alienated collective existence of fully satisfying productive labour and perfect accommodation to the value of social utility. Indeed, on one level Lacan's target in the Genet commentary is a certain vulgar Marxian utopianism in the air in 1950s France according to which the revolution will reconcile humanity with its unruly desires, which are alienated in this view by capitalist social relations. In the broader context of Genet's meditation on *le paraître*, however, Roger's sacrifice indexes for Lacan the necessity with which the sense of our own being must eventually slip from between the signifying forms that make up the world of appearances. As Lacan puts it:

> This subject, the one who represents man's simple desire to rejoin his own existence and thought in an authentic and assumed way – a value that is not distinct from his flesh – this subject who is there representing man, the one who has fought so that something of what we have until now called the brothel can find a place, a norm, a state that could be accepted as fully human, this subject only reintegrates itself, once the test is passed, on condition of castrating itself. That is, (this subject) works so that the phallus is once again promoted to the status of signifier, to that something that can give or take back, confer or not confer, that which is then confused in the most explicit way with the image of the signifier's creator, the *Our Father*, the *Our Father who art in Heaven*.[20]

In his new vicarious brothel identity as Chief of Police, Roger undergoes a kind of consecration that makes possible the reinstatement of a signifying order underwritten, as it were, by a phallic function to which Lacan here explicitly confers the attribute of (perceived) divinity. Roger's castration and subsequent disappearance from the mise en scène ensure that no subject, no matter how authoritative, will ever be capable of manifesting phallic power in his very essence. Power is alienated in the signifier, which means that social authority can only ever be exercised thanks to an attribution, a conferral, that comes from some vague, non-human elsewhere, from the heavens. Power's legitimacy becomes disembodied, transferable, indeed a detachable appendage that could be removed, offered instead to someone else, at any given time. In the light shed by Lacan's commentary, *The Balcony*, with respect to its political significance, begins to look like an allegory for the installation of liberal or constitutional democracy, in other words the operation through which the institutions of Church, military, and (pre-democratic) judiciary are subordinated to a newly sanctioned mechanism for the enforcement of a Law that has now been detached from its direct, iconic, premodern brand of representation overseen by an absolute monarch, for instance.

No longer embodied in noble, semi-divinized persons, social power is now codified, bureaucratized, constitutionalized, rendered as discourse and therefore secularized by paradoxical virtue of a renewed anchoring reference to a 'divine' realm now entirely beyond human reach. For Lacan, Roger's castration emblematizes the renewal of the chasm that divides the execution of power from its representation, the very vexing division from which the brothel's clients, through the enactment of their perverse fantasy scenarios, seek relief. The signifier is now the agency that holds the power over our personal destiny. Henceforth, this power will be confined to an autonomous Freudian primary process in the unconscious, where it is unavailable to the speaking subject for instrumental use. The consequence of this view is that the supposedly revolutionary aspiration for a new humanity unshackled from the signifier's hold becomes instead the worst possible retrograde political fantasy.

But then again, if this reading smacks too much of political history for a properly psychoanalytic intervention such as Lacan's, then we might say that the psychoanalyst's gloss is meant to argue that Genet's play dramatizes the structural or logical requirement for an act of reconsecration such as Roger's at a time of social crisis, when the very functioning of a phallic – in the generic sense of symbolic or cultural – order threatens to collapse, clearing the ground for the advent of the Dictator: a primal father figure exempt from the law of castration who both represents and effectively executes power without producing any residue, divine or otherwise; a force whose very idiosyncratic and irrational will bodies forth the Law without mediation, without juridical codification or administrative accountability.

Here we can cite Genet's reference to Francisco Franco's monument to the fascists' victory in the Spanish Civil War in Catalonia's Valle de los Caídos (Valley of the Fallen),[21] a primary inspiration for the mausoleum image in the play. In this perspective, the mausoleum embodies the necessity with which the police chief's desire to be included in the brothel's repertoire of images – his desire, that is, at once to emblematize and enforce power – must eventually be thwarted by the signifier's power. According to this interpretation, the chief's new status is the same as that of the traditional authority figures, to whom he can offer support and the rehabilitation of their dysfunctional social purchase.

In this scenario, Roger's sacrifice represents the absence of any possible direct embodiment of the Law; the stubborn negativity, that is, that sabotages every iteration of normative power from within. In short, the construction of the commemorative mausoleum in the play underscores the truth that the whole world is a brothel. Giving the lie to the political aspiration evidenced by the off-stage machine-gun fire heard throughout, Roger's dark destiny confirms the truth that there is no more natural, more authentic mode of being purified of untoward enjoyment available outside the brothel walls.

The power of the dildo

I now wish to suggest, however, that even Lacan's reading finally fails to register the subversively comedic force of *The Balcony*. Earlier I argued that Badiou's commentary attributes to the play a nihilistic Nietzschean message about the inevitability of the event's co-optation by the image's lure. As we have just seen, Lacan for his part intimates that the restoration of the phallic order, whatever we might consider its limitations to be, has the merit of circumventing the extension of revolutionary logic to its undesirable, totalitarian conclusion. In this view, the tarnished and hypocritical symbols of the old authority would be supplanted only to clear the ground for something significantly worse: a tyrant who would incarnate without mediation, in the very contingent idiosyncrasy of his person, both the sublime authority and the coercive power of the Law.

To discern exactly where both Badiou's and Lacan's interventions leave something to be desired, a closer look at the details of Genet's description of the police chief's costume will be of help. To be sure, Genet's language suggests something quite distinct from both the image of the imaginary phallus (the anatomical penis idealized; relieved, that is, of its constitutive inadequacy, of its 'normal' state of detumescence), or the phallus-as-signifier (the veil that incites desire, that eroticizes the world by creating or marking lack). Indeed, in its rubbery, eminently modern sex-toy shine, *The Balcony*'s comedic image bears no visible relation to the extant archaeological evidence of the phallic objects used for fertility rites in antiquity, for example.[22] Rather, it resembles to a greater extent the satirical phallic objects used in ancient comedy. Indeed, it is difficult or even impossible to imagine even in our putatively liberated late modernity a solemn community ritual organized around the image of a giant rubber phallus.

In this light, we have no choice but to come to terms with the quite obvious fact that the Chief of Police talks about dressing up as a giant dildo. And what is a dildo if not the embodiment, and in this sense the image, of phallic lack in itself; the exposure, as opposed to the veiling, of an absence of, or gap in, being? More concretely, a dildo materializes the inevitability of phallic failure, of the essential unreliability of male genital jouissance. In Hegelian-Lacanian terms, it embodies the sublime phallic image's speculative identity with the obscene partial object of the drive, the one that reminds us whether we want to be reminded or not of the body's obscene, 'perverse' penetrability, as well as the anatomical identity of virility and micturition. The flipside of the void the phallus works to veil is indeed this object that provokes shame or even disgust. Moreover, a dildo exposes the discomfiting fact that the body image, whose wholesome integrity is much lauded in contemporary mental health discourses, is inherently false; indeed, it is powerless even properly to secure its own borders. Offering incontrovertible proof of the discontinuity between jouissance and what we might call the use value of the body, the function of a dildo could not be further removed from the communal celebration of the social virtue of fecundity attributed to those phallic rites in the ancient world.

This preliminary view of the chief's phallic get-up will benefit from closer scrutiny of what exactly the phallus is for Lacan, especially given that it has proven to be one of his more controversial and misunderstood notions. In his own allusive words, the phallus is 'the privileged signifier of this mark in which the role (*part*) of Logos is wedded to the advent of desire'.[23] As a signifier, the phallus is first and foremost a sound image, usually but not necessarily a privileged word, onto which the subject unconsciously latches to represent to itself its difference from the object that could fully satisfy its primary Other's desire. And yet this conditional or hypothetical satisfaction, this signified that the phallic signifier is meant to signify, can only remain shrouded in latency, as Lacan puts it, simply because it is negated, repressed: banished from our conscious knowledge. This is the sense in which logos is inseparable from an absence arising from the act of repression. The phallus's endemic latency is another context for Lacan's oft-cited contention that 'it can play its role only when veiled'.[24] If there is indeed a phallus behind the veil, that is, then it only vanishes the instant the veil is torn away. The distinction between the phallus as signifier and that which it would appear to signify is crucial because it underlines that the relation between the two is irremediably problematic. In fact, you could say that what the phallus signifies is finally the signifier's tautological self-reference. This is what accounts for the opacity of the signified: the impossibility of its full definition, disclosure or identification; but also its *necessity*, its resistance to being analysed or deconstructed away. For psychoanalysis, this simultaneous impossibility and necessity of the phallic signified is ultimately a reflection of the underlying incompletion of being.

The capacity of the signified to produce effects in the subject's symbolic world is strictly correlative to this same signified's dissimulation in both senses of its unavailability to consciousness and of the marking of its absence in the field of vision. In short, the phallus registers the fact that something has been excluded from the world as a condition of its very construction as an appearance imbued with a convincing impression of reality. More precisely, it signifies the exclusion itself, not what has been excluded. There follows a surprising logical implication. On those rare occasions when the signified manages to emerge – when the real phallus, as opposed to the imaginary or symbolic one, is unveiled – the result is the elimination of the lack that sustains desire and the ensuing claustrophobic collapse of our reality's compelling virtuality. The ideological promise of meaning that lends a modicum of order to the world's representations ceases to function, and the inconsistency of being itself is momentarily revealed. As the structure of desire gives way, the visible world sheds its shaky realism, and we are left only with its obscene remainder, the piece of the real whose repression makes possible psychic life as such. Indeed repression, and the subsequent unfurling of the phallic lure, is the only means available to us for making our imperfect and tenuous exit from the primal, acosmic chaos of unlimited jouissance.

In addition to being a sound image, then, the phallus is also a visual image, one with an ambiguous, oddly redoubled or self-estranged quality. The phallus is neither a dissimulated object nor the thing that dissimulates it. It is rather the image of dissimulation itself, a veil corresponding to the absence of the object that our intuition tells us it is meant to conceal. This is the sense in which the phallus oversees what I have described as Genet's ontology: the only possible access to being in his theatrical world – things of course are no different outside the theatre – is through *le paraître*, a realm of appearances made up of objects that serve only as their own reflections. These reflections try but fail to dissimulate being's inherent self-contradiction, its absence to itself. For this reason, the prospect of the phallic image's unveiling, the tearing away of the veil that effectively *is* the phallus (in its symbolic and imaginary guises), intimates nothing less than the shattering of our psychical world and the extinguishing of the desire that supports it.

It is easy to appreciate in this light why the exposed phallus might become the object of a strict taboo, and indeed why the violator of such a taboo might be subject to punishment. As it happens, this is the reason why Lacan in the development of his phallus concept draws attention to the ruins of Pompeii's Villa of the Mysteries. Gracing the cover of the original edition of *Télévision*,[25] one of its famous frescoes depicts a woman reaching around a tall, columnar object on which a purple fabric has been draped, hiding it from view. Beside the object is a winged figure whose hand, raised over his head, carries a whip ready to crack injuriously on the kneeling woman's extended arms. The image's cultural and historical contexts remain today something of a mystery, not unlike the enshrouded object itself. Whether the fresco is meant to represent ritual marriage preparations, an initiation into the cult of Dionysus, or something else entirely yet to have occurred to specialists, the winged figure Lacan calls 'the demon of Αιδως'[26] is surely meant to dissuade the unveiling of the object while at the same time suggesting as its consequence a painful scar on the body, a kind of literalized castration.

The phallic image sustains the illusion of the existence of what Lacan calls *le rapport sexuel*: the myth of the psychosexual complementarity of the sexes, to be sure, but also, in a much broader sense, the very coherence of the universe, of being as such. The price to be paid for the phallus's unveiling is the painful realization that the desire to apprehend the world as a seamlessly consistent totality is fundamentally irreconcilable with the forms of knowledge and with being itself. The signifier introduces a rift into being that can never be eliminated and that never fails to disrupt our efforts at definitively mapping out our presence within it.

The police chief's rubber costume gains its full significance in this light, a significance left unrecognized in the critical literature, including Lacan's own commentary. 'I've been advised to appear in the form of a gigantic phallus, a prick of great stature',[27] we recall the chief announcing. Who could deny that we have on our hands the image of a giant dildo? The dildo – or indeed the vibrator, which in this context we can take as precisely equivalent – is a privileged ordinary object with which to think through the difference between the phallic signifier or image, the one that lures desire, and the object Lacanian theory names the real phallus: Freud's partial object of the *Trieb* (drive). This latter object holds precisely the *puissance désimageante*, the de-imaging power, that for Badiou characterizes the historical present; as such it can serve to resolve the underlying ambiguity of his analysis. Indeed, the obscene partial object's image-destroying faculty brings us onto the threshold of the event, the same event whose unlikely but nonetheless possible eventuality, in Badiou's misleading view, Genet designs his play to dismiss or deny.

To be sure, in niche retail sectors of the erotica industry, as well as in specific sexual subcultures of today's outwardly permissive liberal enclaves, public display of a dildo may have little discernible effect. If we consider the logic of the world of appearances in general, however, especially with respect to this world's dependence on the implicit, legitimizing look of some idealized personification of authority, we begin to see how a dildo's exposure can be quite literally world-shattering. It is difficult to imagine someone deliberately leaving a sex toy out in full view during the visit of some party in a position of power over them, for example a work supervisor who writes regular performance reports. Moreover, what percentage of men would feel fully comfortable in their virility at the discovery of a vibrator they did not previously know their female partner possessed? And who can envision a dildo as the centrepiece at a table around which high-level diplomatic negotiations are being conducted? Such occurrences are surely quintessentially comedic, but only in retrospect, through the frame of cultural representation, or if they do not personally implicate you.

In short, the dildo is an object that incites the embodied affect of shame because it exposes the pretension, the imposture of the phallic image, whose paradoxical function is to create lack by dissimulating it; more exactly, by creating the illusion of this dissimulation, the illusion that there is indeed something more to be seen. The shameful object exposes the lack in the Other and, in consequence, the lack in all subjects and in being itself. The dildo is a stand-in for the Freudo-Lacanian partial object (breast, turd, gaze, voice), and for this reason it reminds us uncomfortably of the gap between the signifier and bodily jouissance; that is, the failure of society to integrate enjoyment into its norms and dictates. Any utterance of the Law, any representation of authority, betrays the traumatic stain of enjoyment in its eventual failure to obey the terms of its own edict. Relatedly, the dildo makes visible the non-complementary character of men and women, male and female, masculine and feminine. It bespeaks the absence of any cosmic, unifying principle that would make the world appear fully and completely before us, once and for all, thereby reconciling humanity with its own species-being. Not only does *le paraître* fail to correspond to what we might wish to consider the objective real; also, appearances seem at a remove from themselves, reflecting only their own reflections.

From revolutionary to populist hero

These details of Lacan's development of his phallus concept shed new light on *The Balcony*'s complicated and enigmatic conclusion, of which I am now finally positioned to offer an alternative interpretation. Within the world of the play, the visual image of the Chief of Police in a giant rubber dildo costume throws a wrench in the brothel's perverse libidinal economy. As I have suggested, this economy functions to rescue the authoritative purchase of traditional social institutions at the historical moment of their thoroughgoing delegitimization. Rendered ridiculous by the prospect of his appearance as a dildo, the chief effectively discounts himself, albeit only momentarily, as a potential candidate for the position of Hero, the point of identification that would allow the social body to reconceive of itself, post-insurrection, as an organic whole. The comedic moment of the phallus costume makes necessary the re-emergence in the play of the figures of Bishop, Judge and General, now engaged in a public relations campaign to rehabilitate their sagging authority. As the brothel clients dressed as the old order's icons pose for the photographers, they create the new celebrity images being demanded by the people. The citizenry have now abandoned their political investment in the rebellion, which has now been successfully co-opted or abandoned in favour of the reassuring, if simulated, status quo of social relations.

This is the immediate narrative context leading to Roger's self-castration. We are brought back to the opening triad of scenes in the brothel, with their concern for exploring the meaning of the clients' elaborate private rituals with the girls. Now, however, it is Roger who gears up for his new performance as the Hero, donning the uniform of the Chief of Police in order to die symbolically as a martyr for the restoration. Tension soon arises, however, as we realize that Roger is taking his role too seriously; he truly, literally wants to die, taking his place in the mausoleum buried deep within the bedrock underneath the brothel and built, we are informed, thanks to countless but willing hours of slave labour in the worst conditions of exploitation. As brothel worker Chantal coaxes him unsuccessfully to leave, his allotted time in the mausoleum scenario having now expired, Roger turns his back to the crowd and severs his organ, after which time he is dragged offstage, receiving no further mention in the dialogue. The police chief, for his part, proclaims victory: 'Though my image be castrated in every brothel in the world, I remain intact,' he proclaims. 'That plumber (Roger) didn't know how to handle his role, that was all.'[28] Then, as the chief descends the steps of the mausoleum and the three authority figures are declared 'free,'[29] Irma prepares to shut her place of business down, switching off the brothel lights. 'In a little while, I'll have to start all over again,' she says, 'reallocate the roles, assume my own'. Nothing of significance seems to have changed, and the text concludes with a reference to yet another off-stage 'burst of machine-gun fire'.[30]

The Balcony's weirdly anticlimactic conclusion resists any univocal interpretation, to be sure. In light of what we have considered, however, it is difficult not to conclude that, not unlike the patient in analysis before they receive their own message back from the Other 'in an inverted form',[31] both Roger and the Chief of Police have misconstrued the nature of their bizarre, vicarious castration. Further, I would suggest that it is on the basis of these characters' ignorance of the significance of their actions that both Lacan and Badiou offer their ultimately off-the-mark analyses. For an authentic psychoanalytic interpretation surely must suggest that Roger, by cutting off his genitalia onstage, has attempted to repair the damage of a different, properly psychical castration. That is, Roger's literal castration is in reality merely imaginary, an attempt to recreate an untarnished body innocent of sexuality, one that of course never existed. His pseudo-act is a reminder that the male organ, in its semi-autonomy and propensity for 'dysfunction', is already, in itself as it were, evidence of the 'castrated' comedy of human sexuality. Finding himself (as he says with relief) 'intact',[32] the Chief of Police for his part seems now to have finally succeeded in establishing for himself, through Roger's descent into the mausoleum, a postmodern phallic image with which to symbolize the restoration of the social order. The chief's authority is now properly recognized among society's guiding repertoire of sacrosanct images, which have now evidently been re-established as desirable points of popular identification.

Having achieved this incarnation as an image through the intermediary of Roger's sacrifice, the Chief of Police is free to carry on in the world as a 'normal' man, one whose psychical castration allows for the properly sexual enjoyments of which the idealized phallic image, for the reasons of structure I have been trying to outline, must remain innocent. In this sense, Roger's decision to become complicit with power at the play's conclusion allows for the perpetuation of the illicit simpatico that binds the law to jouissance, thereby dissimulating the inconsistency of being. More simply, Roger's castration is just for show, a mere image of castration that rehabilitates the phallus's distracting and depoliticizing lure. What Badiou's and Lacan's commentaries fall short of spelling out is that it is not enough simply to expose the illicit enjoyment that undergirds the functioning of legitimate power. Rather, as in the properly comedic image of the Chief of Police dressed as a giant dildo, the two must be shown to coincide in their essential but uncanny identity. In this sense, the chief's 'castrated' image in the mausoleum is simply a ruse of postmodern power, one that supports the image-intensive rehabilitation of the classical authority figures by adding a more spontaneously 'relatable', falsely democratic, and in this precise sense populist avatar to their historical iconography.[33]

His image now enshrined in the mausoleum, the chief now has an alibi with which he can exonerate himself of power's inherent criminality. Any potential accusation can be referred back to the distracting, depoliticizing lure embodied in the commemorative monument. He may now claim that abuses of power are not his doing because in his image he is just an ordinary 'castrated' guy like anyone else. In this precise sense, the function of the mausoleum into which Roger descends is to transform the scandal of enjoyment into the edifying ideal of sacrifice, in this way obfuscating the violence that makes up the repressed generative principle of the social bond, and substituting updated ideals of patriotism and belonging for concrete histories of contestation and dissent. Crucially, however, because these strange events in the play have been preceded by the strange comedic moment of the phallus's unveiling, we are now acutely aware of a devastatingly ironic tone. This tone, insufficiently appreciated in Badiou's and Lacan's interpretations, results precisely from the jarring discrepancy between what the play shows us as it draws to its conclusion and what we know the play itself 'thinks' about what it shows.

The Balcony provides no direct evidence of what might have taken place if the Chief of Police had been allowed to parade around town, outside the brothel as it were, in his giant dildo costume. What is clear, however, is that immediately after this seemingly off-hand, obviously comedic but also ambiguous event, things turn rather serious indeed, and the prospect's (potentially) subversive consequences are instantly blocked. Roger's gruesome sacrifice and the unveiling of the mausoleum reintroduce the ponderous tone of high tragedy to proceedings. Despite the change in the symbolization of power effected by the Hero's self-immolation, there is nothing more to say about what happens than that things go back to the way they were. The machine-gun fire that we hear once again remains outside the realm of (visual) representation. The rebellion is left without an alternative guiding image with which it might be figured to the people. The vague glimpse of an opportunity for genuine social transformation disappears from view, just like the theatrical interiors of Madame Irma's brothel as she shuts off the lights.

At the deceptive, evanescent turning point of his play, Genet tears away the veil, exposing an unsettling phallic-comic object that provokes laughter, but also opens up, however fleetingly, an anxious space for the potential occurrence of the emancipatory event. *Contra* the interpretations of both Badiou and Lacan, Genet's play makes eminently palpable a lost opportunity for social transformation, leaving its unsettled audience wondering if the Nietzchean return is in fact eternal, and prodding them to take the risk of testing out the possibility of change, obscure but vivifying, in what we call the real world. The final word must go to Marc, a revolutionary in the 1960 version cut from what became the canonical edition, who expertly distils the agenda of *The Balcony*'s political aesthetic: 'May we create poems and images that do not satisfy (*comblent*), but rather annoy (*énervent*)!'[34]

4

Residue of modernity, wound of being: Genet on art

This chapter pivots around a peculiar anecdote recounted by Genet in a series of short pieces engaging with visual art, the works of Alberto Giacometti and Rembrandt van Rijn in particular. The anecdote, which depicts Genet's encounter with an ugly stranger on a train, will inform my argument about the ethico-political consequences of the residue of scientific modernity, considered from both psychoanalytic and aesthetic perspectives. The discussion takes as its point of departure Lacan's asseveration that Descartes's method of radical doubt is both the quintessential formulation of the reductive impetus inherent in modernity and a conceptual condition of possibility for the advent of Freudian psychoanalysis. Central to my concerns is the seemingly contradictory development in Lacan's teaching of the late 1960s of his notion of *objet petit a* as both a kind of (negative) frame for lack and a (positive) placeless surplus. These two modalities of the object join forces to bring to ruin any pretension to what Lacan names 'the universe of discourse' and Genet calls 'the fullness' or 'the plenum (*le plein*)'[1] of the world. Each of these expressions indexes the deluded claim that the network of signifying appearances, which effectively delivers what is ontologically available to the speaking being, cohere in the form of a completely realized unity.

Placed within the context of Lacan's approach to modernity, Genet's encounter with his stranger on a train bears extraordinary, if not entirely unprecedented, witness to the libidinal, properly substantive side of scientific modernity's radical and unresolvable subjective impact as inaugurally signalled by Cartesian philosophy. This, then, is my contention: Genet's essays are profoundly, if inexplicitly, psychoanalytic in the precise sense that they rearticulate in aesthetic terms the historical-conceptual necessity of Freud's introduction of his concept of the libido, along with Lacan's subsequent formulation of his notion of jouissance, specifically with respect to their parallel subversion of scientific modernity's hardly extinguished dependence on a classical ontological assumption regarding both the fullness and consistency of being. To provide context for this claim, I will begin with a summary overview of the notion of the modern, focusing on those elements of this intimidatingly broad term that are most relevant to this chapter's main interest: the striking sympatico between Genet's and Lacan's assessments of modernity's uncannily transformative consequences.

Though it is customary to associate Genet's work with both modernism and modernity, the complications inherent in these divergent terms will benefit from some unpacking. Orbiting around the central notion of a break with tradition understood as the immediate, organic connection of a subjective function to custom or ritual, modernity has been defined in various and interrelated ways. Economically, it has been understood as emanating from an emergent mercantile capitalism and its later development into industrial and financial structures. Socially, modernity has referred to the disintegration of the fixed hierarchical identities of feudalism and their replacement with more abstract, mobile and exchangeable monetary valuations of both goods and persons. Philosophically, reason is invoked as integral to modernity, be it in the form of the scientific empiricisms of the European seventeenth century, which rigorously distinguish between observed fact and moral categories, or else the critical-instrumentalist varieties of rationality by means of which a direct line is drawn from the self-interested bourgeois values of Enlightenment to the bureaucratically banalized evil of the Jewish Holocaust.[2]

For its part, modernism has more distinctively aesthetic connotations, usually characterized by an oppositional or even explicitly destructive commitment to novelty and innovation. From the arid rectilinear spaces of Le

Corbusier's architecture to the labyrinthine pathways of memory in Proust's work, the intolerable weight of history is cast off with the desire to begin again ex nihilo, with only the eternal ideality of geometry or the fathomless sensuate associations of consciousness as guide. In both modernity and modernism, the merciless questioning of tradition, of cognitive business as usual, is always central to the agenda.

Science, or Cartesian hysteria

The impetus to scrutiny and interrogation characteristic of the modern arises out of the agency of a radical negativity whose paradigmatic articulation is surely Descartes's bold methodological definition of subjectivity as doubt. In this light, it should not have come as a surprise over half a century ago when Lacan, connecting the dots between the *Meditations* and *Studies on Hysteria*, identified a rigorous parallel between the Cartesian's 'that perception may not be real' and the hysteric's 'that cannot be my desire', in so doing defining modern subjectivity in association with what fails to appear in the phenomenon. What is most novel in the modern, that is, is the implicit assumption of a position that does not avail itself to representation. From this placeless place, a tear in the fabric of tradition and culture, neither the validity nor the consistency of phenomena can convincingly hold.

This is the sense in which, *contra* Charles Taylor for example, the nature of modernity is in fact *a*cultural. In other words, modernity is a development in generic human time rather than a differentiated anthropological category specific to a particular social or intellectual tradition.[3] Taylor's misleading culturalization disconnects modernity from its great, though not absolute, socio-historical condition (capitalism) and paved the way for its postmodernist relativization, which took the form of a celebration of multiple and alternative modernities.[4] Doubtless this relativization was consummately noble in that it was articulated from the vantage point of the recipients of a decidedly ignoble colonialism and the sufferers of its putrid legacies, which are still of course very much alive today. The downside, however, was the elaboration of a false contradiction between a European or Euro-American modernity virtually reduced to its colonialist and racializing perversions, and a panoply of relativized, non- or alternative modernities, which may too easily be dismissed as mere superstructural excrescences of a late capitalist base whose fragile liberal ideological support is now succumbing once again to the fascination of right-wing populisms and even overt fascisms.

For Lacan, by contrast, the historical phenomenon of modernity is inseparable from the properly conceptual advent of modern science. In Lacan's view, modern science is defined by the gesture with which thought separates itself, in its ambition of mathematical formalization, from any conception of either the observable physical world or the function of subjectivity psychologically defined (by notions like consciousness and intentionality, in particular). Though modernity is indeed an historical phenomenon in the sense that it occurs at a particular moment of the human experience in particular places rather than others, there is no logic immanent to history that by itself conditions its coming into being. The act of isolating the cognitive function from the empirical givens of both nature and consciousness is what grounds the reference to Descartes as the emblem of both modernity and science in Lacan's teaching. Discounting its final, face-saving reference to God, Cartesian method, in its procedure of radical doubt, engenders a concept of thought as pure, absolute cognition abstracted from its requirement to refer to anything but itself.

With the advent of modern science, the duty of reference is not the only thing from which thought is set free, however. For Lacan, in addition, thought is emancipated from the conception of being. Indeed, in his suggestive, radicalized reading of Descartes's famous cogito, Lacan renders being as (a) mere thought, one from which any anchoring to substance has been pulled up. 'I think the thought whose content is "therefore I am"' is one way to paraphrase Lacan's subversive take on the cogito.[5] The signature gesture of both modernity and science of reducing being to thought is in the most rigorous sense an intellectual condition of possibility for Freud's subject of the unconscious as defined by Lacan. The subject is made equivalent to a void between signifiers; the 'that which', that is, that one signifier signifies for the next. In essence, modernity for Lacan concerns the evacuation of substance as quality from the subject; this subject's negative redefinition as deprived of essence, as unamenable to determinative or exhaustive predication.

If the subject lies between signifiers instead of residing in one or many of them, then it must take the form of an epistemological limit. What is 'subject' in what we call the individual is therefore not what we can never know about them, in other words some positive quality that exists somewhere beyond our knowledge, like the identity of the stranger sitting across from Genet in the anecdote to be considered shortly. Rather, the subject is the very modality of knowledge's failure to know, an epistemological glitch that also exhibits an ontological dimension. The insufficiency of knowledge that defines the subject is at the same time the impasse that mars its being. And this remains the case even after we acknowledge that the difficulty is figured as lack in the first case and as excess in the second.

In psychoanalytic terms, the unconscious subject comes to be during infancy in response to a missing signifier in its primary Other's speech; the Other's inability, that is, fully to articulate its enjoyment in words. For Lacan, we are always-already aware of the split in the Other; the unconscious emerges first as the Other's unconscious. Even in the earliest years of life, the infant senses an unsettling discrepancy between the primary caregiver's words and their being; between what they seem to want to say and what is betrayed by their facial expressions and physical gestures. This enjoyment between the lines of speech manifests as a traumatic, surplus excitation in direct association with the absent, unspoken signifier. In consequence, an immanent dynamic between a 'too little' or insufficiency at the level of psychical representation and a 'too much' or surfeit at the level of bodily excitation comes to define the same unconscious subject approached from two different perspectives. Contrary to what the laws of classical logic would suggest, however, these two distinct perspectives, the lack and the excess, neither contradict nor invalidate one another in their equally accurate descriptions of the Freudian unconscious subject.

According to Lacan, Descartes in his philosophical meditations had already arrived at this insight about the unexpressed and inexpressible quality of the subject's being, without however recognizing its troubling epistemological and ontological consequences. The philosopher thought he had discovered through his method a relation of implication between thought (knowledge) and being. In this view, being is conceived as a logical consequence of thought. In Lacan's view, however, Descartes began unwittingly to expose the disjunction that inheres both between knowledge and being and within each. To posit against the cogito's manifest meaning that thought can only fail to think the speaking subject's elusive being is insufficient. Lacan's contention regarding Descartes's latent message is more radical: this failure of thought is already what there is of being in itself.

There is no being beyond thought that thought would impotently fail to grasp. Rather, knowledge's impotence directly delivers the subject's being as essentially beset by the excessive and contradictory relation that being entertains with itself. If knowledge and being are encumbered by an impasse that effectively separates each from itself, then the rigorous categorical distinction between thought and being finally can no longer hold. Just as the experience of being occurs in tandem with a failure of knowledge, the moment of epistemological impasse is itself an encounter with being as such. In sum, the disjunctive non-relation of the unconscious is at once an insoluble epistemological conundrum and a disorienting contortion of being.

Lacan claims that modern science refounds the subject as without ground, deprived of a safe harbour in the world of representations, in so doing opening up a space for Freud's concept of the unconscious. Lacan does not argue, however, that psychoanalysis can operate properly without any conception of substance at all; indeed, it is to this question that he turns with increasing intensity in the latter stages of his teaching. This is also where the link to Genet's writing on art becomes significant. In their distinctive literary idiom, Genet's texts enact the same drama of modern subjectivity that Lacan evokes in his reference to the role played by the Cartesian revolution in the emergence of psychoanalysis. This is the drama of the subject's reduction to (a) nothing, to be sure, but also its subsequent 'reincarnation' as a very peculiar, formless and trans-individual, properly libidinal substance. As I will explore below, Genet's writing bears witness to how this substance forces us to redefine the human as that which we cannot subjectively support. In short, Genet's essays describe the residue of radical modernity's reductionist absolutism. From Rembrandt to Giacometti, modern art progressively exposes this residue: greasy globules of being at the bottom of the stock pot left forgotten on the ontological stove.

If the impossible desire of modern science is to eliminate the cumbersome and illusion-generating sensuous substrate of human existence, in the process rejoining the matter of nature to the forms of thought, then we can describe what Genet discovers on his train voyage as this substrate's return in the real. 'What does not come to be in the symbolic appears in the real,'[6] Lacan famously says in reference to the hallucinations of Freud's Wolf Man. For its part, however, modern science is not inherently psychotic. Within science's conceptual world, the return in the real results rather from the imperative to symbolize everything, to articulate *physis* (physical nature) with neither remainder nor contradiction through strict and exclusive use of mathematical formalization. This is indeed modernity's defining conviction for Lacan: nature is a language that can be written in logical form without leaving behind anything unsymbolized, indeterminate or undefined.

Before turning to Genet, it will be helpful to explore two questions. First, how in Lacan's view does this revolution of science leave its mark on the intellectual landscape in which Freud founded psychoanalysis some two and a half centuries later? And second, how does Freud's conception of the libido reformulate the terms of classical metaphysics? By way of addressing the first question, Lacan audaciously claims that the twentieth-century science of linguistics, beginning with Ferdinand de Saussure's path-breaking work, is a logically necessary outcome of the quintessentially modern project to create an all-encompassing, absolute system of writing. In this precise sense, linguistics is a scientific project par excellence. To speak of language as structure as understood in the discourse of structuralist linguistics is to assume that it can be formalized independently of its subject-effect, which takes the form of a persistent and ineradicable gap in the signifying chain for which the Freudian name is the unconscious. For Lacan, the relative historical contemporaneity of the Saussurean and Freudian projects at the turn of the twentieth century is no coincidence. 'What does language itself speak of when it is untethered (*désarrimé*) from the subject, in so doing representing its radicalized structural void?' asks Lacan. 'In general, it speaks of sex,' he replies to himself, 'of a speech whose silence represents the sexual act.'[7]

The formulation is paradoxical, to be sure. How does science, in its aim to articulate the laws of nature in purely objective terms, wind up speaking of sex, which we generally assume to be what is most subjective or idiosyncratic in the speaking being? Even more preposterously: How can the notion of a silent speech be anything but the most flagrant of contradictions in terms? We should first acknowledge that Lacan is not claiming that psychoanalysis, with its theory of sexuality, fills in some lacuna left open, by ignorance or neglect, by the structuralists of language. In other words, psychoanalysis would not simply compensate for some presumed inability or unwillingness on the part of linguistic science to broach the topic of sex. The suggestion is more radical: the scientific discourse of linguistics, or more precisely the structuralist objectification of language as a functional totality of symbolic differences, directly forces, at a properly conceptual level, the invention of psychoanalysis. Indeed for Lacan, it is as if the hysterical symptoms of Anna O. or Emmy von N. had been directly triggered by their perusal of Saussure's *Course in General Linguistics*. This overly literal scenario's chronological impossibility should not blind us to the crucial theoretical point it is meant nonetheless to convey. In conceiving of language as a complete system of bi-univocal, synchronic signifying relationships – stable, one-to-one connections between signifiers and signifieds, abstracted from their relationship to time – linguistics innocently brings sex onto the scene, not in the late-Foucaultian sense of an 'incitement to discourse', of sex speaking of itself in an endless truth-seeking confession, but rather negatively as silence, as a conspicuous absence that never properly materializes in either *langue* or *parole*, language or speech.

The very 'structuralizing' impulse of linguistic science, in other words its conception of language as amenable to schematic unification, finally exposes the project's immanent limit. Whittled down to its essence, the Lacanian argument posits that linguistic structuralism produced the logical necessity of the psychoanalytic concept of sex understood precisely as the unsayable, which does not mean, however, that sex can never be evoked or insinuated in speech. With Freud's introduction of his notion of the libidinal drive, sex becomes the unarticulated or unexpressed excess (note the paradoxical conjunction of negation and surplus) that always (potentially) accompanies the utterance, but without being demonstrably discernible – verifiable, to use the key term of the empiricist ideology that defines a concept of science very different from Lacan's – in any of its component signifying parts. Sex is the uncanny substance that is never manifestly present in, but at the same time never entirely absent from, the act of speech.

The troubling pragmatic implications are well known, if too infrequently explicitly acknowledged, in the age of #MeToo. There is no objective third party outside the intersubjective relation who could ascertain whether this or that utterance contains, in itself as it were, sexual content. Further, as witnessed already by Freud's first analysands, direct sexual language using standard anatomical vocabulary does not engender arousal. Conversely, the most innocent, seemingly non-sexual speech can be understood, in the right circumstances, as an aggressive erotic provocation. Causing no end of trouble for relationships and for the law, sex emancipates speech and silence from the constraints of Aristotle's law of non-contradiction. Sex is what speech cannot say, but manages to get across, unpredictably, nevertheless.

More rigorously put, sex is the ambiguous extra meaning in the utterance whose presence or absence is conspicuously undecidable, unverifiable in both the statement itself and in the enunciation, at least when this latter term is defined psychologically as a transparent intention. The premise of sex's admittedly paradoxical absent presence in language grounds the claim that the unconscious subject is what resists all forms of modern scientific reductionism. I must add, however, that this statement is valid only on condition that we understand this reduction to imply reduction to form: *all* pre-existing form, that is, from Saussure's universal network of linguistic signs, to the symbolic propositions of classical and postclassical logic, and even to the endless networks of binary code in the ever-expanding applications of information technology.

The essence of *ousia*

Given the wedge he drives between his idea of the unconscious subject and the notion of form, it makes sense that Lacan, beginning in the late 1960s, would shift his discourse away from, but without abandoning outright, the properly modern and abstract terrain of Cartesian cognitivism and towards the distinctly premodern idiom of substance and essence best conveyed in intellectual-historical terms by the Greek term ουσια (*ousia*). This is where I turn to the second preliminary question mentioned above. A warning: readers growing impatient for analysis of Genet's texts may find this section rough going and may choose to jump to the next. The Cartesian reference in Lacan serves primarily to buttress a properly logical conception of the Freudian subject as a lack in the signifying order, in the realm of appearances or representations. By contrast, the critical return to classical metaphysics in later-stage Lacan functions instead to develop the weirdly unextended substantiality of this same subject, a certain quality of non-sensuous plasticity, that somehow overflows and finally subverts what it carries by way of form.

If Descartes takes pride of place in Lacan's logical approach to the unconscious subject, then Aristotle plays the equivalent role in the other, parallel conception. An introductory foray into Aristotelian ontology will be helpful here. In his *Categories*, Aristotle defines what he calls primary substance (*prota ousia*) as that which is neither 'said of' nor 'in' any subject.[8] To be sure, these last phrases are specific to the *Categories* text; as might be expected, their meaning has been subject to considerable debate through the centuries. For my purposes here, I will assume in a quite uncontroversial way that the qualifiers in Aristotle's definition refer respectively to the accidental and essential predicates of a given subject. That is, what is 'said of' the subject may apply in some contexts but not in others, whereas what is 'in' the subject pertains to that subject essentially, in all possible circumstances.

For Aristotle, everything that is not a primary substance specifies one of these substances in the way that a genus relates to a species or a particular shade relates to a colour, for example. Though the *ousiai* are in this sense the basic, irreducible entities of Aristotelian ontology, their status as substances is grounded, counterintuitive though it might seem, in their logical priority over anything that can be said about them. For Aristotle, fundamental or ground-level being ('being qua being' in a more philosophical Badiouian vocabulary) can only ever be a 'that which'. This means that being for Aristotle is the unspecified, and in this sense abstract, stuff about which a particular knowledge claim can be made. Aristotle's conception of primary substance is what allows him to describe it as a *hypokeimenon*, in other words as the underlying entity that persists in a being subject to change over time; to becoming, you could also say.

With his pedagogical reference to these features of the most foundational of Western metaphysical traditions, Lacan however does not wish to assert their direct, unqualified relevance for psychoanalysis. To be sure, as I have had occasion already to remark in previous chapters, the subversiveness of Lacan's teaching with respect to the philosophical canon almost always results from his strategy of intervening in the fundamental conceptualization of classical notions rather than from arguing for their obsolescence or rejecting them outright, as the deconstructionist alternative has tended contrastingly to do. The case here is no exception. For Lacan, the problem with Aristotelian ontology is not precisely that it is 'metaphysical' in the pejorative sense fashionable not so long ago in the heyday of Derrida's work for example. Aristotle would not go astray, that is, where he assumes that there must be some quality or category of being that logically precedes, and remains unexpressed by, any predicative claim that can be made about it. The difficulty lies rather in Aristotle's consideration of being as such, which assumes by default a quality, however generic or non-predicative, of unity, of oneness. In other words, Aristotelian ontology advances a happy coincidence or simultaneity of existence and essence as well as, we can say by (Cartesian) extension, of thinking and being. For Aristotle, *ousia* is the ground of being, the material support that lends to the existent an essence that remains intact through the vagaries of its becoming. It is the unqualified substance that allows a river, taking the conventional Heraclitean example, to remain identical to itself through the wild torrents of the rainy season and the lazy meanderings of the dry.

Rather than subscribe to this canonical interpretation, Lacan instead connects the Aristotelian *ousia* to his own notorious concept of *objet petit a* which, in his seminars of the late 1960s, he endeavours to define mathematically as the radically incommensurable, as the quantity that remains intrinsically hostile to number or denumerability. Referencing such concepts in the history of mathematics as the golden ratio and the Fibonacci sequence, for example, Lacan defines *a* as the residue or leftover of the One. Explicitly assumed in this definition is the idea that a certain mark or construct of unicity as well as its immanent subversion are inherent in any activity of symbolization or numeration. Mathematically defined, *petit a* is the non-denumerable (non-) value – indistinguishably positive and negative, greater and lesser than – that remains as the inherently inconsistent by-product of any procedure of counting. As value's immanent subversion, it is 'not susceptible to "more or less"', says Lacan, 'can be introduced into no comparison, no "greater or lesser" symbol, not even "lesser or equal"'.[9] If all value is relational, if the worth of an object can only be expressed in relation to that of another, then *a* is what throws the spanner of non-relationality into the network, destabilizing and finally undoing it from within.

The Lacanian object stands here for a disruption in the mythical continuum of being, a disruption that has always-already occurred. In this sense, *a* holds the status of an *a priori* of the most absolute kind. Indeed, the use of the term 'object' to designate Lacan's *petit a* is misleading, and doubly so. Not only can there be no experience of an object in the absence of this object's prior self-alienation or immanent division in and by *a*. Also, the positive 'object', the objectal substance, is simply the other face of the subject conceived as lack. For psychoanalysis, subject and object are not the names of two conceptually distinct entities; they are rather two different modalities of the same twist or contortion, the same paradoxical lacking excess, inherent in the very fabric of being.

Lacan's attack on classical metaphysics is thus sidelong, covert. To be sure, Aristotle was on to something in his *ousia* discourse with the idea that any subject-object requires some ontological base for the display of its phenomenal manifold, for the unfurling of its predicative qualities. Like an empty set, ousia is pure 'there is', an exclusively notional being without verifiable existence, about which thought can claim precisely nothing. Indeed, there is something prior (in the sense of transcendental) and indefinite in the subject that cannot be expressed, that resists description, never fully coming into being. None of this is problematic for Lacan. The difficulty rather lies with how this support in being is conceived. Must *ousia* be a positive, and in this sense physical, substance, Lacan effectively asks? Does the subject really have a substantive existence *as* the unexpressed? Moreover, must the subject have a form, assuming the concept of form to imply a minimal degree of unity or order, in short an identity, as this last term is commonsensically understood?

In short, Lacan's answer is 'no'. Substance is coextensive with being's self-difference, with what in being is in fact *in*substantial. Substance is discontinuous, and the stuff of which it consists has come unstuck from itself. Substance as difference in this precise sense is not to be viewed as the difference between this and that appearance of being. Rather, absolute difference is difference as such, the prior difference that comes in-built inside every phenomenon as its non-self-identical, negative surplus, as the something extra that nevertheless fails to take (a) form. This difference is not precisely a content without form, but rather a kind of form without form, or content without content, one that renders the distinction between form and content inoperative and nonsensical by effectively invalidating the field of reference of both terms.

Lacan was acutely aware that the aspect of his definition of *objet petit a* that depends on a figure of negation – non-appearance, resistance to the count, non-identity, inexpressibility and the like – can lead us astray in so far as it can detract from the object's inherent link to jouissance: sex understood as embodied experience, to put it in less recherché terms. For Lacan the link is essential: 'there is jouissance only of the body,' he declares.[10] Though Lacan may not have wanted to suggest that *a* is exactly the same thing as jouissance, the two notions are intricately linked in their common dependence on an admittedly counter-intuitive deconstruction, to use the term loosely, of the distinction between lack and excess. The missing signifier in our primal Other's enigmatic speech and the accompanying traumatic excess of bodily excitation, which together define us as subjects of the unconscious and install the fundamental fantasy around which our lives take form, are like two facets of the same coin, two modalities of the selfsame psychosomatic agency. As is the case with light in physics, which requires contradictory but also complementary wave and particle iterations, the subject of the unconscious is both an absence or discontinuity in unconscious cognition and a symptom-forming excess at the experiential level of the body. Jouissance is the agency in the human biological organism that ensures its incommensurability with any other organism as well as its own biologically defined being. It repulses any attempt to place it in relation to anything outside itself. In this precise sense, jouissance is inherently *a*social (lacking in any connection with the social) as opposed to *anti*social (detrimental to social links presumed already to exist). There is no signifier, or sign even, capable of directly representing the subject at the level of its jouissance.

Not only does Lacan in the strictest terms connect enjoyment with corporeal experience, but he also ties both to the very concept of matter and to the realm of ethics. Indeed, Lacan argues that the essence of the subject is the body that enjoys. As we will discover in the upcoming engagement with Genet's art essays, however, precisely how we are to understand this experience might come as a surprise. For it is only a seeming contradiction that we can legitimately qualify this corporeal experience as out-of-body, 'body' understood here along the lines of these roughly analogous notions: the pop-psychological trope of the body image, Freud's concept of the (ideal) ego, or neuroscientific philosopher Thomas Metzinger's idea of the PSM (perceptual self model): the unconscious, virtual sensuate matrix that constructs our perceptions, our very experience of reality.[11] The enjoying body is what excludes the possibility of any relation involving the subject strictly speaking and, moreover, forms the conceptual foundation for a properly materialist ethics. And this ethics features a striking simpatico with the consequences Genet draws from the encounter with his stranger on a train.

Stranger on a train

We may now finally turn to Genet to inquire into his literary evocation of modernity's residue of jouissance and to develop the implications of this residue for the materialist ethics just mentioned. Genet recounts his anecdote in two separate pieces whose publication dates span almost a decade. 'The Studio of Alberto Giacometti', which no less a figure than Pablo Picasso considered the best essay ever written about an artist, was composed in 1957, but only first appeared the following year at L'Arbalète, the house run by Genet's long-time publisher Marc Barbezat. Exactly when Genet wrote the second piece, bearing the cumbersome title 'What Remains of a Rembrandt Torn into Little Squares All the Same Size and Shot Down the Toilet', is impossible to ascertain. The essay featured among a suitcase of unpublished manuscripts which Genet, in a fit of despair after his lover Abdallah Bentaga's suicide in 1964, tried to destroy. 'What Remains' eventually appeared with Genet's consent in an issue of Philippe Sollers and Jean-Edern Hallier's seminal Parisian avant-garde journal *Tel Quel* in May 1967.

Within the context of Genet's work as a whole, these two essays, alongside the closely related 'Rembrandt's Secret' published in the magazine *L'Express* in 1958, introduce a novel candour. The texts bear witness to a dolorous epiphany that would reorient Genet's lifework, guiding its course right up to the moment of his 1986 death. Collectively, they mark the oft-noted post-novel shift in Genet's work, forever altering his now even more fraught relationship to the written word. From this point onward, Genet not only struggles to rationalize ethically and politically the work of the writer in a world beset by social injustice and deep economic inequalities. Also, he goes as far as to renounce the novels that had transformed him, by the end of the 1940s, into something of an international literary superstar.[12]

Before turning to the account of the train incident itself, it will be wise to consider the implications of its curious association with Genet's engagement with fine art. The experimental, double-columned form of 'What Remains', the likely inspiration for Derrida's similar side-by-side coupling of alienatingly dense commentaries of Genet and Hegel in *Glas*, juxtaposes Genet's recollection of his encounter on the train with his reflections on Rembrandt's later portraiture. In this unusual essay, Genet sets the narration of an autobiographical interpersonal experience against a probing, if idiosyncratic, interrogation of the Dutch Golden Age artist, showing complete indifference to the distinct nature of his two subjects, specifically to the question of the significance of whether or not each is 'mediated'. That is, Genet broaches the problem of how to evoke his comparable responses to the old man on the train and Rembrandt's Jewish Bride as if the fact that the latter consists of an artwork and the former an event of lived experience held no implications whatsoever for his investigative method.

Genet's guileless unconcern for the conventional distinction between presentation and representation has two significant consequences. First, it shifts attention away from an interest in qualitative differences between perceptual objects, along with the degree of their inadequation with 'reality', and towards a focus on the subject's problematic placement within the field of vision, in other words the nature of their relation to the appearances composing the visible as such. Genet's musings on this or that work of Rembrandt or Giacometti strip away all art-critical or art-historical specificity in their alternative focus on the effects of various (re)presentations on the subject of vision and the vicissitudes of their desire. Relatedly, the discussion's timbre becomes noticeably internal, loosely phenomenological. Genet is less interested in describing what he sees for the sake of the description itself – its accuracy or evocativeness, for instance, although Genet is certainly not uninterested in questions of form and technique – than in tying particular attributes of the objects to their respective impact on his body and his general state of consciousness. The possessive adjective is misleading here, however. Suggesting a (perhaps) surprising affinity with Kantian aesthetic philosophy, Genet's depiction of his reaction to what he sees is resolutely impersonal, assuming implicitly that any beholder with an ordinary capacity for attention or sensitivity will be affected by the phenomena he evokes in precisely the same way.

But Genet also wants his discussion to figure the subject of vision as more than simply an embodied, desiring patient of visual-perceptual stimulation. Crucially, Genet moves beyond the issue of his receptivity to images of and in the world around him to centre on what becomes his central concern: the viewer's response to the surfeit in intensity of psychosensory input over the mind's capacity to process or organize it. Genet's reflections proceed under the assumption that our engagement with the field of vision will deliver an encounter with the same excessive and ecstatic experience of jouissance that Lacan conceptualizes for psychoanalysis. Sensory exposure to particular images can trigger a psychosomatic response that overwhelms us, traumatizes us even; it transforms the world of appearances into a dangerous manifold that requires strategies of defence in order to become visually negotiable. In ethical terms, Genet's writing implies that we are duty bound to acknowledge the disruptive possibility of jouissance in the visual field along with its numerous consequences for the way we think about our desiring relation to what we see.

Though seemingly unremarkable and outwardly banal, it is no exaggeration to say that the event on the train serves up to Genet a painful epiphany whose effects transform his very being. The anecdote is set in a third-class carriage travelling in the lower Rhone valley somewhere 'between Salon and Saint-Rambert-d'Albon'.[13] Seated across from Genet is an unfriendly and unbearably ugly old man with a 'dirty moustache' and a 'spoiled mouth' who aims 'gobs of spit' onto the floor of a 'compartment already dirty with cigarette butts, paper, crusts of bread'.[14] Genet casts the man's presence as the source of an infection, evoking a 'rottenness' that begins 'to gangrenate' his 'former vision of the world'.[15] These initial observations already signal the overarching themes of disintegration and shattering, of subjective undoing or destitution, that permeate Genet's prose.

Though nothing in the nature of a narrative event takes place in Genet's relating of the episode, a fortuitous meeting of glances suddenly triggers the striking insight that every human being is not simply worth every other; can be interchanged with, substituted for, any other. More counter-intuitively, Genet senses that any given individual person actually *is* every other. The quintessentially modern idea that we are all of equal inherent value in relation to some abstract category of personhood or citizenship that transcends our situational particularities – familiar in the European tradition since at least the anti-aristocratic, liberal-revolutionary egalitarianism of the Enlightenment – is here supplanted by the more radical and genuinely uncanny notion that there are no individuals as such. Everyone is in effect the same person, though 'person' here is an equally deficient term.

The details of Genet's description of the seeming non-event from which his realization derives are light on narrative information and heavy on abstract speculation. The transformation takes place in an atemporal instant, to the point where it seems not even to qualify as an experience in the term's conventional understanding. Genet's consideration of the old man's impact on him in two separate essays – we might assume there were other drafts and approaches destroyed in the aftermath of Bentaga's suicide or on other occasions – suggests something of the difficulty he may have experienced articulating its significance in prose. Indeed, the inadequacy of language to capture the real is a dominant theme in Genet's writing, which constantly places, in properly Cartesian fashion, the validity of its assertions into radical doubt. The language is taught, terse, but also thick with resonance; it is also markedly idiosyncratic, difficult to link up with any degree of certainty with other literary or philosophical discourses.[16]

Genet describes the man in the train carriage as not only 'dirty' and 'mean' but also 'very ugly' and even 'ghastly (*épouvantable*)'.[17] Evidently, the impact of the old man's repulsiveness is not something that can easily be overcome, through some Platonic procedure of abstraction towards some beautiful essence of the human for example. Though Genet writes that 'anyone ... can be loved beyond his ugliness, his stupidity, his meanness',[18] the insight plainly costs him; it fosters an affective state not of serenity or peace, but rather of wrenching disillusionment. Comparing his apprehension of the old man to the way Giacometti looks at the subjects of his figural artworks – the visual stance or attitude, that is, that gives form to the artist's extraordinary vision – Genet adds that the motivation for the outlook he shares with Giacometti has nothing to do with what he calls 'goodness'.[19] Neither beautiful nor recognizably human, what Genet sees in the old man is also categorically disjoined from that consummate category of practical reason. The key implication is that whatever the substance that Genet finds in his Other might be, its identity cannot be expressed in the terms of any of the humanist discourses according to which the existence of a human life may be justified, rationalized or valorized.

Further, though the strange matter he finds in his neighbour – the thing he calls 'that precious point' – is an object of 'recognition' for Genet, this recognition proves to be quite peculiar. Indeed, it stems from a 'solitude'[20] that results not from a gesture of differentiation or individuation, but rather from a peculiar logic of equivalence and identity. This detail is particularly intriguing in that it casts by implication the whole discourse on recognition in liberal political philosophy, taking its inspiration from Hegel's famous master–slave dialectic, in a distinctly oblique light. In general terms, recognition has been viewed to inform the conflicted relations inhering between individuals and social groups within a democratic field as they struggle for the validation of their distinctive identities or ways of life within a legal-juridical apparatus of rights and responsibilities that provides formal equality between citizens but not genuine, concrete social equality. In this context, 'recognition' names a dialectic that pits individual and social differences against an abstract, universal agency presumed capable of integrating those differences within the general political framework. With time, the claims of emergent groups force the system to reformulate the terms of inclusion, since the universal structure is never concretely universal, and depends instead on a process of selection that operates surreptitiously, often in direct, though covert, violation of the terms of the law. As the foundation of ethical self-realization or as a means of eliminating institutional subordination, the imperative of recognition lies at the root of the most influential critical theories of justice in the liberal tradition.[21]

With Genet's insight, however, this liberal logic, even and perhaps especially in its avowedly left-materialist vein, ceases to pertain, since what is recognized is very clearly not predicated on a concept of either individual or social (group) difference. What Genet sees in the repulsive old man rather obliterates difference and individuality as these terms are commonly understood. Genet is led to the unsettling insight that not only is his own being directly the other man's ugliness, but also everyone else's is too. The secret identity of every individual human turns out to be this single, decidedly *in*human substance that effectively alienates every being from its own humanity; from every attribute, that is, that one would reasonably wish to associate with the species generically conceived. The logic of identification that buttresses the ideology of recognition falls away when what is recognized not only differentiates itself from what partakes of humanity, but also renders inoperative any criterion by which differences are identified between persons and collectives. In parallel with Lacan's reframing of Aristotle's *ousia*, the concept of humanity is separated off from the complete set of its possible predications. Unlike in Aristotle, however, this is done in Genet in a way that deprives being of any phenomenal unicity. The unbearable ugliness of the old man on the train is simply the worldly appearance of a non-phenomenal, characterless and generic (in)human substance coincident with our species-being's difference from itself.

Solitude and the non-relation

For Genet, the extraordinary accomplishment of Giacometti's artwork lies in how it 'restores' in us the capacity to perceive a sameness in the other where 'the human being is brought back to the most irreducible part in him'.[22] In paradigmatically modern fashion, what is perceived in the other human being is a residue of the process by which what is merely contingent, circumstantial, situational or contextual is mercilessly stripped away. This leftover remains after 'the accident is annihilated (*anéanti*)',[23] as Genet succinctly puts it; when all that is inessential and unnecessary has been chiselled off the stone block of being. The difficulty, of course, is that when the process is complete there is nothing verifiably existent left to be seen, no *physis* left over to be sublated into form. This gesture of logico-phenomenological reduction long since associated with modernity and the modern is pushed so far in Genet as to negate the relation as such. There is no possibility of a relation to another to the extent that the subject can entertain no proper relation to itself. Genet's idea of solitude, so strongly developed as to be worthy of the status of a concept, offers an original and consequential anti-humanist and anti-historicist insight. Whereas the world's 'visible manifestations' are ordered by a mechanical and pitiless determinism invulnerable to human will or action, Giacometti's body of work, in Genet's view, seeks 'to discover that secret place in ourselves from which an entirely different human adventure might possibly begin'.[24]

Genet's distinction pits the rigid determinism of an order of appearances governed by a pitiless historical law against the dynamic unpredictability of an irreducible and trans-individual human substance which is both nowhere to be seen in the field of vision and resistant to the forms of knowledge. On the surface of his discussion, history's indifferent causal chain relates to Genet's solitary, invisible region just as the inhuman relates to the human. That is, all the ugly evidence of human depravity that accumulates during the first half of the twentieth century (and beyond) ambivalently determines the need for a more edifying account of what makes up our species-being. But Genet's suspicion of humanist ideals insistently returns as he wonders if the new adventure to be born from historical tragedy will be 'moral' in nature; inspired, in other words, by a 'nostalgia for a civilization that would try to venture somewhere beyond the measurable'.[25]

For Genet, Giacometti's art bears unflinching witness to modernity's historical horrors. Refusing to look away, it struggles to convert the illusory and retrogressive, utopian desire for escape to some unknown beyond into a painful and properly aesthetic acknowledgement of what appears to be inhuman in humanity. Modern art's turn away from contextual determinations and historical causalities aims at placing the beholder in a visual (and tactile) position from which it becomes possible to 'discover what remains of man when the pretence is removed'.[26] An artist like Giacometti or Rembrandt creates works that hold the power to force us, should we allow them, to encounter the essential solitude of objects and persons, in other words that element within them that does not avail itself to entering into relation with any other entity. In Genet's account, the modernistic jettisoning of artifice in Giacometti's art functions to separate the object out from the full panoply of its situational determinants, any conception of utilitarian value, all individuating psychological factors (most importantly intentionality or affect), and even form itself.

In ontological terms, the artist aims to sever all of the object's relations in the view of achieving an absolute, unmediated sovereignty that finally estranges it even from its own being. Embodied in the artwork, this hostility to relationality and the consequent alienation of being then impose themselves on the beholder. If a Giacometti sculpture forces us to abandon all sensuous awareness of other objects, for instance, then this ascesis also has the effect of disclosing the work's strange absence to itself. The art object's creation and subsequent persistence in time bear witness to the torsion point in being from which art emerges and which it functions to conserve within the disorienting contours of its materiality. The solitude of both the artist and the artwork paradoxically discloses the incompletion of even the non-relation itself. If every relation fails to cross a zone of negativity in being, then the reverse is also true. The non-relation acquires a strange positivity or presence that finally allows something of the relation to occur: a relation, that is, imbued with its own discontinuity, its own non-relation with itself.

Moreover, Genet brilliantly captures how the material form of Giacometti's artworks manages to open up our conception of historical time by embodying the disorienting spatial and temporal effects of this weirdly embodied discontinuity. One day, walking into Giacometti's Montparnasse studio, Genet apprehends two canvases that 'seem to be in the midst of walking, coming to meet (him), never stopping this motion towards (him)'. Indeed, the paintings depict heads that appear to come from the 'depths of the canvas'.[27] Genet attributes the 'beauty' of the sculptures to 'the incessant, uninterrupted to-and-fro movement from the most extreme distance to the closest familiarity'.

The impossibility of fixing the art object's distance from the beholder also corresponds to its indeterminate and nomadic positioning in time. The artist must become 'not a sort of eternal present, but rather a vertiginous and uninterrupted passage from a past to a future, an oscillation of one extreme to another'.[28] When put into practice by an artist like Giacometti, this uncommon temporal disorientation results in a work that unmoors the beholder from the here-and-now in precisely the same way. It would be a mistake, however, to infer from Genet's account of the artwork's spatial and temporal mobility that these qualities deliver an experience of continuity, either in the intimate and subjective sense of Bergsonian *durée* or in the the sense of cosmic unity that Freud claimed never to have experienced in response to the 'oceanic feeling' that Romain Rolland famously described to him.[29] Rather, space and time become dislodged from themselves, revealing a zone of floating, peripatetic negativity enclosed within the medium, but not of it.

This, then, is Genet's startling claim in the trio of essays: any singular work of art effects 'the historical abolition of the one who is looking'.[30] It is not just the artwork that is made to elude the clutch of history, but its beholder as well. The irreducible, non-historical nucleus that Genet identifies in the artwork ricochets back onto the viewer, forcing them to acknowledge how their 'own' being – being does not belong to us in the ordinary sense – exceeds what can be described as historical in precisely the same way. Also, Genet turns decidedly off the existentialist path with this idea that we are already – *a priori*, as it were; before the launch of any volitional project – something both more and other than the total accumulation of our lived experience or the full temporal sequence of our biographical situations, materially defined. Against the grain of today's ambient New Age psychological meditation culture, which advances ideas of stillness and presence, what becomes inaccessible at this non-historical moment is precisely the immediate 'now'. As the object's being is isolated and discerned, Genet concludes, the beholder 'ceases to be present'.[31]

The elusive but putatively accessible state of whole being sought after by the contemporary post-religious spiritual subject seeking relief from the scattered and unfocused world of late capitalism becomes in Genet not simply impossible to grasp, but more importantly non-existent, an illusion. Genet chooses the past perfect tense to evoke the event on the train, suggesting that it could not have been experienced immediately, that it could only be lived as having already happened or as yet to occur.[32] Indeed, an encounter with Giacometti's or Rembrandt's artwork has the subject experience the very antithesis of the eternal present we are incessantly enjoined to enjoy. Instead, an 'uninterrupted and vertiginous … oscillation' between past and future overtakes us and, as Genet elusively continues, we never cease to 'withdraw into an undefined past and future'.[33]

Rather than gain tangible access to the normally fleeting moment, during Genet's encounter time as such ceases to flow. No longer witness to a succession of discrete or continuous nows, we rather become, more radically, non-present in time. The past and future fold into one another. Eternity becomes immediate, subverting the anticipatory quality of temporality, in other words the idea that we are always waiting or striving for something else. An object or substance remains, to be sure, but it can no longer be described as an object of desire. In Genet's own terms, all 'affective or utilitarian' connections to being 'are abolished'.[34] There is no longer use or exchange value, no more psychology when the object acquires a quality of unmoving, if nonetheless harrowing, indifference.

The wound of being

In an extraordinary essay that merits in-depth engagement, William Haver seizes upon these elements of Genet's art essays that subvert our intuitive understanding of space and time. Ingeniously, he develops from them what he calls a social ontology, and it bears some striking similarities to the one for which I am arguing in this chapter. An overview of Haver's discussion will provide an opportunity to bring some refinement to the conception of the non-relational variety of being that Genet's theme of the wound aims to evoke. In the Giacometti essay in particular, the wound becomes a sign for Genet's sense of the shared identity of subjectivity and ontological negativity, and art becomes a means of shedding light on this identity, of encountering it in the guise of a failure of knowledge. 'Beauty has no other origin than a wound ... that everyone keeps in himself,' writes Genet. And Giacometti's art aims 'to discover that secret wound of every being, and even of every object'.[35]

For Haver, sociality in Genet is constituted in difference and separation. Hostile to both communication and community, it enacts 'the immanent articulation of the relation of non-relation'.[36] Concise but technical, Haver's phrase captures the paradox by which, for Genet, what is most essential and incommunicable about a person, what is most distinctive, individual and untransferable, is not only what renders them abject, but also what is shared universally by 'all sentient being'.[37]

Haver is correct to specify that despite some circumstantial evidence to the contrary, Genet does not assume the existence of an originary unity of being that would then succumb to some process of phenomenal dispersal by means of which distinct individuals appear. In this mistaken view, the encounter with the old man on the train would serve to restore or reconstitute a lost ontological unity. Rather, Genet's thinking (as does Lacan's, I would add) presupposes what Haver, in another succinct expression, calls an 'atemporal disjunct simultaneity' between identity and difference whereby difference is already immanent to, or included within, identity. With this formulation, identity becomes inseparable from its own internal difference. The logic is topological rather than temporal: there is no dialectical movement in time between moments of identity and difference; instead, the one is always-already – transcendentally, that is – implicated in the other such that no categorical distinction between the two terms can legitimately be made.

Despite the striking lucidity of Haver's formulations, however, some critical specification can nonetheless be made. Indeed, the argument goes on to conclude from the admissible premise that in social being 'there is no inside, no outside' to the misleading conclusion that there is 'only the outside, sheer exteriority'.[38] By way of a psychoanalytic rejoinder to this assertion of an absolutely external being with the power to eliminate any trace of interiority or self-affection from the subject, we can again invoke Lacan's notion of *extimité* which, rather than situating subjectivity purely in the realm of alterity, insists instead on the uncanny interconnection of the proper and the alien. For psychoanalysis, in other words, it is a question not of erasing the distinction between inside and outside, founding in the process some putatively consistent and self-present field of otherness, but rather of rendering the distinction ambivalent, undecidable: the foreign is inside me at the same time that what is most 'mine' is unsettlingly 'out there'.

This subtle but significant revision to Haver's Genetian social ontology also requires a qualification of its approach to the matter of multiplicity. 'The principle of sociality ... is a principle of multiplicity,'[39] Haver asserts. Just as there is no absolute exteriority in being, however, neither is there a pure multiplicity untarnished by the mark of unity. Here another famous expression from Lacan's later teaching can bring welcome nuance. With his introduction of the phrase *Y'a d'l'Un* in his seminar in the early 1970s, Lacan wishes to address precisely this question of the mutual implication of unity and multiplicity in the conception of being. A colloquial contraction of the difficult-to-translate phrase *il y a de l'Un* ('there is some One' or 'there is some of One'), Lacan's expression conjoins the partitive article *de* with the signifier for unicity, capitalized to underscore the apparent contradiction brought about by conjoining in a single concept both the part and the whole.

This distinction between pure or absolute multiplicity and what could be termed, after Haver, the relation of non-relation of the multiple and the One would remain somewhat arcane if it did not bear consequences for my engagement with Genet's writing. More specifically, it sheds crucial light on the thematic of ascesis that runs consistently through the work, but finds perhaps its most arresting formulation in the train episode's various presentations. Though Haver justifiably draws attention to the Eros-abating and world-shattering disillusionment occasioned by Genet's encounter with the old man, there is no suggestion in the essays that the resulting state of abject indifference can grant indefinite immunity to the charms of seduction.

In line with influential currents in queer theory that celebrate the prospects of impersonality,[40] Haver's reading implies the possibility of a sociality of pure, indifferent promiscuity fully liberated from the effects of repression and idealization, as if Genet's traumatic realization on the train represented some final, decisive exit from the experience of sexual desire as commonly understood. To be sure, Haver himself discovers conflicting evidence, observing in Genet's essays what he astutely calls 'an ambivalent nostalgia for the erotic enchantments of the world'.[41] In its illusory attachment to the enticing and endless appearances of 'the predicate' of being, the erotic is indeed 'a lie'.[42] It is not amenable, however, to definitive eradication.

Towards sublimation

A reference to the psychoanalytic concept of sublimation can bring further refinement to Haver's important reading and will serve to support my own claim about the general affinity of Genet's work with psychoanalysis. When Lacan describes sublimation as the practice that 'raises an object … to the dignity of the Thing',[43] we might justifiably wonder at the apparent incommensurability: the Thing, stuff of the disgusting, pulsating jouissance that deprives me of the sense, the very image, of my own being, becomes the very foundation of my dignity, my worth. Things become more clear, however, with the addition of the proviso that this worth does not accrue from the viewpoint of the Other. Indeed, the Lacanian object of sublimation, in sharp contrast to Freudian sublimation's dependence on social approbation, acquires its dignity from the point of view of the Thing itself, as if this Thing had the capacity to bestow upon the object a position within the field of signifying relations. This is the paradox of sublimation: at the same time that it creates an impossible reconciliation between the signifier and what ordinarily resists signification, it exposes the signifying system's non-coincidence with itself, in other words its dependence on that which it functions to abscond and obscure. Genet's discourse on the ontological wound is the consummate act of sublimation in that it creates a new signifier to index what remains irremediably intrinsic, incommunicable and non-relational: or solitary, to use Genet's preferred term.

Sublimation is the obverse of idealization. Idealization is the operation through which indifferent libidinal substance is objectified, thereby acquiring an erotic value by virtue of the signifying relations it entertains with other objects. By contrast, sublimation requires us to work from the substance from which no relation can be forged, to which no signifier can be ascribed. And yet, seemingly impossibly, sublimation manages nonetheless to create a signifier for this substance, undoing in the process what is ordered in the so-called symbolic order. In sublimation, the artist creates something out of what appears socially as nothing, starting from a placeless place that has no coordinates, in between the forms with which the social world takes shape.

Here again we can invoke Haver's essay to underscore the importance of this aspect of sublimation that creates a new signifier. This signifier produces neither a new meaning nor a newly consistent modality of being. Rather, it marks out and condenses into form the common indwelling incompletion of both meaning and being. With uncommon lucidity, Haver argues that (for Genet) the artwork concerns the specific 'something of the word that resists interpretation and the understanding absolutely, something that philosophy cannot recover for intelligibility, something that at once provokes and interrupts thought'. Art does not stand there asking to be interpreted or understood. Alternatively, it is 'another experience of identity and equality',[44] and the duty of someone like Genet who sets himself the task of writing about it is to evoke that experience, to create a text to be placed alongside the work of art, not above it. A psychoanalytic view can add to these observations the insight that the text is equally a 'work of art', in other words an act of sublimation, or what Genet would describe as a poetic act. This act creates a new form to signify precisely the resistance to understanding that Haver evokes. This slight shift in perspective has the salutary effect of evacuating the mysterious 'something' in the Haver quote of any positive content, indeed of any quantum of being. There is no enigmatic substance or quality in the art object that thought fails to think; art viewed as the object of sublimation rather becomes the embodiment of the constitutive impasse of both thought and being.

Haver goes as far as to qualify this quantum of being in the artwork that escapes thought as 'the ontological priority of the political'. This priority is then invoked to assert the 'impossibility of establishing a ground that would sanction any political order' or justify any particular politics.⁴⁵ This move strikes me as ill-advised because it safeguards an ontologically pure realm both political and aesthetic in relation to which any specific political agenda can only appear as degraded or debased. To be clear, it is not a question of reasserting some essential ground for political action, which could be legitimated in some putatively objective fashion through, for example, the exercise of a practical rationality whose procedural telos would be some determinate concept of the Good. Rather, I wish here to signal the difference between conceiving of the political's priority in being in a critical way as what any concrete political programme can only fail to express, and alternatively in an affirmative way as the explicit avouchment of the impossibility inherent in any such programme. In other words, the awareness of this impossibility becomes the content of the political programme itself. Whereas the former conception dissuades political action by focusing on the grounding or legitimation it lacks, the latter reframes that same lack as the very principle of political intervention, effectively occupying the space of political sovereignty as a means of leaving it empty, open and undefined.

I will have occasion to develop this point in the next chapter. To conclude this one, however, we can take the opportunity to extend our refinement of Haver's important reading of Genet to address the related thematic of being's 'extensibility' in the influential work of Leo Bersani. For Bersani, inspired in part by the psychoanalytic work of one-time Lacan student Jean Laplanche, Freud's text both describes and occludes what he calls 'the natural extensibility of all being'.⁴⁶ This being is constituted not through a violent or imperialistic imposition of self on Other, but rather through a more subtle extension of subjectivity in a continuous process of constitution and shattering of selfhood. On my reading, Genet's ontology is incommensurable with the Bersanian reading of Freud because of the emphasis Genet places on what we might call his singularity's wild heterogeneity, its hostility to the very notion of selfhood as such.⁴⁷ The quality that most essentially defines the Genetian wound is precisely its resistance to incorporation with the self, however provisionally this self is defined. As demonstrated by the trajectory of Bersani's work, a more 'extensible' ontology can lead to notions of impersonal community or sociability such as the one that might characterize a certain world of gay or queer men, for example.

In a patently different vein, Genet is at pains to stress that his sense of humanity's universal essence, to use rather too pompous a phrase, is anything but an encomium to what he calls brotherhood. 'Each man was myself', Genet writes, 'but isolated, temporarily, in a particular shell (*écorce*)'.[48] For Genet, being is the source of a discontinuity in the social relation that renders it volatile and fragile. Being engages in the weakening and severing, not the establishment, of ties between objects. Being is fundamentally non-relational; it renders discontinuous my relation both to the world and to myself. However, these qualities fail to prevent these relations from persisting in their discontinuity. For both Genet and Lacan, the object of art and its act of creation remind us that the relations we do manage to construct between ourselves and the world are finally unsound, provisional and nonexclusive, bound to a base level of irreducible ontological incompletion.

5

Postcoloniality meets indeterminate negation: The Screens

An ontology of defecation

In the penultimate scene of Genet's final play *The Screens*, a French sergeant recounts from the realm of the dead the last moments of his life. We are in the midst of the colonial system's death-throes in an unnamed Arab locale that resembles Algeria in the years immediately prior to the play's publication in 1961. The Sergeant has left the encampment to get away from his lieutenant; he is looking for some privacy in order to take a shit. Assuring himself that he has not been followed, and also that there is no viper hiding within its depths, he crouches atop an inconspicuous hole, shoving the lower portion of his uniform down to his ankles. Then, 'just at the moment when (he's) pushing and (his) gaze begins to tremble (*vacille*), just at the moment when something is veiled … and takes off (*fout le camp*)',[1] he dies in a manner unspecified in the text, victim of a brain aneurysm, perhaps, or possibly rebel sniper fire.

There follows a strange monologue in which the Sergeant speculates about the subjective experience of excretion and its inherent link to the production, or revelation, of a gaping emptiness, a fault in the fabric of knowledge and being. Miming his final defecatory exertions for his laughing fellow dead people onstage, the Sergeant attempts to make sense of the episode by recalling others in the same situation. 'I've seen officers shitting – higher officers, general officers!' he exclaims. 'Their eyes: emptied. Not just empty, but emptied, i-e-d. The stars on their caps, no longer stars when the eyes are emptied.'[2] The Sergeant is fascinated but also disturbed by evacuation's strange power to strip even prestigious military personnel of their identities. The void created by the act swallows up 'your rank of sergeant or captain', he specifies, along with its various signifiers, including 'uniform ... stripes, (and) decorations'.[3] Together with the digestive tract, the field of signification associated with military insignia gets emptied out, leaving only the acute sense of a space from which the rightful contents have been flushed away.

In Lacanian terms, the Sergeant's scatological vignette suggests the idea of the symbolic order's evanescent suspension: a fleeting interval of time during which the horizon of meaning giving shape to a network of signs disappears, sucked into a gaping hole as if by the force of gravity. In the Sergeant's military context, hierarchies of power cease to function without the emblems that confer determinate positions on the chain of command. Decorations legitimizing authority and commemorating honourable acts of bravery become meaningless, even ridiculous when they are shorn of their symbolic power. In semiotic terms, the metaphorical bond that attaches a signifier to a signified dissolves away just like the expression in the eyes of the Sergeant's defecating officers. It is as if, for Genet, the signifying form were shitting out the last remnants of its connection to content, to the very possibility of signification, exposing in the process its empty contingency and irreparable incompleteness. For a moment, a spectrally positive mark of the unconscious appears in its disruptive and paradoxical negativity, subverting the efficacy of the system of differences that organizes any social formation of meaning and power, and neutralizing the effects of the cut of castration that conditions the very possibility of signification.

Condensed into this abjectly comedic setting, narratively marginal yet conspicuous for its position near the play's end, is the fundamental triadic structure jouissance – excess – void. This is the structure against which takes shape in this unwieldy and complex play Genet's meditation on the tenuous constitution of the world of appearances. The indelicate enjoyment in voiding, made manifest in the emptying out of the Sergeant's eyes and bowels, produces an abject surplus, the 'turd half out'[4] to which the Sergeant alludes and which can find no place within the order of signification. Curiously, however, the scene's details discourage the interpretation according to which the void and the surplus would entertain, as one might spontaneously assume, a zero-sum relation as symmetrical opposites. In this intuitively persuasive view, the emptied-out volume would equal the space taken up by the excreted object. As we discover, however, the turd's production fails to neutralize all of the numerous elements of negativity referenced in the scene: the hole itself, the absence of light, the lieutenant whom the Sergeant suspects may be following him but 'wasn't there',[5] and finally his own death, which supersedes the momentary vacillation of consciousness that accompanies the enjoyment in the effort of excretion. Indeed, death arrives just at the moment when the Sergeant looks forward once again to contemplating 'the beauty of war's gestures' with an 'eye that knows how to decipher service records'.[6] Death interrupts the anticipated precarious reconstitution of both aesthetic and symbolic orders, leaving behind both a contemptible excess and a yawning hole. This hole is animated by a ghostly negativity that goes without a proper object on which to operate its power of negation.

No distracting comedic interlude, this scene can be viewed to ground Genet's notion of the dissimulated but impossible truth of being-as-appearance. In more concrete terms, the baroque stagecraft of *The Screens* mobilizes a generous multiplicity of giant articulated *paravents*[7] arranged in a variety of configurations on multiple levels on the stage and onto which characters draw images reflecting aspects of the action. Two crucial observations should be made in this regard. First, it is (almost) always the Arab characters engaged in the rebellion against European colonialism who draw images on the screens. And second, the scene with the Sergeant takes place on a platform representing the realm of the dead and occupied by screens that remain empty.

Manifestly a meditation on the politics of decolonization,[8] *The Screens* additionally formulates through literary means Genet's mature theory of the creative act as a specifically feminine form of sublimation from abjection. As I will explore in detail in this chapter, this act refounds the image as not only impossible, and therefore self-annihilating, but also as revelatory of a transcendental (in the sense of *a priori*) deficit that thwarts both epistemological and ontological fullness. *The Screens* is interested in the recursive process by which, time and again, the world of appearances dissolves and reconstitutes itself, endlessly confronting its failure to constitute a coherent world, and then attempting to put itself back together only to be torn asunder once again.

In part, the play animates a conventional colonizer–colonized binary. Whereas the European characters invoke the values of national identity, administrative hierarchy, aesthetic beauty and historical continuity, the Arab rebels unite around representations of violence, ugliness, rotting, crime and evil. The symbolic offensive against the hegemony of colonialist ideals takes place on two different fronts, however. Whereas Genet associates the revolutionaries led by ostensible hero Si Slimane and his female ally Kadidja with the activity of alternative image-creation on the screens, the central triad of characters – the Mother, Saïd and Leila – stand for a more radical, non-relational or absolute negativity, one that shifts the locus of difference from the interval between identities to identity itself. Against the historical backdrop of early North African postcoloniality, *The Screens* asks a question that transcends historical specificity: Is it possible to create a new kind of image, one that opts not to lure us with the promise of a faultless, fully actualized totality? An image, in other words, that could resist the co-optation of postcolonial power by the structures of domination? Hegemonically, images dangle before us the prospect of completed knowledge and realized being by creating a neutral, empty space meant to be fleshed out by fantasy; the image frames a void against which an ideal can be unfurled. In *The Screens*, Genet instead tries to invent a practice of image-making that somehow betrays the image's promise to convey identity and meaning through its exposure not of a neutral lack, but rather of a more radical ontological deficit, or lack-in-being.

Genet's final theatrical work asks if the repetitive cycle of destruction and reconstruction of hegemonic image systems is condemned to reassemble the same structures over and over again. Answering in the negative, it offers a theatrical figuration of repetition that foregrounds the intervention of a particular kind of symbolization. By indexing the locus of a debt in being, the symbolic act carves out a space in which can be nurtured the fragile possibility of the new. Written and rewritten during the final bloody years of the Algerian revolution, the play presages the victory of the nationalists and the reconstruction of an independent Algeria led by a regime hardly different from the vanquished French colonial administration in its obsession with the militaristic display and exercise of power. With its impossibly large cast of loathsome Arab antiheroes, epigons of ugliness and betrayal, *The Screens* dissects the mutual implication of signification and idealization in a merciless attempt to affirm the possibility of creating a new kind of self-destroying image or anti-image. This is the image that would manage to break free from the complicity that enmeshes the negativity of repetition with the unacknowledged enjoyment binding us to the force of worldly power.

Jouissance after the revolution

The contours of the ontological argument that bolsters Genet's theatricalization of the poetic act of sublimation are first suggested in details of the 'indications' that precede the first scene. Depicted onstage is a rectangular outdoor courtyard surrounded by an array of unevenly placed black planks forming platforms at varying heights along all three sides. During the play, numerous three-metre-high multi-panelled screens, some to feature hand-drawn images suggesting objects and settings, are wheeled out from the wings in various configurations, but always placed next to 'at least one real object'.[9] Genet names two of these objects, a milestone and a pile of coarse gravel, stipulating that they are to be present onstage already as the audience enters the house. Just before the play begins, a screen is wheeled out from stage right and placed behind the two objects, which receive only cursory mention as they play proceeds.

At first glance a deliberately enigmatic whim of high-concept stagecraft symbolism, the arrangement gains in significance when viewed through the lens of psychoanalytic theory. A milestone, of course, demarcates a point of reference from which a differential set of values, distances in this case, can be determined. Like any standard, it represents an originary mark against which values can be measured as a means of enabling navigation or wayfinding, for example. A properly human intervention, such a mark engenders psychological intuitions of space and may conjure retroactively the imaginary ideal of a pure natural landscape devoid of signifying forms. The other two objects, gravel mound and screen, stand for the by-products of the milestone's creative organization of a network of differentially determined values. More precisely, they embody the fact that the signifying mark emerges in an attempt to compensate for a properly transcendental negativity; a void or absence not in the network of signifiers, but rather in the very fabric of being itself.

In psychoanalysis, the correlate of this absence is the missing or impossible signifier that would resolve the enigma of the Other's desire; the representation, that is, that would resolve the inconsistency created by an enjoyment that distinguishes, unsettlingly, what the Other says from what it enigmatically wants. The human reliance on symbols – the elementary binaries of presence and absence, signifier and signified, substance (gravel) and void (screen) – is the effect of a rupture or convolution in what we intuitively, though mistakenly, experience as a continuum on the level of space and time. The primary signifier, what Lacan at one stage of his teaching calls the *trait unaire*,[10] is not the cause of the symbolic order's inherent excess/lack; it does not perform what Gilles Deleuze and Félix Guattari call a 'disjunctive synthesis'[11] of substance (enjoyment) and void (desire). Rather, the dialectic between the signifier and the excess/lack is already a (failed) response to a logically prior, indeterminate and properly ontological negativity, occurring 'before' the emergence of the forms of knowledge with which desire finds its tangled articulations. This is what I think Genet tries to articulate in an enigmatic statement about a redoubled void, which features in one of his major texts on the theatre. A playwright's 'verbal architecture', according to Genet, is meant to draw out from 'the illumination that shows the void' an 'appearance that shows the void'.[12] The statement makes sense only if we assume that the two voids are not the same. That is, theatrical practice should reveal a negativity more foundational or transcendental than the one that stages the desire constitutive of psychic life, the desire that constructs our ordinary sense of reality. If 'illumination' signals the space of ordinary reality structured around a central void, then the theatre must go further, exposing through a deliberate manipulation of appearances how this second-order absence is merely an attempt to compensate for a more primordial deficit in being itself.

Within the theatrical logic of *The Screens*, the milestone is the sign of the dehiscence or splitting of the world of appearances from itself. The screens form backdrops for the creation of images that stand in front of, and therefore dissimulate, an originary ontological rupture. They can be qualified as metatheatrical in the sense that they redouble the theatre's own replication of the phenomenal world, making visible the ambiguous empty background against which all possible elements of what we call reality take form. As he does with *The Balcony*, Genet premises *The Screens* on the conviction that the theatre simply reproduces the unconscious transcendentalism constitutive of subjectivity. This is the law according to which our only access to reality passes through the screen of fantasy, which is activated by the idealization of a special, that is to say phallic, signifier. The function of this signifier is to obfuscate the inherent negativity in being and to condition reality in accordance with the dialectic of desire.

Curiously, however, Genet specifies in his prefatory directives that the mound of gravel is not to be the only real object visible to the audience. Privileged by virtue of both its presence onstage before the action begins and its juxtaposition with the milestone and the first screen, the gravel mound is subsequently displaced by other objects – 'wheelbarrow, bucket, bicycle, etc.' – that 'must always' accompany the screens. The function of each of these, Genet writes, is 'to establish a contrast between its own reality and the objects that are drawn (on the screens)'.[13] This additional detail adds a crucial nuance to *The Balcony*'s prior message about the groundless multiplicity of images forming the fabric of human reality. In *The Balcony*, the phenomenal world balances precariously between the endlessly reflective void engendered by the numerous mirrors and the political reference embodied by the phallically authoritarian Chief of Police. In *The Screens*, by contrast, the mound of gravel destabilizes this balance, introducing a disruptive surplus element right from the outset. It is as if appearances in the later play had overshot their mission, exceeded their mandate, producing an excess of stuff that fails to materialize into identifiable form. Indeed, not unlike (Lacan's version of) Aristotle's *ousia* explored in Chapter 4, the gravel serves as a reminder of the residual substance that never quite manages to coalesce into phenomenal form. In consequence, this form is marred by its incomplete realization as a faulty incarnation of what it was supposedly meant to be. For Genet as for Lacan, reality becomes itself by virtue of its very incompleteness, of its incapacity fully to become itself.

The chief's dildo-like phallus costume from *The Balcony* anticipates the appearance of the gravel in *The Screens*, which figures as a new, more radicalized iteration of the same function. Both objects signify the ruin of the phallus, its latent inability persuasively to figure the constitutive exception to the rule of existing power relations. But the comparison can be extended: *The Balcony*'s phallic police chief, specifically in his ambition of immortality as rendered in the mausoleum, together with the multiplicity of reflecting mirrors onstage, become in *The Screens*, respectively, the milestone and the screen-on-wheels of the inaugural mise en scène. The crucial difference is that the excess of dissimulated, unsignified jouissance is figured straight away in the later play. Whereas *The Balcony* investigates the dynamic, at once libidinal and social, by which a system of political authority can restabilize itself after a period of incipient rebellion, *The Screens* rather inquires into the ambivalent moment of an apparently successful revolution, when the question arises as to the possibility of the construction of a new and less oppressive order of signification, one that would be supported by images of a genuinely different kind.

Hysteria's sublation

The interrogation of this possibility of a new kind of image requires a return to the matter of the specifically feminine ontology that this book began to explore in Chapter 2. Indeed, Genet's meditation on the poetic act in *The Screens* reflects a specifically feminine response to the impasse of being. Revisiting his portrayal of the brothel in *The Balcony*, Genet in the later play explores the political impact of the feminization of the phallus as it shifts the nature of the relation between transgression and the law. *The Screens* acknowledges the inherent duality of femininity's relation to the world of appearances in the clear but complex distinction it draws between the two main brothel women, Warda and Malika. Warda, the elder of the two, is heavily invested in her identity as a prostitute on the level of being-as-appearance. Genet's dialogue and stage directions highlight the obsessive attention she brings to her looks, specifying how her ultimate aim is to transform herself into a mannequin or skeleton, in other words a pure, empty form on which clothing, jewellery, decoration, adornment – the full array of Genetian *paraître* and *parure* – could be displayed. The signal detail of this desire is Warda's unique infatuation with dental hygiene. 'Me, I've worked for years on my tooth cleaning (*décrottage*) with a hat pin',[14] she says, emphasizing how this activity is central to her project to incarnate something like the Platonic ideal of the brothel whore. In their dramatic context, Warda's pristine dental gaps stand for her long-standing design to become an appearance, a perfect image or screen, deprived of any support in meaning or substance. Genet goes so far as to indicate that Warda is not even particularly interested in engaging with clients. Though she wants to attract them, to lure their desire with her excessively ornate personal display, we see her slip away behind a screen only with Saïd, whose manliness and virility the play will constantly undermine.

By contrast, Malika prides herself on her productive efficiency and pragmatism in the brothel. We see her disappear on numerous occasions with soldier clients from both sides of the conflict. Malika boasts that it is she, not Warda, who is responsible for nurturing the brothel, for transforming it into a respected if illicit village institution. Unlike Warda, who makes clear that she is above such vulgar concerns, Malika acknowledges the brothel's commercial vocation; she has no qualms about mentioning the monetary compensation she receives in exchange for her sexual labour. Whereas Warda's numerous sartorial layers lend her a heaviness indexed by her 'leaded petticoats',[15] Malika's adornments open up and disappear at the vaguest sign of male arousal. 'A man comes for me', she says, and 'my belt unbuckles'. In similar circumstances, however, 'when a man's meat calls *me* to the rescue', as Warda delicately puts it, her articles of clothing 'pile up on (her) shoulders and (her) buttocks', as if to defend themselves from phallic attack. Indeed, the reference to what Malika, with even greater flair, calls 'the meat that gets a hard-on'[16] draws unmistakable attention to the agency of the phallic signifier in the distinction between the two women. Whereas the display Malika creates to attract men's attention clearly aims to enable phallic jouissance, Warda's thick adornments are contrastingly ambivalent, standoffish, hysterical: masculine attention is sought after only to be dismissed as inadequate and pushed away. In short, Warda's address to the phallic signifier is imbued with the knowledge of its inadequacy; her unconscious vocation is to embody the phallus construed as the identity of image and being. This is the stance that empowers her to enjoin the agency of the masculine subject who is supposed to 'have it' and then to reject this agency as ineffectual or surplus to requirements.

The play's contradistinction of the two sex workers invites comparison to an often-overlooked detail of Lacan's formulas of sexuation, which usually appears in the seminar transcriptions below the formulas themselves. Lacan univocally defines the masculine subject as a lacking signifier $\mathcal{S}$ in its address of a problematic object of fantasy (a) that causes their desire. By contrast, femininity is marked by an inherent ambivalence or duality, its subjectivity posited, as Chapter 2 explored in some detail, as the impossibility of coherent totality (*pas-toute* or not-all). In Lacan's so-called mathemes, this impossibility is figured by a crossed-out feminine definite pronoun. From $\bcancel{\text{La}}$ ($\bcancel{\text{The}}$), two distinct vectors set out: one destined for the phallic signifier (Φ) and the other for $S(\bcancel{A})$, which Lacan defines as a signifier that 'marks the Other as barred'.[17]

Of course, much has been written in the decades since Lacan first presented the formulas about the somewhat notorious other jouissance 'beyond' the phallus that he associates with femininity.[18] The phrase has proved to be misleading. Lacan renders masculinity as a signifying absence, and therefore as a properly fantasmatic (non-)relation. In other words, masculinity is a form of subjectivity that cannot exist outside of a functioning fantasy frame. This implies that it features a degree of autonomy with respect to the symbolic order, that is to the cultural scripts and constructions that order and facilitate sexual access to women (or of course men). In this precise sense, it is masculinity, not femininity, that is 'beyond the phallus'. By contrast, Lacan defines femininity bivocally in relation to two distinct *signifiers*. As has often been noted in the better commentaries, the corollary of this is that the feminine subject is more fully subjected to the symbolic order, more radically circumscribed within the realm of appearances, than is the masculine subject.[19] The crucial detail for my purposes here, however, is that these appearances come in two distinct kinds.

As far as *The Screens* is concerned, we can simply remark at this initial juncture Warda's affinity with the notion of a feminine subjectivity that 'duplicates itself (*se dédouble*),'[20] as Lacan puts it. Femininity's duality stems from its capacity both to acknowledge the phallic signifier's support in (phallic) enjoyment and to kick this support out from under this same signifier. Femininity is double in the precise sense that the phallic signifier it requires to engage with a man – or more precisely, to engage with phallic jouissance, which does not necessarily require the anatomical possession of a penis – also serves to signify that this same signifier 'doesn't have a signified',[21] in other words that it has no semantic support, no stanchion in substance or being that could rescue it from radical, baseless contingency.

Here is a clichéd but illuminating example: Why do most women (and many men) love a man in uniform? Psychoanalysis offers a straightforward answer: because his uniform signifies the man's precise, determinate position in the social order, a position imbued with prestige and symbolic meaning, especially as viewed from the position of femininity. In this sense, the uniform is 'more than a uniform' in that it anchors a whole semiotic field, lending it both ontological depth and epistemological consistency. The aspect that renders this perspective distinctively feminine, however, is the fact that, from this same position, the uniform is also 'just a uniform', a male stripper's costume at a hen party or gay club, for example. In this latter case, the costume has no 'signified', no objective connection to the social status or position of the wearer. The same appearance that represents symbolic authority for femininity can also, with a subtle shift in point of view, represent its representation, in other words that same authority rendered as pure, groundless display, shorn of its special status and symbolic effectivity. In this way, femininity holds the power to disclose the elemental performativity of the phallus; to theatricalize it, you could also say to underline the connection to Genet's theatre.

The properly psychical fact that a feminine subject does not depend on the phallus to enjoy comes with a consequence, however. She (or he) loses their bearings in the symbolic order, which as a result becomes unmoored, groundless, inconsistent, unorientable. Genet signals this topological disorientation in *The Screens* by luxating the direction of the characters' looks onstage from the scenography's spatial arrangement. In the latter half of the play, when the characters in the realm of the dead on the uppermost platform address their living counterparts below them onstage, they look upwards instead of down.[22] Femininity deprives phallic jouissance of its exclusive and exceptional ontological importance, its anchoring of the species as a whole to being. Indeed, from the (non- or rather not-all phallic) feminine perspective, the phallus can take on the vulgar guise of a signifier for 'masturbation', what Lacan also calls in *Encore* the 'jouissance of the idiot'.[23] We should not misunderstand his phrase as a pejorative comment on the value of onanism, however. Rather, Lacan's description of phallic jouissance implies not only sexuality's generically maladaptive connection to reproduction, but also and more specifically masculinity's inherent inability to move beyond what can only remain an essentially masturbatory entanglement, mediated by fantasy, with the sexual partner.

Warda's trajectory in *The Screens* advances towards a properly feminine destiny in its attempt, and subsequent failure, to embody a perfect phallic image, to become a unique, absolute appearance or a pure, unified surface. But the feminine, and more specifically hysterical, enterprise to weld appearances to being in this manner has the paradoxical effect of exposing the transcendentally-determined inconsistency of both appearances and being. From the outset, Warda's obsessive fervour for display reverses the conventional understanding of the relation between a prostitute and her client, positioning the man as the more contingent and vulnerable of the two partners. Moreover, Warda's intensive aestheticism has an immediate and counter-intuitive political impact in that it grants her immunity from the kind of revolutionary romanticism that for Genet can only detract from the prospects for anti-colonial victory.

Congratulating herself for her twenty-four years of experience as a 'talented' whore, Warda subversively masculinizes Beauvoir's famous feminist question, asking of no one in particular, 'What is a man?' and then providing her own answer: 'A man remains a man.' Adding that 'it's he who strips naked in front of us like a whore from Toul or Nantes',[24] Warda implies that these Lorraine towns are not known for the resplendence of their strumpets. Even after having removed multiple layers of clothing, Warda remains strangely done up, innocent of the nakedness – the 'real', sub-sartorial exposure – revealed by her paying guests when they strip down to nothing. But Genet also makes clear that there is nothing to be discovered underneath Warda's ornate skirts and sparkling petticoats, except perhaps nothingness itself. 'My adornments!' she exclaims. 'Underneath, there's not much left.'[25] We understand that whatever exists beyond all the finery carries the same lack of essence, the same ontological weightlessness, as what lies on the surface. To be sure, Warda's ferocious dedication to the image of the glamorous harlot collapses, flattens the very distinction between surface and depth.

Even more intriguingly, however, *The Screens* specifies that Warda's vocation, which we might otherwise misconstrue as narcissistic aestheticism or blithe superficiality, lends her an unexpected seriousness. Moreover, this seriousness foments scepticism about the true political commitment of the anti-colonial revolutionaries. This becomes clear when Genet sets Warda's self-professed lack of depth alongside her dismissal of brothel colleague Malika's investment in the legend of the play's revolutionary hero Si Slimane. Malika has heard from numerous sources, everyone from 'a Kabyle from Saada' to 'a butcher in the medina', an unlikely story about Slimane's magical insurrectional prowess. By all accounts, he has appeared 'on his horse in sixteen villages at the same time', while 'in actual fact' he was merely 'resting in the shade, at the side of a road'. Warda squarely rejects the account's veracity, declaring to one of her clients that the rumour is worthless, good only 'for the joy of words, the delight of conversation'.[26]

For Warda, empty words are one thing, but war is another; victory requires an entirely different relation to discourse. 'If we had the misfortune to take the homeland (*la patrie*) seriously', Warda says, 'then farewell to our misfortunes, farewell to our pleasures'.[27] Though Warda is certain of the strategic worthlessness of ludic conversation, her own investment in the revolution features a marked ambivalence. A moment later, Malika associates the seductive pull of the rumour, the 'hope' it offers to the nation's dispossessed, with the sensuous escape she offers Ahmed, one of the brothel clients. 'If you go up with me', she tells him, 'I'll give you the gift of gifts', by which she means the idle daydream of national sovereignty that lies 'underneath (her) belts, underneath (her) fasteners'. In contrast to Malika's promise of revolutionary fervour fuelled by 'hatred of foreigners',[28] Warda insists that only death lies beneath her adornments. In sum, Warda's seriousness encourages a literalist consideration of both language and the image: both are to be taken strictly at face value. The notion that beyond there may lie some elusive desideratum – revolutionary saviour or ontological guarantee, for example – she steadfastly rejects.

About halfway through *The Screens*, however, the war's momentum suddenly shifts, the Arab fighters now set to emerge victorious over their French oppressors. The transformation rearranges the libidinal dynamic between the brothel and the broader community, further distinguishing Warda and Malika from one another. We learn that Malika's dedication to the brothel's pragmatic function of providing local men with sexual release has enhanced its aesthetic glow, but at the price of granting it a sort of shameful singularity that separates it off from village life. By contrast, we discover that Warda's devotion to the image of the perfect harlot has rather attenuated, paradoxically to be sure, the aura of transgressive scandal around her, effectively integrating her into the life of the community. Warda's destiny in the play expresses a specifically feminine logic by showing how the inevitable failure of the hysterical project to incarnate being in an absolute appearance has the effect of shattering this appearance into countless distinct forms. As a result, (feminine) being is revealed to be not only multiple, but also inconsistent and even contradictory, irremediably beset by a free-floating and reflexive negativity.

Warda's death is the occasion when *The Screens* reveals the full significance of her devotion to aesthetic display. From up on the platform of the dead, Warda watches her living brothel sisters wash and decorate her body, incarnated by a second actor for the purposes of the scene. This literal twinning of Warda's body across the divide separating life from death already intimates the Lacanian theme of feminine *dédoublement*. As the women complete the preparations for her funeral, the stage notes stipulate that Warda is 'adorned (*parée*) in an extraordinary fashion', her get-up featuring a 'large gold lace dress covered with blue roses', a face painted entirely in white, and shoes 'made of huge pink roses'.[29]

Despite its obvious magnificence, however, the point of all this posthumous glorification is to underline by opposition Warda's failure to become during her lifetime the 'gilded mannequin'[30] or 'skeleton draped in gilded gowns'[31] that she had worked so tirelessly to become. To underline the extent of her disillusionment, Genet has Warda rip up her skirt in a fit of frustration. Warda has wanted to melt into, indeed to become, a screen by eliminating the empty, reflexive gap of (feminine) subjectivity and fulfilling the masculine demand for a sexual relation with the impossible Woman. In her attempt to incarnate the apotheosis of the glamorous prostitute in her ultimate appearance and singular essence, Warda unwittingly reveals the conceptual identity of reality and representation. That is, essence is revealed to be just another appearance, a signifier like all the rest. In Lacanian terms, Warda becomes S($\cancel{A}$): in this context, evidence that the distinction between essence and appearance is situated within the world of appearances themselves.

Moreover, *The Screens* spells out how Warda's failure has been precipitated by the war's imminent end. As the violence winds down, her former clients, their bodies scarred by battle, no longer have the strength even 'to lift (her) leaded hem'. So weak are her enfeebled johns that she is forced 'to cut a slit for them in (the) front'[32] of her brocade skirts to assist them in their purchased acts of now-compromised virility. But the play also specifies that if business in the brothel is no longer what it used to be, if the clients arrive not in excited anticipation but with 'their teeth clenched',[33] then this cannot solely be on account of the conflict's physical toll. As one might expect, throughout her life as a prostitute Warda has been reviled by the village women for monopolizing the attention of their men. Now, though, she is saluted rather than shunned, receiving social invitations even from the most respectable of ladies. The soldiers' attitude has also changed. Though they still visit the brothel, albeit in smaller numbers, now they do so shamefully, hiding their frequentations from public view. As Malika observes, the clients now 'make use of the night as a veil'.[34]

As for the war, a soldier explains that the Arabs 'are no longer fighting for fun, but to win'. The gauzy aura of revolutionary romance has dissipated; the struggle has become serious business: 'pleasure must exist alongside war', the soldier adds, 'not within it'.[35] Viewed through a psychoanalytic lens, these changes in the balance between pleasure and duty attest to a shift in the collective masculine relation to enjoyment. The discipline of military strategy, the desire to emerge victorious, the suspension of a merely ludic and aesthetic approach to armed conflict, attenuate the agency of the only seemingly dichotomous fantasy figure of the virgin/whore, what Lacan called *La femme*. Indeed, Warda describes the transformation of the brothel's status and function as a kind of emancipatory sublimation:[36] 'Men used to come from far away to see me ... pick my teeth with my big hatpins', she observes, indexing her former function as an empty frame for masculine fantasy. With victory on the horizon, however, the soldiers 'come to fuck me', she says, as they would any other available woman up for a casual encounter, in exchange for money or not. Previously entranced by her melding of adornment and emptiness, the soldiers now lack 'respect for (her) riches'.[37] In short, Warda has lost her status as an exceptional woman; she has failed, as she must, in her project to embody the irrealizable apotheosis of femininity. Her failure manifests the impossibility of assembling the feminine into a single, coherent and knowable whole. More theoretically put, she demonstrates that there is no signifier, no symmetrical alternative to the phallus capable of unifying the inconsistent but actual infinity of feminine being.

The inclusion of Warda within the community disrupts the illicit complicity that affixes the perpetuation of existing social and aesthetic orders to unconscious, unsignified enjoyment. Indeed, this complicity captures the general sociopolitical function of the brothel in Genet's theatre, as presented most famously in *The Balcony*. Near the later play's conclusion, Warda looks back nostalgically at the time when she could gaze at herself in the mirror 'for hours on end while yawning',[38] not having to find a useful purpose in legitimate society. So ordinary has she become in the dawning postcolonial world that she even considers giving up the brothel to become a nurse, here figured as a kind of epitome of the essential worker, trusted but taken-for-granted buttress of the social order. Just a year prior, a battalion chief from the colonial army visiting the brothel had to sew back the buttons on his uniform himself. Now, however, Warda knows how to 'thread a needle, sew in a patch, cut on the bias'.[39] Relatedly, *The Screens* links the practical injunction that rules the transformed order to the exposure of the corruption that secretly undergirds the ideal of justice. The *qadi* (Shari'a court judge), whom we later see escorted to prison for shady dealings, laments the shift in social power away from those who 'knew how to make things more beautiful'. As what Ommou ironically calls 'this justice so beautiful'[40] rots away, things can only go to hell in a handbasket from the perspective of the Islamic magistrate. Explicitly connecting the unpalatable undersides of seemingly unrelated ideals of justice and beauty, *The Screens* elucidates the dependence of social transformation on the exposure of the occluded corruption that fuels our subservience to these ideals' oppressive power.

If Warda's aesthetic project strengthens the anti-colonial forces by attenuating the transgressive lure of the brothel and the romanticism of revolutionary dreaming, then Malika's dedication has the opposite effect, causing the whores 'to return at last to (their) solitude' as well as their 'truth'.[41] Whereas Warda's impact compromised the sanitary cordon separating the brothel from the village, Malika's pragmatism engenders the 'solid stuff (*le solide*)' that builds up around the house of ill repute, which becomes 'thicker and thicker'. When Djemila worries about their increasing isolation from the community – soon it will be impossible 'to go to the post office or anywhere else'[42] – Malika scolds her: 'If you don't have the strength, don't be a whore.' Indeed, Malika is so confident about her value as a prostitute that she alone is 'tall enough to support the entire brothel on (her) shoulders'.[43]

In *The Screens*, Genet sheds light on the complicity between Malika's businesslike attitude and the machinations of colonial power when he has her engage in a flirtatious exchange with a dead French general. Despite their distance from one another across the divide, they manage nevertheless to stretch 'threads of saliva' between them 'so fine and gleaming'[44] that they can even vanquish death. Belying her confidence in the brothel as a going concern, however, there are signs that Malika's prowess will not be recognized by the younger generation in the new conditions of independence. 'Keep your thighs crossed', the grocer's son tells her, adding 'I've been particularly attracted to Swedish girls of late'.[45] In Lacanian terms, Malika's commitment to the financial health of the brothel maintains the hegemony of the phallic signifier. Her actions strengthen the force of repression that keeps jouissance beneath the threshold of both signifying intelligibility and social legitimacy. The effect of Malika's dedication is the enhancement of the prestige of the phallus, whose function here is to perpetuate the illusion of the social status quo's frictionless consistency. The grocery clerk's newfound erotic interest in Scandinavian women suggests that Malika's work ethic has only enhanced the enslavement of local men to idealizing fantasies that perpetuate the very values to which colonialism subjected them.

The contrast Genet develops in *The Screens* between Warda's and Malika's distinctive modalities of feminine being exposes a fundamental paradox. Warda's inevitably frustrated project to hypostatize and unify the feminine in an ultimate, essential image has the effect of subverting the phallic signifier's prestige. This subversion discloses the truth that the phallus's only distinctive characteristic is its resistance to the revelation of its own contingency, and by extension the inconsistency of any possible regime of intelligibility together with its lack of grounding in well-ordered and fully realized being.

Nomadic negativity

If Warda's hysterical desire serves to reveal the contingency of the phallus, then *The Screens* uses Saïd, Leila and the Mother, the play's marquee family of abject antiheroes, to explore how a particular practice of image-making can expose a nomadic negativity that disunifies being. The full significance of the play's celebration of abject appearances is best appreciated in relation to the idealizing backdrop against which these appearances gain their corrosive agency. The Arab trio's theatrical abjection is contrasted with a long-standing Genetian target: the nationalist fantasy of a certain image of France, figured by aestheticized paragons of ancestral nobility and military glory. At one point in the play, for example, reproaching one of his soldiers for having sloppily knotted his cravat, a French lieutenant stresses the importance of carrying a mirror or, lacking one, using 'the eyes of your comrades'[46] as a substitute.

Each soldier's impeccable attire is reflected in that of the next, composing in this way a unified brotherhood bound by mutual identification under the approving glance of the Lieutenant: a group in the strict Freudian sense. But the ideal exception figured by the Lieutenant – his look is a constitutive symbolic point external to the brotherhood itself – is redoubled by an abject one that threatens the group's cohesion and for this reason requires constant policing. Hence the Lieutenant's questioning of the solider Pierre who, not coincidentally, winds up affiliating with the revolutionists in the afterlife after being strangled by Saïd's mother. 'I'm asking whether you're an Arab?' the Lieutenant demands to know. Dismissing Pierre's insistence that he hails from Boulogne, the Lieutenant judges that 'the Orient casts its halftones' on the soldier's complexion, pronouncing like some vulgar Cartesian that the soldiers must 'represent a sharp (*nette*), precise France'.[47]

In a passionate speech, the Lieutenant goes so far as to prioritize the creation of an image of French militarism above even victory over the Arab insurrection, giving voice in the process to what could very well be Genet's own view of the overarching cause of the colonial system's collapse in North Africa. At the precise point in the play when the French forces begin to lose the upper hand, the Lieutenant maintains against all evidence that 'France has already conquered'.[48] Indeed, France 'has offered an indelible image', he declares; one can rest satisfied in its contemplation despite all the maimed soldiers returning with their 'missing feet, lost kidneys, torn-off balls, noses eaten away, and faces blasted'.[49] The argument is not without a contradictory aspect, however, and it suggests the kind of double consciousness psychoanalysis associates with fetishism. To be sure, the Lieutenant's description of the battle-worn French soldiers carries a note of visceral abjection comparable to the misery of the Arabs, whom they have seen 'dragging in the mud, living on peelings'.[50] As it turns out, the polished leather and rod-straight cravats of the soldiers' uniforms mask a kind of postcolonial death-wish; the sharp image of a pure France is shown to be secretly complicit with a suicidal infatuation with bodily mutilation.

The Screens works assiduously to distinguish this redoubled or fetishistic practice of image-making, which conceals destructive violence under a veneer of military honour, with the revolutionaries' transparent and ritualized displays of war's horrible carnage. On the French side of the conflict, the grotesque underside of patriotism remains not exactly invisible or unknown, but rather improperly acknowledged, lacking the form that could integrate it within the field of official representations. Within the logic of the play, that is, the Lieutenant can evoke the mangled soldiers in words, but only if, on the level of the image, he has ensured that the regiment's pre-battle beauty reflects the glory of France. Certainly, the Lieutenant could not draw attention to the abjection of defeat without causing irreparable damage to the national image, which he is duty bound, as he sees it, to perpetuate.

Contrastingly, Genet's play makes clear that on the side of the Arab insurrectionists victory depends on precisely such a practice of unedifying image-making. Kadidja, leader of the village women, associates this practice not with ideals of ethnic identity, military glory or national character but rather with evil, which she enjoins to 'impregnate'[51] her people. Freshly shot dead by the son of Sir Harold, one of the play's *pied-noir* landowners, Kadidja, holding a candle, receives the testimonials of a parade of Arab men who, one by one, recount their gruesome and despicable acts of war while drawing in charcoal their representations, 'monstrously enlarged', on a giant screen. Lahoussine depicts a bloodstain to render the rape of 'one of their girls', for example, while Larbi sketches 'steaming'[52] guts to figure the disembowelment of an enemy soldier. By the end of the scene, there are further sketches of smoking pistols, stolen money, a decapitated Norman head and an exploded lemon grove, all of which suggest the creation of an alternative image repertoire that exposes rather than conceals the crimes of war.

The long line of critics who accuse the later Genet of glorifying violence, anti-colonial and otherwise, entirely miss the point.[53] Granted, Genet insists on distinguishing between hegemonic and emancipatory violence: France's colonial crimes and the crimes of the Arab fighters are not ethically equivalent in the context of the outrageously unequal power relation that shapes their interaction in the colonial situation. But the deciding factor lies elsewhere, in the definition of two qualitatively distinct practices of image-making. While one serves as an edifying alibi for an ultimately self-destructive project of racializing, nationalist self-assertion, the other insists on exposing those aspects of emancipatory struggle that we would prefer not to acknowledge, those that resist integration into official histories or pious commemorations. The creative practice of Kadidja's Arab rebels dissuades, *avant la lettre* as it were, the construction of retrospective narratives whose function is to exalt the founding of the postcolonial nation through the disavowal of the crimes thanks to which that nation came to be, even if these narratives seemingly inevitably come to be reconstructed in the postrevolutionary return to relative social stability.

But *The Screens* adds crucial nuance to this presentation of the value inherent in Kadidja's curation of her alternative gallery of crime. Genet juxtaposes in the scene in question the anti-colonial fighters' drawings with Saïd and Leila's thievery, surely a requisite oppositional tactic in conditions of extreme racialized inequality. The couple's criminality makes no distinction between the two sides of the conflict, however. Indeed, we know by this point in the play that Saïd, a quintessentially Genetian paragon of betrayal, has probably provided the colonial forces with valuable intelligence about the insurrectionists' acts of subversion. Genet dramatizes this friction between the creation of images of evil and the more radical variety of negativity embodied by Saïd and his family in a tense exchange between Kadidja and the Mother, who never wavers in her unconditional support for her son and daughter-in-law's deathly abjection. Unlike the rebels' acts of violence, this abjection could never find a corresponding screen image because it lacks the redemptive reference to the nationalist cause. As the last of Kadidja's witnesses departs, unable to produce a drawing for lack of space on the screen, the Mother makes her appearance. She comments on how, unlike Kadidja with her continuing concern for the revolutionary cause among the living, she herself must 'spend her nights communing (*en tête-à-tête*) with the dead'. We take the Mother's remark that, in spite of Kadidja's demise, her 'indignation is still fresh'[54] as a subtle animadversion of the incendiary anger with which Kadidja has gone about expressing her support for the insurrectionists' crimes of war.

We learn from the old woman Ommou that while Kadidja's soldiers have been drawing their grotesque images on the screens, Leila has been stealing her fellow Arabs' dresses and coffee grinders with the help of Saïd. Kadidja can now recognize the gulf that separates her creative vitality from the Mother's less easily defined desire: 'I know you're on intimate terms with what no longer has a name on earth',[55] Kadidja tells her as she watches the Arab men chase her away with her blessing. Though she fails to finish her sentence, we understand that Kadidja considers the Mother's affinity with the dead to be a threat. The reason may not be clear, however, since neither woman, to risk an understatement, has shown herself to be a friend of the colonial regime. We are left to wonder what prevents them from joining together in solidarity in the anti-colonial cause.

Consideration of key details of the play reveals a convincing answer. Kadidja has been busy replacing the dominant figural repertoire with alternative images of what, from the perspective of colonial discourse, represents evil, effectively substituting one regime of signifiers for another. In contraposition, the Mother has shown herself to be an advocate for something that resists both figuration and formalization. Like death, the act of thievery leaves behind not merely a neutral absence (of a purloined object, of biological life), but rather a place from which something has been removed: an ontological deficit, if you will. The grotesque representations of Kadidja's bloodthirsty Arab fighters engineer a counterhegemonic imaginary designed to corrode the nationalist and racializing values of colonialism. Instead, the Mother offers only something that 'no longer has a name', as Kadidja puts it, which implies of course that it did have one in some probably mythological past but was subsequently lost. If Kadidja's grisly cartoons corrode the oppressive colonial images they replace, then the Mother's deathly stance indicates the image's corrosion of itself, in other words a kind of positive rendering of that corrosion, the marking of the image's withdrawal into the void. The Mother's unassimilable presence renders inherent, and thereby internalizes, the external opposition (victim–oppressor, colonizer–colonized) whose terms Kadidja instead seeks to reverse. Within the logic of *The Screens*, Kadidja must banish the Mother because the Mother's deathliness discloses how the hateful alterity that must be destroyed is not some external discrepancy that threatens knowledge's coherence from without. Rather, for the Mother, otherness can only be a projective displacement of an inconsistency inherent in the forms of our knowledge, in the very fabric of being itself.

Concerning the endless catalogue in both dialogue and mise en scène of the abjection of the play's accursed Arab family – Leila is the ugliest woman in the world, so ugly that she has to wear a hood; Saïd marries her only because she is the only woman in the village he can afford, and in any case he plans to go to France to work in the Le Creuset cookware factory to earn enough money to get a better one; the Mother barks like a dog and is shunned by the rest of the village women – it is essential to note Genet's insistence on this abjection's status as an appearance. In short, abjection in *The Screens* does not take the form of a 'fallen (*chu*) object',[56] in other words some intermediary or liminal psychical substance in between the categories of subject and object. Rather, it is an image, a signifier. The entity with which the Mother is on intimate terms may be unnameable, but Kadidja nevertheless names it as such. The care with which Genet connects the representation of abjection to the screens onstage requires us to distinguish the Genetian abject from Julia Kristeva's, famously formulated in *Powers of Horror* as an unrecognizable non-object, inassimilable to the ego and bearer of 'a weight of non-sense'[57] external to signification. The Kristevan abject's externality to the order of the signifier has its agency confined to the dramatic affects of revulsion and disgust, affects that require the intervention of the elaborate rituals of purification by defilement described with reference to the work of anthropologist Mary Douglas, for example.

According to Kristeva, these rituals evince a quasi-psychotic separation of the symbolic rite from the filthy object, and provide in this way a glimpse at an abjection distinct from the order of language and representation. By contrast, Genet's theatrical practice enacts a sublimation from the abject, the effect of which is an altogether different kind of purification that goes beyond the inclusion of the prohibited quasi-object within the symbolic order. On the road to nowhere in particular, or perhaps to 'the land where the monster lives',[58] Leila enjoins Saïd to persevere in his decision 'to refuse the brilliance of darkness, the softness of flint, and the honey of thistles', indeed to go 'right to the end (*jusqu'au bout*)', adding that the love that motivates her is destined not for her husband, but rather for 'fire'.[59] Here we witness how, in a redoubled negation, Saïd's family's stance goes further than the merely oppositional practice of Kadidja and her soldiers. Opposition, after all, preserves rather than obliterates the relation between the function of negation and that which it negates. Saïd and Leila's subversion of romantic sentimentality even transfers this embrace of the non-relation to the realm of the couple. Indeed, they become a kind of emblem for Lacan's idea about the non-existence of the sexual relation: Saïd refers to Leila as 'his shadow', which he carries and drags along, adding that he can no longer separate from the 'misfortune'[60] she represents for him. Saïd is attached to his wife, she is a burden to him, but this attachment connects him only to his own difference from himself, to the shadow that situates his identity in the space of the Other.

The most central point of the scene, however, is its correlation of our antiheroes' perseverance in the sublimation of abjection to a process of elimination, subtraction and stripping, the very same process I described under the heading of the Genetian modern in Chapter 4. The more Saïd and Leila evoke images of their misery, the more the landscape as evoked in the dialogue is voided of content and the identities of the characters disjoined from themselves. 'There is really nobody. Not a living thing. Nothing,' Leila says, looking around her. 'Even the stones are now nothing but stones.'[61] Identity is revealed to be the gap between a thing and itself, the 'nothing but' that separates the first mention of 'stones' from the second in Leila's judgement. Because she belongs to the 'same race' as the botanical irritants, Leila can stick her buttocks in a grove of stinging nettles without getting blistered. 'There are (the nettles)', she says, 'and then just nothing'.[62] Miming the gesture of hanging up 'something invisible' on an 'invisible nail', she proceeds to shed her belongings and qualities, indeed all of the predicates of her identity: 'dignity', 'sadness', 'severity (*gravité*)'; her 'herbal teas', her 'softness', even the 'hood (*cagoule*)' she wears to spare the world of her homeliness. Having reached the end of her list, she trails off, wondering aloud if anything remains. 'A smile,'[63] she responds to herself, perhaps in a reference to Lewis Carroll's Cheshire cat, but also introducing a note of levity that lessens the weight of all the abjection which, we recall, is composed merely of appearances. The further along Leila advances in the signification of her abjection, the more her qualities, all of them, are cast off, revealing in the process a gaping void ambiguously conjoined with a ghostly, ineffable presence.

Genet's choice of Leila to figure the shedding away of predication such that only an empty essence remains recalls the link to femininity or, more precisely, to a specifically feminine form of sublimation that exposes the groundlessness and inconsistency of the world of appearances. As I have previously argued, this inconsistency in representation is the result of a logically prior ontological discontinuity. Leila's endless exuviation of her qualities exposes only the image of a deficiency in being, like the match the insurrectionists use to burn down a *pied-noir* orange orchard, which becomes 'tender and good' only once it is 'white and black and twisted by fire'.[64] Femininity equates ethical value not with the name that would properly describe a particular feature of existence, but rather with the paradox by which the multiplication of these descriptors reveals only the incompleteness of both substance and form.

The image that refuses to form

The final tableau of *The Screens* offers the most detailed account of the difference between the two types of image theatricalized in the play: the one, which functions to screen, in the sense of dissimulate, the inherent inconsistency of the social world; and the other, which manages to reveal the image's self-difference, working against its very being as an image. Three distinct levels appear onstage as the scene begins: the uppermost, as in previous scenes, populated by characters who have already died; the second representing a prison and grocery; the third depicting a domestic interior, the village square, and the brothel. Various characters on the upper level, including the Mother, Kadidja and Warda, pull up chairs to await the arrival of Saïd and Leila, whose radical stance of redoubled negation – targeting colonialism, certainly, but also the oppositional ideals of the revolution, indeed of the ideal *tout court* – is applauded among the dead. On the lower level, the group of European colonials we have come to know, now so war-torn as to be 'almost naked',[65] discusses the future of the dying French-colonial *départements*.[66] In standard-issue decadent-colonial fashion, they express their pessimism about any new nation's capacity to perpetuate existing standards of culture and civilization or else invent worthy new, postcolonial or indigenous ones.

As Saïd finally arrives (Leila is known to be dead but still has not broken through the screen separating the dead from the living; she seems to be caught in some kind of purgatory), a debate breaks out between a group of old Arab revolutionary fighters, still alive down below and hanging out outside the brothel, and the women in the realm of the dead, feminine veterans of anti-colonial invective and sabotage. In a gesture of conciliation, the former want to forgive Saïd for his betrayal of the anti-colonial cause and integrate him into the official memorialization of national victory. But the latter refuse the gesture, goading Saïd on to resist, stirring him to become instead a symbol of pure opposition to any cause or ideal, any relation of solidarity or, perhaps best expressed, to the relation as such. In the final moments of the play, Saïd steps offstage, a gunshot rings out, and we hear what we assume to be a falling body in the wings. Though the conclusion of *The Screens* figures Saïd's destiny as ambiguous – Is it really Saïd who was shot? In any case, was he not already supposed to be dead? – Kadidja, ensconced among the dead, can nevertheless assert: 'He'll no more be back than will Leila.' And the Mother, wondering aloud where her son could be, suggests that he might be found 'in a song'.[67]

Another of the play's central disputes, this one occurring between the defeated colonialists and the dead nationalist revolutionaries, hinges on the question of the nature of the substance with which the image is constructed. As the (European) academic says, the Arabs[68] have become accustomed to dependency after a century of French domination; indeed, 'their only memories are of poverty and humiliation.' Questioning whether a tradition of art and culture can 'be born for the purpose of enshrining so many facts which (the Arabs) themselves would like to forget', he responds in the negative, claiming that postcolonial culture is 'doomed to decay'.[69] The missionary introduces a dissenting nuance into the discussion, however, when he insinuates that it is precisely because of the absence of an edifying historical ideal among the formerly colonized that they will ultimately emerge victorious. From his perspective, the strength of the revolution lies in the idea that it has managed to 'deif(y) abjection'.[70]

Of course, colonial discourse judges as deficient a tradition that in its estimation, compared to the European, lacks the self-attributed artistic and scientific triumphs thanks to which it grants to itself a higher degree of cultural advancement. But the point of the exchange is not merely to negate this glaringly false judgement by appeal to indigenous accomplishments, for example; in other words by constructing an alternative assemblage of ideals with which the formerly colonized might edify themselves. Genet rather aims to take out the very gesture of repressive idealization by means of which selective historical memory becomes the foundation of national identity. Here we can add to my previous contention the idea that abjection, a key quality of the generic Genetian aesthetic but taken to new heights in *The Screens*, includes in this instance a specific act of sublimation. The function of this act is to seize upon a representation that is normally subject to the repression that conditions the creation of the image. Repression works to keep this representation beneath the threshold of visibility. Instead, with sublimation, this representation is positioned in the place where the rightful, functional image is meant to be, becoming in the process what we might call an impossible image. This is an image that reveals its own failure to constitute itself, one that figures only the inevitable decomposition of the desirable perceptual reality that it is meant to construct.

As its final scene proceeds, *The Screens* refines this elusive sense of an image that refuses to become itself. Ommou, perhaps the most radical figure in the play's pantheon of insubordinate (and eventually dead) women, attacks the revolutionary veterans' project to erect 'a monument to the war dead', which they will inaugurate 'while listening to (a) patriotic speech'.[71] This last detail reveals how Genet revisits in this play the Franco-inspired mausoleum motif of *The Balcony*, only here he issues a staunch and explicit negation of its repressive logic. 'You and your pals are the proof that we need a Saïd', declares Ommou on behalf of her sisters beyond the grave, making clear their opposition to the veterans' 'high and harmonious' commemoration, which would hearken what she memorably calls the 'esthetics of decease (*l'esthétique du décès*)'.[72] By contrast to this making-beautiful of a lived experience of violent conflict, to this affirmation of a redemptive value for sacrifice and suffering – in short, to a transposition of life-affirming values from the here-and-now to a projected afterlife – Ommou asserts an alternative need for 'an emblem that rises up from the dead, that denies life'.[73] For Ommou, the dead are meant to intervene in lived historical time by inserting subversive interruptions that compromise the intelligibility of cultural discourses, ruthlessly exposing in the process their contradictions and inconsistencies.

But surely Genet's most telling insight regarding the complexity of the challenge posed by this project of sublimation from abjection relates to the difficulty of distinguishing what Ommou calls the 'emblem', the alternate type of symbol she wants Saïd to become, from any standard-issue image. A sceptical question can be asked in this connection: Will any representation, no matter how abject, not become just another ideal when it is placed in the proper discursive space, the sacred place of cultural identity and meaning? Are the forces of idealization not so powerful and obfuscatory that they can transform even as wretched and unedifying a character as Saïd or Leila into an imperious wellspring of positive inspiration? Genet answers in the negative, exploring in the final moments of *The Screens* Saïd's rejection of not just the veterans' offer of reconciliation but also, and more importantly, the purely oppositional symbolic project that Ommou envisions for him.

As the dead await his mysteriously delayed appearance among them, Saïd acknowledges that his improbable purgatorial popularity has granted him considerable influence over the course of events. Nevertheless, he insists on telling off all entreating parties as they gleefully impart their advice on how he should move forward: 'to all of you, I say shit (*je vous dis merde*),'[74] he says by way of summing up his stance. Saïd shows himself to be a radical negationist to the end. Indeed, he negates even Ommou's desire to transform him, along with his spouse Leila, into an image, even if this image is to be assumed in a decidedly peculiar way, through a kind of taking-leave of oneself or subjective evacuation that would take place 'through (the) mouth or asshole',[75] as she specifies. Saïd's resistance to Ommou's project of negative sanctification involves a redoubling of negativity. Very precisely, this absolute variety of negation is both indeterminate and non-predicative: it operates on no field or domain, and relates to no object distinct from itself. Moreover, it marks a novel enmeshment with affect through its explicit linking of subjectivity to corporeal orifices; those places on the body, that is, where enjoyment superposes itself upon a void.

This seemingly impossible attempt to figure enjoyment, to find a form with which to embody the impossibility of its figuration, marks a crucial distinction with respect to the normative relation between the image and commemoration. The ultimate agonistic exchange of views in *The Screens* pits Ommou's idea to transform Saïd into a positive emblem of negation against the recently dead Sergeant's claim that the 'atrocities (*saloperies*)' he committed during the war have made him 'luminous'.[76] With respect to the latter, the figuration of remembrance is conditioned by the curious epistemological contradiction characteristic of repression. To his delight, the Sergeant is informed that a memorial plaque has been installed in a dead-end street in the tiny French village where his uncle owns a mattress factory. The academic puts his finger on the logic of the fetishistic splitting that informs the dynamic of post-war idealization when he claims that, though 'no one knows what (the Sergeant) did except that he died', it is clear nonetheless that 'one can't build on what he did'.[77] In other words, though the precise nature of the Sergeant's actions during the war may not be on the public record, we know that if these actions had been known, a plaque could never have been mounted in his honour. I should specify that this last statement only holds for the historically dominant image regime. For it is precisely to the possibility of the commemoration of that which cannot be commemorated that Ommou devotes her afterlife.

Only the Arabs, then, or more specifically the constituency of characters that orbits around the Mother, Saïd, and Leila, can build an emblem on actions that are neither edifying nor glorious. Further, only this alternative kind of image manages actually to preserve memory, not in the empirical sense of retaining an accurate record of what actually took place, but rather in the sense of resisting the repressive gesture of denial that falsely attributes redemptive value to the senseless violence of war. Paradoxically, only the self-destroying emblem succeeds in preserving memory. By contrast, conventional images effect an obscurantist idealization that attributes value and meaning to actions that in fact carried neither. Celebrating his plaque, the Sergeant avers that his 'beauty served as a setting (*écrin*) for (his) cruelty', which he calls 'that jewel'.[78] Here the image is explicitly qualified as an aesthetically pleasing lure that cordons off a libidinal zone of sadistic jouissance. By stark contrast, what

Ommou calls the emblem subversively inserts an abject signifier in the place where we expect to find the beautiful, with the result that this very place – the locus of idealization, the frame of ideological fantasy – is shown to be a screen whose function is to abscond from visibility not any particular object, but rather the faultline that breaks the continuity of being.

This is how *The Screens* leaves its exhausted, bewildered witness: Leila and Saïd are neither dead nor alive; the last events onstage are Kadidja's 'gesture expressive of doubt'[79] and the exit of all the remaining characters, carrying away the screens. These final details distil Genet's insight that the void haunting the world of appearances is more, or rather less, than a neutral absence: it is somehow inhabited, virtually, by a subtraction. Like Kadidja's gesture, its signifier is positively negative. As a *marked* negation, the sign of loss as such, it acquires a kind of destabilizing and destructive, vacuum-like gravitational pull. Despite its many ambiguities and perplexing details, *The Screens* asserts unambiguously that its antihero couple, supported by the Mother, will refuse every value, perhaps especially the value of valuelessness. Their hostility towards the consecration of the merely oppositional negation offered them by the well and truly dead will continue indefinitely. Saïd and Leila persist at the play's conclusion as spectral presences, their absence figured by the enigma of their non-appearance in the afterlife. Their destinies affirm the reflexive, peripatetic and objectless variety of negation that Genet wants to invent in his play. By their insistence on issuing, again and again, signifiers of abjection, they pull out from under the world of appearances its false ontological support of disavowed enjoyment. In so doing, they reveal the contingency, fragility and incompletion of discourse's construction out of a constitutively, indeed transcendentally, missing form: the primally repressed signifier of the unconscious.

6

The image of absence: Prisoner of Love

Though it contains numerous references to Lacan and psychoanalysis, this chapter focuses on a close reading of elements of Genet's masterwork *Prisoner of Love*, the memoir that offers his most mature and thoroughgoing account of the poetic act, the act that reveals the fundamental incompletion of being. The greater focus on Genet is motivated by the text itself: with the Palestinian resistance (and to a somewhat lesser extent the Black Panther movement in the United States), Genet finally finds his great cause, and the full intellectual weight of his long-standing interrogation of the at once destructive and creative power of the image is brought squarely to bear on a specific historical and political conjuncture.

Of course, *Prisoner* is hardly the first work in which Genet broaches particular social contexts. As I explored in Chapter 3, *The Balcony* comments on early- to mid-twentieth-century European fascism, and *The Screens* reflects on the early years of the torturous process of decolonization in North Africa. In keeping with the candour of the essays and interviews collected in *The Declared Enemy*, however, which span the period from 1964 to 1985, *Prisoner* is decidedly less coy than the two previous works in its references to historical actuality. Hence the sense that Genet's last work represents an unprecedented achievement in his oeuvre: it combines the dense intellectual rigour and critical speculation of his previous output with a newfound attention to geopolitical specificity. What results is a spellbinding practical demonstration of the power of the poetic image to reorganize and finally subvert the process by which historical experience becomes sedimented in discourse. As Félix Guattari aptly puts it in an admirable essay, Genet creates images that are 'generative of a real (*productrices de réel*)': new, unforeseen realities that also contain their own negation.[1] Though this chapter can be read independently, the references to Genet's ontology will benefit from prior engagement with the rest of the book.

Missing cards, absent ancestors

The initial pages of Genet's memoir announce its abiding concern for the connection between image-making and historical representation with a striking meditation on the subversive agency of chance. In a world like Genet's in which being is unfinished, causality must necessarily feature elements of unpredictability, indeterminacy and contingency. Unsurprisingly in this light, *Prisoner* returns insistently to games of chance, most memorably to an unusual scene of card playing among the fida'iyeen (Palestinian resistance fighters; literally, warriors) in the Jordanian camps. Genet engages in a long and complex description of the card game, saving the key piece of information – that there were no cards, that the soldiers 'had played at playing'[2] – for the end of the passage. Sternly watching is senior Fatah official Dr Mahjoub, who provides a Marxist rationale – card playing is 'a bourgeois game for the bourgeoisie'[3] – for an activity also proscribed by Islam for its incitement of disorder both social and metaphysical. The latter is linked to gaming's incendiary reliance on chance, which belies the premise of a consummately ordered universe fully available to divine knowledge. To be sure, the theme of chance has a long history in Genet's work, figuring as a sign for the incompletion of being as well as the subsequent subversion of any putatively natural or determinate order of causality.

Two young fida'iyeen in camouflage, 'still quite young but with downy mustaches on their upper lips to show how tough they were'[4], size each other up before taking their places on benches set up beneath the trees around the camp. A third fida'i takes a pack of cards from his pocket 'with a movement … seeming to belong to some rare ceremonial'.[5] A solemn atmosphere of ritual now established, the players proceed to mime a game of poker with remarkable dedication to the illusion, one of them even feigning to drop a card, then picking it up 'so nonchalantly' that it reminds Genet 'of a film in slow motion'.[6] The competition is fierce, insults in Arabic criss-cross over the table, and a formal handshake brings an end to this 'dreary ceremony',[7] which resembles 'dry masturbation'.[8] Genet senses that the spectacle is put on at least in part for him as a kind of silent protest against Dr Mahjoub's prohibitionistic authority; he surmises that the fida'iyeen experience the absence of playing cards as an addict would the absence of cocaine. For Genet, all the fuss to produce such a highly contrived spectacle has the effect of engineering only an 'absence of images',[9] in other words a paradoxical image of absence itself. This memorable figure's periodic recurrence through the memoir affixes Genet's idea of the gesture to the recognition and marking of the haunting absence of something that should be there, but has instead been absconded from sight.

In a complex passage on the challenge posed by chance to Dr Mahjoub's political conviction and conventional morality, Genet juxtaposes the card game with the image of a hand throwing dice. At the moment when the dice are thrown, Genet writes, 'the hand is turned over' like 'a bird swept along on its back by a squall'.[10] Genet then links the bird image with the cultural significance of the eagle, which can be found in Christian contexts hovering 'over a lamb grazing unaware', and in classical ones carrying Ganymede to Zeus for the latter's aesthetic delectation. Though the card players may 'try to be clever and conceal their hands from one another', it is nevertheless 'Zeus who decides'[11] their fate in the game.

This evocation of divine power, be it in the form of Christ's resurrection or Zeus's pederastic appetites, raises the issue of God's desire, in other words the question of whether or not he plays 'at dice with the world', as Genet puts it. The commentary uncovers the theological sleight of hand by which contingency can be remediated through its ascription to divine will after the fact: if God is 'Everything', then the dice game's outcome must be the product of His fancy, and 'presto, chance's name is Providence'. But the text goes on to scrutinize this simplistic logic. Indeed, the winning player's victory begs the question 'why me?', Genet reasons, and the consoling premise of divine necessity is then sullied by the enigma of God's unfathomable intention. Though any worldly happening can be ascribed to God's omnipotent will, the ascription fails to illuminate His motivation, to rationalize the divine will itself. Similarly, faith in the existence of a divine power cannot dispel all intimations of contingency: 'Did God come to exist by chance?'[12] Genet asks, separating out the question of belief from the problem of how God Himself came to be. In the midst of all this speculation about the meaning of God's existence and the nature of His desire, Mahjoub's prohibition against gambling comes to resemble a desperate plea for the restoration of a semblance of cosmological order. If Islamic faith conventionally rests on the possibility of submission to a self-present, if inscrutable, divine will, and if orthodox Marxism relies on an unshakeable conviction in the proletariat's glorious historical destiny, then games of chance, in their revelation of necessity as a mere retrospective gloss on a more fundamental law of contingency, must be outlawed at all costs. Genet's depiction of Dr Mahjoub introduces a ruinous element of uncertainty into the watertight ideological systems of both Marxism and Islam, at least in their most conventional (or vulgar) forms.

An equally compelling image of the disruptive power of the negative immediately follows in the form of Genet's appreciation of the ghostly celebration known as Obon or Bon. In this old Japanese custom with Buddhist and Taoist roots in China, family members honour the spirits of deceased ancestors through music and dance. According to Genet's explanation of the tradition, celebrants believe that the dead return in the form of the deliberately awkward movements of the members of the living who mimic them. For weeks prior to the event, for instance, children practice their limps for an imaginary race with the dead, which comes to a sudden end when 'shin-bones, skulls, thigh-bones and finger bones fall to the ground, and all the living laugh'. The custom is 'an act of irony and affection' that gives the dead a 'taste of life',[13] Genet concludes.

The parallel images of card game and Obon ritual involve a carefully choreographed set of actions organized around an absence made eerily conspicuous. Though neither the cards nor the ancestors are of course materially present in the world, neither can we say that they are fully absent, since the actions taking place around them – limping children, the gestures of shuffling and laying down imaginary cards – are unintelligible without taking into account their performative virtual presence. It is hardly a revelation to point out that this foregrounding of absence in *Prisoner of Love* serves to highlight the statelessness of the Palestinians, a condition shared historically by the Jews until the eventual success of the political Zionist project. But, more significantly from Genet's point of view, the indexing of absence also suggests the problematic identity of the Palestinians, a people whose origins, unlike that of the Jews, is mysterious and without material record; whose feudal social structure, dominated by a small number of rival dominant families, has discouraged the development of ethnic or national solidarity; and whose historical territory has suffered a basically uninterrupted history of occupation: Roman, Ottoman, British and finally Israeli. Like the card players and Obon celebrants, who both lament and enjoy the absence of cards or loved ones, the melancholic nostalgia of Genet's Palestinians will occasionally succeed in turning the pain of exile into a light-hearted and celebratory commemoration of absence itself. Such celebration marks the elusive possibility not of a final reconciliation with being's disruptive incompletion, but rather with a less decisive and triumphant, but nonetheless cathartic and joyful, acknowledgement of its unmasterable effects.

The Obon ritual returns in Genet's powerful recounting of Palestinian diplomat Leila Shahid's story of the return of a group of refugees to their birthplace of Maaloul after the Nakba, the 'catastrophe' of Zionism's brutal displacement of the Palestinians. In the violence leading up to the creation of the Israeli state, Jewish terrorists had mined the villagers' land, blown up their houses and then planted a forest where the houses once stood. For a few hours, 'much less time than the Obon dead are allowed in Japan', the returning Palestinian villagers get drunk and share stories as their 'imaginary village comes to life',[14] improved in some of its details on what had actually existed before the expulsion. Like Genet's Obon ritual, however, the celebration cannot be reduced to a nostalgic desire to revive the dead or return to the past. In fact, for Genet, the Palestinians' forest feast could not be more different from Israel's realization of its Zionist dream. At its root, the Arab revelry does not reflect 'the sort of longing that precedes the struggle for a real return'. Instead, it resembles the persistence of pagan fairy customs in Brittany which, as Genet attests, have survived suppression 'by the Romans and then by the Christian clergy'.[15]

None of these strange, ghostly celebrations – Japanese, Palestinian, Breton – take return, restoration or redemption as their aim. Rather, they enact a performance of the trauma of loss which, through repetition, loses something of its traumatic quality, becoming instead an ambiguously joyful re-enactment that puts into question the very ideas of ownership and home. In quintessentially Genetian fashion, the Palestinians' revelry in the Zionist forest constructs a poetic image not of the village itself, but rather of its unrecoverable absence. Instead of compensating for ontological incompletion, of filling out the hole in being, the image in this instance rather frames it, making it materialize – negatively, as a second-order subtraction – from the void.

As I have tried to argue throughout this book, such images become in Genet's hands the figural short-hand for a deep ontological conviction concerning reality's interrupted self-realization. However, they are also clearly intended to counterbalance his overt, historical criticisms of the Palestinian resistance as insufficiently committed and politically naive. Yes, the military camps housing the fida'iyeen have a theatrical or film-set air about them, and even the direct actions the fighters perform seem designed more to bring media attention to the cause than to generate concrete geopolitical change. Yet, on another level of Genet's analysis, the theatricality is precisely the point. In this perspective, the resistance's true significance lies not in the attempt to wrest historical Palestine from the Zionists, nor even to disrupt the complicity of Euro-American capitalism with the neo-feudal autocracies of the Arab Gulf states, but rather to draw attention to the ontological scandal that disqualifies all claims to unmediated identity and pure origin. *Prisoner of Love* never manages to resolve the insoluble contradiction between, on the one hand, its concrete political advocacy in favour of the Palestinian cause and, on the other, its abstract, philosophical argument concerning being's irremediable malformation. Nevertheless, the text ultimately prioritizes the latter in its insistent return to its memorable poetic images. As Genet argues poetry must do, these images figure their own undoing, revealing how every object that comes to exist in the world of appearances does so in the most paradoxical way: by having failed fully to come to be.

A supernumerary orange

Of all the images in *Prisoner of Love* that betoken Genet's conviction about being's indwelling fault, perhaps the most compelling is the pyramid of oranges he sees in an Istanbul market during a layover on the journey that would unite him with the Palestinians. Genet's attention is initially caught by the vendor, a youth with 'the gift of the gab' and an ambiguous aura of seduction, whose 'hand move(s) swiftly from his eyes to his teeth to his crotch, then very rapidly back to his black hair, teeth and shining eyes'.[16] Just as he senses that the young man's provocative gestures are designed to 'disturb rather than charm', Genet notices a strange, supernumerary orange inexplicably suspended in the air a foot or so above the top of the fruit pyramid, hanging there 'motionless despite the bustle of the street'.[17] Noticing his puzzlement at this violation of the laws of physics, the vendor, showing Genet 'a few more teeth', flicks the orange, which begins to swing 'from right to left'.[18] A group of Turks around Genet bursts out laughing as he finally realizes that 'the orange (is) hanging from a invisible nylon thread attached to the (kiosk's) awning'.[19]

Though the orange on the thread is clearly an element of excess over the geometric regularity of the pyramid below it, Genet intriguingly associates this excess with its apparent opposite. When a malicious customer selects an orange from the bottom of the pile, Genet remarks, the merchant 'know(s) how to whip' one out and 'replace it with another that fills the void without putting the construction out of balance'.[20] The pyramid structure contains both an evanescent absence and an enigmatic excess, both of which Genet links to the seller's dexterity in replacing the extracted piece of fruit as well as his unsettlingly insinuating gestures. At one point in Genet's narration the text suddenly shifts with a remark on the preponderance of the idea of levitation in Turkish culture as well as Genet's own ecstatic experience, evoked in the immediately preceding passage, coming out of a long period of debilitating depression. Viewed as a hybrid ontological metaphor, Genet's associations link the discontinuity of the pyramid of fruit – the extra orange floating above it and the gap that opens at the bottom when a piece is removed – with the experience of enjoyment, both Genet's own out-of-body experience (to be explored later in this chapter) and the discomfiting suggestiveness of the vendor's louche movements. Broaching again the phenomenology of embodiment, Genet makes another wild associative move with a mention of his interest in Sufism, more specifically the thought of Bayazid Bistami, the Sufi he 'revere(s) the most'.[21] Bistami is associated with the doctrine of *fana*, or mystical union with Allah in death, as well as with *sukr*, an ecstatic school of Islamic mysticism whose name signifies intoxication. Linking these disparate, otherwise-confusing references is the idea that jouissance – the ecstatic, often-unwelcome, intrusive or even traumatic experience of the body – occurs at a place of structural discontinuity, of a fault in being.

Also crucial to note, however, is Genet's inclusion in the construction of his literary image of an explanation for the uppermost orange's gravity-defying feat. Asking after Genet's national origin, the provocative merchant goes on to reveal the secret of the orange '*en charabia*'[22] – in bizarre, convoluted or nonsensical language – referring to his contraption as 'a little miracle'.[23] There follows, again without logical transition, a passage on 'dreams of power' as figured in legends and fairy tales. These narratives, always featuring a noble or heroic protagonist, are designed in Genet's view to elicit the storyteller or listener's identification and to valorize taking 'the road to power' over a liaison with 'the loveliest and most naked of young girls'[24] whom the hero, a man of course, might come across along the way. Unsurprisingly, Genet takes his distance from such clichés, stating that he would 'do better to go back and marry (his) mother and become king of Thebes'.[25] Despite their jarring suddenness, Genet's juxtapositions not only connect the lure, the power of attraction, of the pyramid of oranges to the desire for social or political prestige as reflected in dominant cultural narratives. In addition, they associate this connection to enjoyment, suggesting that jouissance is the glue that holds the structure of power together, accounting for the fascination it exercises, just like the invisible thread that creates the illusion of the floating orange. By extension, the tragic destiny of Oedipus at Colonus, where he blinds himself in horror at the discovery of his incestuous liaison, and which Lacan himself took as a figure for the outcome of analysis, for the traversal of fantasy, becomes a figure for interpretation. Interpretation here signifies the demystification of narratives of power and the subsequent eradication of the unacknowledged enjoyment that sustains their hegemony and influence in the discourses of culture.

One of the key images with which Genet relates to his own person this properly analytic process of identifying and eliminating enjoyment from the body is the house he dreams of building on a hillside overlooking the Mediterranean near Antakya in Turkey's southernmost Hatay province, home to the ruins of the ancient Greek city of Antioch. For Genet, the seductive promise of comfort is a danger both ethical and political against which both he as author-witness, and the Palestinian resistance as a political movement, must struggle without compromise. Despite its origin as a sort of official, Arafat-sanctioned chronicle of the revolution, *Prisoner of Love* is chock full of criticism of the Palestinian leadership for betraying the cause's principles in favour of personal material gain. But Genet also struggles quite brutally against himself as he discovers an inviolable limit to his ascetic refusal of the repose offered by home, nation, genealogy, selfhood and identity, indeed by any conventional understanding of origin, truth, presence or certainty.

The first mention of the house occurs adjacent to a lament for the deference shown by many fida'iyeen, despite the avowed Marxism of several of their factions, to the aristocratic figures of the great Palestinian families. In the text, Genet relates the visit of a number of these families' grand ladies to the Palestinian wounded in south Lebanon. Bedecked in their gold jewellery, they tend to the wounded as if protected by silk cushions. In a memorable image, Genet writes that the ladies simmer in their distanced fellow-feeling like goose meat in its fat being prepared for a cassoulet. Self-critically, Genet cannot resist comparing himself to these ladies who 'contemplate their people from their chaises-longues, through pearl-handled lorgnettes' as he imagines himself in his prospective Turkish retreat watching 'the sea and Cyprus in the distance'.[26] Though he insists that the resemblance never troubles him, he admits nonetheless to being, in relation to the fida'iyeen, 'always on the other side of a boundary', never on board with 'the whole'[27] of himself. This key passage reveals Genet coming to terms with the limits of engagement, of fellow-travellership, as his partisanship butts against a core of subjectivity that remains stubbornly unintegrated and alone.

The attachment to the Turkish villa is further analysed in a subsequent passage in which Genet relates – in the third person, underlining the theme of self-expropriation – his lifelong project to divest himself of property, to suppress all affective bonds to worldly objects. Genet specifies that by property he means 'a certain number of objects, or buildings, or lands, or people, external to oneself, which a proprietor has at his disposal to use, enjoy (*jouir*), and abuse'.[28] The direct association of property with jouissance, explicit in French, was frequently observed in his early teaching by Lacan, whose point was not that the experience of sexual enjoyment is akin to the experience of ownership, but rather that the alienation of jouissance – the fact that enjoyment takes you outside yourself, to the point that it is more readily discernable in the Other's body than in the proper body – incites a desire for appropriation, for the annihilation, potentially overtly sadistic, of its unsettling exteriority. By wishing to eliminate his attachment to objects, Genet endeavours to cleanse himself completely of enjoyment. The result, however, is that he finds himself invaded – 'one can only wonder via what orifice' – by an overwhelming 'desire for a house, a solid fixed place, an enclosed orchard'.[29]

The text's vagueness on the actual existence of the Mediterranean villa underlines its properly psychical quality, its location 'inside' Genet, but in 'a part of the body that doesn't exist'.[30] Immaterial, grounded in inexistence, but at the same time oddly corporeal, the house muddles the distinction between inside and outside while also marrying the contrary qualities of quiddity and insubstantiality. The endpoint of Genet's ascetic experience is contact with the 'total void' concealed by 'the inside of (his) house' or, more vaguely, by an 'uncertain place'.[31] Revealingly, this key series of images superimposes two figures of emptiness. The absence that fuels the desire for objects paradoxically fills a more primordial void, one that intimates the collapse of subjectivity as such. In the attempt to purify himself of the bonds of attachment, Genet discovers desire's inexhaustibility: the object, in its status as absent or unattainable, is the only thing that stands between us and psychical disintegration.

From the psychoanalytic perspective, the function of the house near Antakya for Genet is finally to create a certain psychical distance from the identity-shattering acknowledgement of enjoyment. This becomes clear in the various places in the text where Genet imagines himself contemplating the view over the Mediterranean, observing a 'naval battle (he) would have liked to see from (his) window with drowned men floating on the now still waters'.[32] Though it is never made clear whether or not Genet actually witnessed such a battle – the text is generally uninterested in historical facts in the objective sense – there are allusions in the text to the Turkish-Hellenic conflict, and there could be a link more specifically to Turkey's invasion of Cyprus in the summer of 1974.

In any case, Genet vividly wonders if the project or fantasy of a Levantine retirement home with a view has as its origin 'a desire for a shell or the joy of having (his) spirit swim in fiction like a body on water'.[33] Protection, settlement, safety, isolation, calm, the notion of a safe harbour, but also fiction and by extension his own literary activity ('more noble' but 'less true'[34]), these ideas are set against Genet's uncharacteristic military reverie, which turns the spotlight on dead male bodies floating on the Mediterranean after the last gun has been fired. No doubt there is an element of sadism here, as if Genet were asserting the equivalence of the desire for security and protection and an unrecognized morbid pleasure that gets off on images of war and death. In sum, however, the Turkish villa beautifully figures the paradoxical logic according to which the most determined attempt to evacuate the body of enjoyment leads inexorably to the discovery of an intractable fantasmatic nucleus the acknowledgement of which fundamentally alters Genet's relationship to, and experience of, his own embodiment. In an illuminating example of the act of sublimation's curative effects, Genet relates that the unrelenting torment of his desire for the Mediterranean retreat only subsides when he decides to build a house not for himself, but rather 'for a young Arab'.[35]

Maronite enjoyments

Genet's direct politicization of his intuition concerning the nefarious impact of unacknowledged enjoyment is nowhere more evident than in his analysis of Maronite Christian culture in Lebanon and the sectarian Phalange (Kataeb). The Phalange's political organization in the 1930s was partly inspired by Italy's National Fascist Party, and its militia was modelled by founder Pierre Gemayel after Hitler's *Sturmabteilung*, the Nazi Party's original paramilitary wing. *Prisoner of Love* sets the convention of the assumed nom de guerre among the Palestinian fida'iyeen, which substitutes fantasy and self-creation for the determinations of family history, against the discovery of 'some deep genealogy' among peoples and nations engaged in the search for their 'singularity', their 'roots'.[36] Genet's example is the attempt of some Lebanese Maronite Christians to describe themselves as Phoenecians as a means of distinguishing themselves from the Syrian Arabs who invaded Lebanon in 1976, partly in order to stop the growing influence on regional politics of the various Palestinian factions. Genet further relates his own memory of watching Phalangist soldiers in 1970 marching in formation while singing 'a hymn in honour of the Immaculate Conception', looking 'delicately stupid' and exuding an 'apparent virility' that seemed nonetheless 'tragic'.[37] Suggestively, the text then pairs two seemingly random images to bring out their fetishistic value, one of which seems rather out of context: the two sons of a newspaper seller gripping their golden Virgin of Lourdes medals, and a Malian on the banks of the Niger clutching his gri-gri, which takes the form of a red woollen purse that contains 'a few magic words in Arabic'.[38]

Intimations of the deep complicity between religious faith, social and political power, the desire for identity in difference, and idealized (and therefore repressed) sexuality becomes more explicit as Genet recounts another memory of early 1970s Lebanon. In this one, he notices a Phalange militia member kissing a young woman 'between her tanned breasts' where there shines not a medallion of the Virgin, as one might expect of a Maronite, but rather a 'gold gibbet, studded with diamonds and rubies'. As Genet observes, the young soldier's tongue seems 'to swallow the pearl'[39] that is also featured among the clustered jewels. The apparent eroticism of the scene is belied, however, by three other Phalangists who, also present at the scene, react by 'bow(ing) their heads for this communion', and by the young woman herself, who takes her leave 'chastely' after offering the militiamen a characteristically Maronite blessing: 'May Jesus protect you and His Mother give you victory.'[40]

The passage vividly uncovers the strong connection between the obfuscation of libido embedded in Maronite custom (the observation is far from limited, however, either to Christianity in general or its Maronite sect in particular) and the cruel militarism that arises out of the aspiration to ethno-religious purity. For Genet, the geopolitically significant manifestation of this link is the deep Islamophobia that guides the Phalangists towards a de facto military alliance with Israel against the Palestinian refugees in Lebanon. This alliance reached its criminal culmination in the notorious massacres in the Beirut camps of Sabra and Chatila on 16 September 1982, of which Genet was famously one of the first European witnesses. The insight is indeed deeply psychoanalytic: if sex is what harbours the incompletion of being, and by extension the impossibility of undivided identity, then its repression, in this instance the disguise of enjoyment under a cloak of religious mystification, is required to maintain the illusion of national coherence and belonging. 'I was getting to know them better,' writes Genet, referring to the Lebanese Christian militia and gearing up for his coda. Driving home his point about the evident yet unacknowledged libido embedded in the culture, Genet recalls how the 'thick lips' of the Kataeb militiamen 'clung to medals of the Virgin on gold chains, and lingered over the hand of a Patriarch devoutly masturbating the shaft of his golden crozier.'[41] In these last images the specifically masculine or phallic character of the repression is memorably brought to the fore.

Ethical commemoration

Much of the work of *Prisoner of Love* consists in creating commemorative images of both the Palestinian resistance itself (along with the Black Panther movement) and those of its agents with whom Genet came into contact.

A prime example is the affectionate portrait of Hanna Mikhail, to whom the text refers by his nom de guerre Abou Omar. Mikhail was a Christian, Ramallah-born, US-educated politics professor and friend of Edward Said who left academia in 1969 to assume positions in the PLO and Fatah, and whose disappearance at sea in 1976 during the Lebanese Civil War remains unexplained to this day. Like the leper whom the Cid famously kissed, a figure whose identity has been obscured by the tradition going from the eleventh-century epic poem, through Corneille's classical tragedy, and up to Bizet's opera and beyond, Mikhail for Genet is 'one of the anonymous heroes'[42] of the Palestinian resistance, one whose deeds call out for celebratory literary memorialization. To be sure, Genet is interested in the process by which particular details of events survive to become part of the historical record. His text is clearly meant to intervene in this process, altering the parameters against which the Israeli-Palestinian conflict has been remembered by countering the insidious and still-familiar Zionist narrative whose function is to cast off the trauma of the Nakba into history's dustbin of truths inconvenient to the powers that be.

I wish to argue, however, that the more consequential theory and practice of what Genet calls poetry aims rather at the creation of a distinct kind of image that moves beyond the symbolic acknowledgement of forgotten personages and events, important though this commemorative work surely is. As I explored in Chapter 5 à propos of *The Screens*, Genet accomplishes this by inventing images that disclose the inherent non-being within the image itself. *Prisoner of Love* tethers its mention of the Cid kissing the leper to other examples – Polynices 'replaced by Antigone' and 'the wolfhound by Hitler'[43] – to underscore how the survival and perpetuation of one image tends to require the suppression of another. Two possibilities ensue. The first involves the creation of a counter-image to reverse the process of selection that decides which of the two representations survives in the fullness of its significance and the glory of its prestige. Consider the figure of Ariel Sharon, the Israeli general and future prime minister found complicit in the Sabra and Chatila massacre by an Israeli judiciary inquiry in 1983, 'replaced by' (to use Genet's phrase) the image of Abou Omar, for instance.

The second chooses to focus instead on the very gesture by which the dominant image's perpetuation creates a void left behind by the subordinate image's erasure. Replacing remembrance of the event or personage is a sort of testimony to the impossibility of fully signifying the real of being. This second strategy does not deprive the first of its ethical and political legitimacy, however. In literary form, Mikhail lives on very memorably indeed in the pages of Genet's book and the minds of its readers. The point is rather that the creation of a counter-image, one that aims at the subversion of dominant historical narratives, does not escape the illusionary logic imposed by hegemonic regimes of visibility. The author of *Prisoner of Love* obsessively highlights how his testimonial misses the mark; literary representation is a pale imitation of a fullness of being that does not exist. This is to say that images themselves create the illusion of the authentic reality that they fail convincingly to depict; this means of course that there would be no sense of an authentic reality were it not for the images that are meant to depict it. Relatedly, in the absence of our awareness of the image's inadequacy, we would have no idea of a true reality against which the image could be judged a mere approximation.

Genet interrupts his homage to Mikhail with the recurring image of a procession at the funeral of a Muslim leader, centred on the figure of a 'cradle or football, or if you wish (a) coffin', pitching, dancing and flying above the heads of a crowd that is 'visibly angry but maybe amused by the game'.[44] This general or abstract image echoes Genet's more historically embedded depiction of the funeral of Gamal Abdel Nasser, anti-imperialist and pan-Arabist president of Egypt in the period immediately prior to Genet's first Palestinian sojourn. Nasser's sudden death in 1970 three years after Egypt's defeat in the Six-Day War with Israel shook the Arab world; it figures in Genet's book as the signal event that triggers at once the surge and the demise of the Palestinian resistance. The procession at Nasser's funeral drew over five million people into the streets of Cairo and proved so uncontrollable that foreign dignitaries present for the occasion were evacuated from the area. In *Prisoner of Love*, Genet seizes upon the tremendous resonance of the event across the Arab world at the time. His rich prose moulds the scene into the centrepiece of a remarkable meditation on the image's intimacy with a deathly void.

The Nasser iteration of this recursive image foregrounds one key detail: the coffin held up by the throng of mourners, which the text compares to a rugby ball, in fact 'may be empty'.[45] Assembled in this memorable tableau are the pivotal Genetian notions of the void, death and enjoyment, the latter conveyed by the passionate grief of a people mourning the premature demise of a symbol of Arab resistance to a long and humiliating history of Roman, Ottoman and modern European imperialisms. Despite Genet's clear admiration for Nasser, however, the passage also features an implicit critique of the elevation of the late Egyptian leader into a depoliticizing anti-colonial symbol whose concrete effect was to discourage direct action against foreign influence in the Arab world. But as Genet's complex discussion transitions from the funeral scene to an image of shadow puppetry, a signal tension, characteristic of the text as a whole, emerges between the specificity of Nasser's legacy as a counter-image to dominant Zionist and Euro-American narratives in the region and the passage's more general philosophical significance as a reflection on being's funereal incompletion.

The immediate context is a comparison between the inevitably failed attempt to immortalize the dead through the creation of literary images and the macabre, ghostly qualities of shadow puppets. Through the strange illusion of their autonomy, the puppets expose an unsettling gap between their reality and the one inhabited by the puppeteers, whose voices narrate the story and whose movements give them their disquietingly distinctive life. Genet implicitly links the image of the empty casket in the Nasserite funeral scene with the 'unbridgeable distance'[46] that separates the shadow puppets from their makers and grants them their excessive, spectral vitality. Without a doubt, the puppets represent one of the key motifs with which *Prisoner of Love* aims to embody a paradoxical image of absence; a representation, in other words, of something that should be present, but is not. With the puppets, Genet attempts to incorporate into the image itself, to positivize as it were, the negativity that normally de-realizes the image, that differentiates it from something we could perceive, however naively, as real. If the image, in its very distance from the quality of realism, normally functions to create the illusion of that same 'realistic' reality, then the puppets effect the opposite gesture: they figure the inherent incompletion of being itself. This incompletion is the fault that fictionalizes being, undoing the very distinction between the image and that which it is meant to be an image of.

These reflections on the image of negativity occur in the midst of Genet's heartfelt tribute to Mikhail. In consequence, the doctrine of being's irreducible self-difference acquires a more specifically subjective quality. This is to say that Genet offers something like a negative ontology of the subject, one that equates a subject's essence with the fault in (its) being. Moreover, this ontology has a fierce ethical character that resonates deeply with the ethics of psychoanalysis. For Genet, Abu Omar resembles the shadow puppets in 'their indifference to story and voice alike', the lesson being 'that story and voice are not theirs, and that when we are dead anything anyone says about us is not only literally false but also sounds it'.[47] Certainly, we should be wary of the phrasing's possible insinuation that there is a truth of the subject that would be fully communicable in some better, alternative discourse. Nevertheless, there remains the clear implication that the disparity between puppet and puppeteer, the 'distance' that emancipates the shadow from both the diegetic world of the narrative and the physical reality of the object that casts the shadow, signals the absence within the subject itself, in other words the gap of subjective self-difference.

In this sense death, in its guise as the silence that 'survives everything',[48] inheres also in life as its immanent negation. Indeed, Genet asserts that 'the author too, like those he speaks of, is dead'.[49] In such pivotal textual moments, Genet does not shy away from a radical implication. Despite the importance of putting down in writing, for the historical record as it were, the key details of Mikhail's life – Genet includes a number of circulating theories about his disappearance, singling out the scenario of his abduction by a Syrian patrol boat and his handing over to the Lebanese Phalange, who would have assassinated him, aided and abetted, perhaps, by Tsahal or Mossad – the true ethical imperative is the production in image form of the fissure of being that separates the subject from any signifier that would take upon itself the foolish task of its exhaustive representation. For Genet, death is the name of this elusive, nomadic negativity that, 'as soon as you evoke it by naming it, is transformed'.[50] In this light, ethical commemoration, the kind that would qualify as a poetic act in the Genetian sense, should aim to signify not the signal accomplishments of a life, but rather the necessary failure of literary remembrance; the impossibility, that is, of capturing the essence of a life in prose, or indeed by any other means. Genet's ontology implies that the subject corresponds to a point of rupture or discontinuity in the metaphorical fabric of being. And the image of this fault is the one that intimates a deathly immortality, the uncanny persistence of an insistent absence: 'the skeleton and the skeleton dust to come', as Genet himself memorably puts it.[51]

The eclipse of femininity

Genet further develops this idea some would call dialectical of the identity of an object with its own erasure in a rich meditation on the word 'eclipse'. For Genet, existence is inseparable from its disappearance or dissolution. Though any entity already contains its own negation, in Genet's sense of the term the event of an eclipse fails to obliterate its existence; indeed the thing concerned can 'return regenerated' like the sun, which is 'more visible if the moon eclipses it'.[52] The meaning of the term in question is eminently slippery, and its reflexive form in French can mean, in Genet's own uncontroversial view, either to 'slip away, (to) escape' or to 'disappear' behind 'the brightness of another'.[53] But 'eclipse' for Genet finally does not suggest mere polysemy, in other words a (potentially infinite) multiplicity of meanings. Nor, in ontological terms, does the word simply capture the constant transformations of being, in other words being's endless becoming. Rather, 'eclipse' designates the sovereign void around which the movement of both meaning and being takes place, and which forever stalls the definitive incarnation of any of its instantiations. If things never fully come to be, then neither do they ever truly cease to exist. Being and meaning are in constant flux due to their status as inherently unfinished. In consequence, the negativity responsible for this quality of incompletion acquires in comparison to the state of flux an oddly permanent and even positive presence.

As is characteristic of the later Genet, these abstract thoughts are concretized through reference to radical political movements of the time: 'the Zengakuren in Japan in 1966; the Red Guard in China; the student unrest at Berkeley; the Black Panthers; May 1968 in Paris'.[54] These movements materialize dramatically only suddenly to fade away, then return in brilliant flashes of action or survive with unanticipated afterlives. Of course, Genet also has in mind the brave young fida'iyeen who leave their camps on the banks of the Jordan under the cover of night and penetrate into Israeli territory to meet almost-certain death. Returning to the 'eclipse' discussion, Genet dismisses particular cosmological and geological connotations he associates with the term: the ancient Chinese belief that eclipses were caused by a celestial dragon eating the sun in the case of the former; or, in the latter, planetary orbits and the 'telluric fault lines' that encircle the earth.[55] For 'gravitation, the law that governs the stars', of which the hungry Chinese dragon is a mythological account, Genet substitutes the image of a hollow prison 'full of holes and cavities', each containing a man who 'can imagine ... a time and rhythm different from those of the stars'.[56]

In this complex figural contrast, Genet valorizes the interruption of natural causality as well as its mythological figuration, preferring instead the creation of spatial singularities that allow for invention along fault lines not geological but ontological in nature. With respect to the term's reflexive form, Genet writes that 'to eclipse oneself (*s'éclipser*)' is 'a malicious and somewhat apprehensive (*craintif*) verb' that 'allows every thing to be the star that eclipses the other'.[57] The implied infinite regress ties each and every star both to the act of eclipsing another and to its own occlusion. The suggestion is not only that being and non-being are intimately imbricated into one another; also, and more radically, the negativity effected by the act of eclipsing works to dissimulate a more fundamental abyss of absolute indistinction. Like Genet's counter-intuitive example of the Alawite imam who hides his Alawite identity for fear of being taken, mistakenly, for a non-Alawite, and perhaps for a Jew,[58] the act of dissimulation covers over not a positive quality or identity, but rather another instantiation of indeterminacy, yet another eclipse of being.

Psychoanalytic readers, and readers of previous chapters of this book, will already have noted an affinity between this notion of a feint that masks nothingness itself and the Freudo-Lacanian theory of femininity as fundamentally a question of pretence, one that unexpectedly brings feminine-sexuated subjects closer to the truth of being in its inconsistency than masculine ones, whose sense of an exceptional substantive sexual identity is the true simulacrum, the authentic illusion, within sexual difference. It is hardly a coincidence, then, that in *Prisoner of Love* Genet pursues his long-standing interest in femininity as performance (and not gender in general as performance, note), not only with respect to its particular way of foregrounding the complicity of appearance and void, deception and absence, but even more significantly in how it informs those elements of Palestinian revolutionary culture to which he lends his most unqualified support. In a characteristically dense passage on sexuality within the resistance, Genet links the extraordinary sociality of the fida'iyeen, together with their particular brand of 'understated (*sans emphase*) bravery',[59] to an enjoyment in loss, or more precisely in the loss of the very possibility of loss. In spite of the all-male membership of the groups of Palestinian fighters it lovingly depicts, *Prisoner* qualifies this reflexive variety of loss as distinctively feminine, though in a fashion clearly not exclusive to the female (biological) sex. As might be expected, we discover in this connection yet another reference to death. Here, however, its macabre and funereal aspects are set aside in favour of a sense of lightness and play, which arises from acknowledgement of the inherent absurdity of fighting 'to the death for some land either here or there'.[60]

Genet expands upon these ontological implications of femininity in a section of the memoir that describes a well-known Milanese custom. Passers-by in the famous Galleria Vittorio Emanuele II take a moment from their busy days to spin around three times on a mosaic floor with their heel planted on a representation of the testicles of the horse of the condottiero Bartolomeo Colleoni, fifteenth-century Captain General of the Republic of Venice. As the unacquainted will guess, the gesture is meant to grant its performer some of the stallion's virility. Counterfactually from today's perspective, Genet asserts that 'no woman has ever been allowed to do it'.[61] From this image of virility, or rather the desire for it, the text shifts suddenly to a description of grenades hanging from the belts of male pupils in a Palestinian schoolyard. Each boy, writes Genet, 'show(s) off the double or quadruple monstrous testicles he carrie(s) at his waist or over his shoulder'. Qualifying the sight as 'at once obscene and innocent',[62] Genet remarks on 'the apparent absence of sexual desire' among the fida'iyeen, which he deems 'quite out of keeping with the ordinary life of strong young males'. 'Orgasm is a very masculine noun in French,' concludes Genet, 'but it's scuppered by such feminine nouns as death-agony, death, woman and war.' In the end, it is these latter terms that 'have the last word'.[63]

These seemingly disparate thoughts precede a return to the immediate narrative context, such as it is, which involves *Prisoner of Love*'s recursive account of the time Genet spent with a young fida'i named Hamza and his mother in a refugee camp at Ajloun, in the northwest corner of Jordan.[64] These two are the most pivotal persons depicted in the entire text, and Genet foregrounds the figure of the mother, 'a widow, but very strong', who is 'armed exactly like her son'. Though her authoritative domestic presence draws attention to her status as 'head of the family',[65] she delegates her power and authority symbolically to Hamza in his role as leader of a group of fida'iyeen. Genet's characteristically associative juxtapositions work to sever the attributes of masculinity and virility from their link to substance, to the being of a determinate emblematic subject, in so doing feminizing them in the sense I have been arguing for throughout this book. As I have explored extensively in previous chapters, Freud linked masculine anxiety to the prospect of loss; for the girl, in contrast, loss has always-already taken place. Femininity is thereby imbued with a certain lightness, with the power to remain indifferent to a law whose threat of punishment has no bearing for the subject who has already been punished. But this fact of feminine castration does not grant its subject immunity to anxiety. On the contrary, if the Freudian boy's fear of castration disguises a more radical anxiety that there is in fact nothing to be lost, in other words that his penis fails to count as the phallic One, then the girl has no protection from the abyss, from the ontological catastrophe that the boy's anxiety serves to dispel; no protection, that is, apart from her 'gender performance': the series of masks that, in their inconsistent multiplicity, flaunt the absence of any link to grounded, intelligibly ordered being.

Genet's images put into practice this distinctively feminine dissociation of the phallus from its obfuscatory grounding in the male biological body, in particular the body of the man meant to figure the phallic exception to the law of castration. The overstated or outdated prohibition against women spinning their heel on the horse's testicles in Milan only highlights the possibility that a woman may, 'illegitimately' as it were, acquire the elusive attribute of virility. In this light, the pupils' grenades featured in Genet's other image intimate not only a premature, incongruous adult male sexuality, but also virility's strangely detachable, mobile and transferable qualities, in other words the fact that it is always somehow in excess of, separable from, the subject who is meant to possess it.

Genet's textual depictions of the sexuality of the young fida'iyeen – their lithe bodies and sensuous smiles; their youthful, yet-to-fill-out moustaches; their self-conscious poses, Kalashnikovs placed suggestively between their legs – foreground this same surfeit of care and attention that lends to their sexuality its performative quality and paradoxically desexualizes it, deprives it of its potency by means of a certain feminization. Genet sees among the fida'iyeen what today's gender theory would call a 'performance of masculinity', one that dissociates the phallus from its presumptive link with generation and even eroticism, transforming the prospect of absence from a source of castrative anxiety into a celebration of, and enjoyment in, lack. Psychoanalysis would only add to this availably ambient interpretation the insuperable psychical fact of sexual difference: the 'performance of masculinity' is of course essentially feminine; it is one possible manifestation of a distinctively feminine sexuation. In the hands of the Palestinian fighters, the image of phallic identity becomes a sign for the inconsistency and incompletion of being, to which a non-hysterical femininity has privileged access for the reasons just outlined.

Moreover, by granting Hamza's mother an overtly phallic position in the family structure, Genet subverts the transgenerational logic of patriarchy with the insinuation that a son is fully capable of inheriting the phallus from the maternal line, albeit in a distinctive form. Genet's depiction of Hamza's household entirely sidelines the paternal figure without, however, eliminating the function of the phallic signifier as such. Only a brief mention of the father's suicide attenuates what would otherwise risk collapsing into incestuous fusion.

In Genet's depiction, Hamza inherits from his mother a distinctively feminized version of the phallus, one that indexes its internal or inherent beyond. Here libidinal investment is displaced from its symbolization in a privileged signifier or image as it moves towards a de-eroticized jouissance that celebrates the limitless and groundless play of appearances in their vertiginous identity with the void.

For Lacan as for Genet, however, femininity is not exempt from a more conventional, and properly neurotic, position vis-à-vis the phallus. To be sure, *Prisoner* explicitly links this position to certain official, and notoriously corrupt, elements of the Palestinian state and civil society. In an illuminating passage, Genet vividly contrasts his encounter in her luxuriant Amman villa with a bourgeois lady he calls the 'president' of the Palestinian women with his experience among a group of less privileged old ladies in the Jebel Hussein refugee camp only 'fifty metres away'.[66] He comes upon the latter lounging nonchalantly amid the ashes of their houses, burned to the ground in a napalm fire during an attack by Bedouin soldiers in the Jordanian army. While the lady president can only spout United Nations-sanctioned pieties about the occupation with reference to international law, implicitly framing the resistance's goal as an attempt to recuperate territory lost to Zionism, the refugee women become a crucial figure for Genet's doctrine of the good image, the one that manages to body forth a negativity both placeless and atemporal in nature. There is no denying that Genet's response to the spokeswoman, who 'crudely mangle(s) out an invisible text, forcing the arguments of the Palestinian resistance on (him)', is cruel: 'If the leaders of Fatah appointed you they must be as stupid as you are,'[67] he depicts himself as saying. Admonished by his translator's attendants for his seemingly unwarranted hostility, Genet is clearly triggered by the account's cold legalism and territorial *Realpolitik*.

The tone of the accompanying prose could not be more different, however. Though the old women in the ashes sit between 'five times four smoke-blackened stones', the only remnants of the houses they lived in, they are 'cheerful in misfortune', 'light and graceful', conspicuously unveiled, baring 'their solitude to the bone'.[68] Hospitably offering Genet tea in a blue porcelain cup that miraculously survived the fire intact, the ladies make fun of the Jordanian king Hussein, asking Genet if he wants to 'take him and show him to the French'.⁶⁹ The women's joy in one another's company shines through despite their knowledge that the king's orders resulted in the death of one of their husbands, killed by a napalm bomb and burned to the point of becoming 'clean … as a fish-bone',⁷⁰ his remains lying half-buried in soil too shallow for proper cover. Unlike the bourgeois Palestinian lady, who is invested in the recuperation of territory and property as well as the (retrospectively inadequate, to risk an understatement) efficacy of UN Security Council Resolution 242,⁷¹ the old women have 'the cheerfulness of those who have ceased to hope',⁷² showing themselves 'perfectly' suited to their casual and familiar use of 'modern military vocabulary'.⁷³

Genet's old Palestinian women have come through radical loss with the realization that there in fact had been nothing, apart perhaps from their surviving relatives, to lose. In Genet's eyes, they have realized that the attachment to place and property functions as a psychical buffer against a more profound experience of destitution immanent to subjectivity and ultimately irreducible to even the most traumatic of lived experiences. When one of the ladies mentions the burial ceremony planned by Fatah for her husband, Genet conjures the image of a mobile cemetery, an image that succinctly captures their familiarity with a feminine enjoyment of rootlessness and impermanence. The antithesis of memorialization viewed as the marker of identity and presence, Genet imagines his nomadic cemetery as 'collapsible', 'a kind of war memorial that ha(s) to be dismantled quickly … and the parts carried away'.⁷⁴

The imagery is certainly not without a connection to historical Palestine's nomadic, desert-dwelling Bedouin, a group of Arab tribes whose membership includes the Jordanian soldiers responsible for the destruction of the women's homes and the deaths of at least one of their husbands. No admirer of the Bedouin soldiers' violent persecution of the Palestinians under Hussein, Genet nevertheless pushes the women's jubilant, carefree celebration of dispossession to the extreme by figuring the funerals of their menfolk with tropes evoking the lifeworld of a mortal enemy of the portion of the Palestinian refugee population housed in Jordanian camps. In more theoretical terms, Genet's collapsible mobile cemetery is among *Prisoner*'s most memorable figures for a specific, evanescent and placeless, variety of negativity, one that defines space as both incomplete and unamenable to mapping or localization. Indeed, feminine being goes without any fixed point of reference from which spatial relationships could be determined, particular points defined and in this sense known.

Being and melancholy

Surely the part of *Prisoner of Love* that most intimately connects the groundlessness of feminine being to Genet's own authorial voice is the striking passage evoking his five-year struggle with depression and, more specifically, his awakening from what he evidently experienced as a dark period of creative stagnation.[75] Feminine enjoyment's intimacy with the void of subjectivity, it has been argued,[76] can produce a tendency towards melancholy; melancholia, in other words, is a hardly uncommon modality of *la jouissance féminine*. Genet's evocation of his experience of depression offers images of solitude, separation and detachment, figures that suggest being's point of discontinuity or non-relation; the ontological fault, that is, that psychoanalysis insists on associating with sex. The paradox, of course, is that melancholic affect is anathema to eroticism, and we rediscover here one of Genet's fundamental, and most psychoanalytic, insights. Counter-intuitively, the subject's most unmediated experience of 'sex' corresponds to the eclipse of the libidinal object in its capacity to cause desire. What in everyday parlance we call sexuality emerges from the obfuscation of sex at the hands of the fantasies and idealizations produced by repression, which in this sense is the psyche's way of attempting to compensate for the ontological deficit. In sum, sex has an inversely proportional relation to sexiness: the more directly we encounter the lack in the Other, the impasse of being, the less our reality is granted its charming seductions; the less we 'cathect (*besetzen*)' reality, to use translator James Strachey's idiosyncratic translation of the original Freudian term.

Genet experienced the episode of melancholia recounted in *Prisoner of Love* while passing through Turkey on the way to rejoin the fida'iyeen in 1972. The episode reads like an echo of the 'stranger on a train' encounter I consider in detail in Chapter 4. In the *Prisoner* account, Genet immediately associates melancholic affect with a longing for reprieve from a sense of ontological failure. Living through a 'strange separation' from the world, Genet feels a 'cold reprobation' that keeps him 'from approaching other people'.[77] He compares himself to 'a muslim woman wrapped in a granite scarf' who desperately seeks 'in the eyes of others the thin strand of silk meant to link (them) together, the sign of the continuity of being'.[78]

But this continuity of being, so resonantly phrased, requires a minimal gesture of differentiation in order to prevent reality's collapse into itself; a state of complete indistinction, that is, that would render impossible the interpersonal connections of which Genet finds himself incapable during his struggle. The text figures this indistinction as the inability to differentiate between objects in the world and, more specifically, as the failure of desire: no special object separates itself off from the background, in so doing attracting an investment of libido and creating a psychical world. 'The Egyptian Pyramids had the same value, force, dimensions and depth as the desert, and the desert had the same depth as a handful of sand,'[79] Genet writes of his indifferent state of mind. As was the case in the aftermath of the train episode Genet outlines in 'The Studio of Alberto Giacometti', each object is equal to, exchangeable for, any other. 'The most beautiful boys had the same value and power as the others,' offers Genet, 'but no one had any power over me.'[80] Only the conditioning of childhood remains to indicate that an Egyptian pyramid cannot be put on the foot as if it were a shoe.

As signs of recovery appear, however, Genet finds that 'the world begins to swarm with individuals' who, because they are 'separated', are 'capable of entering into relation with one another'.[81] There follows the pivotal passage in which Genet describes an ecstatic experience of embodiment. Lying in bed one night, Genet looks back on the previous five years of overwhelming sadness and creative frustration, a period whose temporality is so vague and nebulous that he questions its very existence. Just at the moment when he decides to 'rediscover' this 'undifferentiated past',[82] however, Genet envisions a diffuse light shining around him so intense that its brightness persists even after he covers his head with the blanket. 'For a few moments something in me was phosphorescent,' writes Genet. 'I even thought my skin might have become luminous, as a parchment shade does when a lamp is lit.'[83] The reader then witnesses a wild, typically Genetian flow of images and comments – fair-haired hippies dancing barefoot in the snow outside Istanbul's Blue Mosque, prisoners 'suddenly refus(ing) food and barricad(ing) themselves in their workshops', Paul Claudel writing about 'the jubilations of chance' despite being a Catholic 'square (*carrure*)' – all of which suggest the questioning or delegitimization of religious authority or, as Genet puts it, the subversion of the idea of *un Dieu-Un*, a 'One God'.[84]

As *Prisoner of Love* becomes increasingly self-aware of the properties of the image that instantiates the poetic act, Genet consolidates his ascetic emancipation from the attractions of attachment and the solace of rest. He compares his idea of the Mediterranean retirement villa to the 'invisible nun's cell' of Saint Elizabeth of Thuringia, a thirteenth-century religious woman and symbol of charity whom Genet casts as the personification of a falsely autonomous variety of solitude intimate with a certain conception of the unicity of the divine.[85] Indeed, Genet qualifies Elizabeth's cell, whose inner walls only she and God can see, as 'personal and secret'; it takes the shape of a 'Cyclops'[86] for which space is fully transparent to vision. From the perspective of psychoanalysis, it makes perfect sense that Genet would associate Elizabeth's sacred personal space with orality, which he evokes with a reference to a plum tree in the Turkish villa's garden and whose fruit he is unable to eat on account of an uncomfortable feeling of fullness. 'For a long time everything had been in me already,' Genet writes. The feeling causes him to fear 'dying of indigestion' and unleashes a longing for the 'desert without rain in a desert without rain'[87] of Sufi poetry. Evidently, the sense of self-sufficiency suggested by Elizabeth's cell becomes claustrophobic and creates the desire for absence, for the lack that causes desire.

The lesson imparted to Genet by his recuperation from depression is this: apart from desire, there is no alternative remedy to our constitutive inability squarely to face up to the real of ontological incompletion. Not only is the satisfaction of desire through the achievement of identity with oneself impossible, its pursuit leads only to a nauseating proximity to enjoyment from which we desperately seek relief. For Genet, the discovery of desire's inexhaustibility makes him laugh 'and laugh again', but not without a sense of humiliation, which he contrasts with the jubilant sense of the luminescence he experienced earlier lying in bed. The impact is sobering, disillusioning, akin to the moment he discovers the thread suspending the floating orange in the Istanbul market. The pleasure of the illusion can still be appreciated after the enigma is resolved, but the explanation deprives the experience of its effect of fascination, of its power to hold us transfixed, spellbound. The slight Genet feels at the key moment of these parallel experiences makes palpable the inherent and inescapable emptiness of the self, at once a reflection and dissimulation of the ultimate incompletion of being. It also reveals the subjective particularity of the fantasy that tries in vain to establish ontological consistency: 'My humiliation made me aware that it was *my* house, *my* furniture, *my* light, and *my* interior,' he writes, going on to wonder if this interior is merely 'a vague, uncertain place put there to conceal a total void'.[88] For Genet, as for psychoanalysis, the objects we hold most dear as the very signs of our identity finally function to dissimulate nothingness itself, the final barrier that protects us from unmitigated psycho-ontological catastrophe.

The enticingly inexhaustible lure of plenitude persists nevertheless. Desire, charm and seduction return, but this time with their tether to repression's hygienic ideals significantly weakened. In the text, Istanbul is celebrated not for its historical significance or religious monuments – 'Golden Horn … Galata, St. Sophia, St. Ireneus, the Blue Mosque, the Red Sultan'[89] – but rather for its seediness and fakery: 'the gambling alleys, the black markets, the false cripples, the false archaeologists'.[90] In the same vein, Genet lauds legendary national founder Kemal Ataturk not for bringing secular enlightenment republicanism to a cosmopolitan but thoroughly feudal Muslim empire, but rather, in his excessive Europhilia, for forcing Turkish men to urinate standing up. The unedifying effect enlivens the atmosphere of the distinguished city with 'graceful arcs of urine and saliva suddenly and accurately spouting from between teeth, moustaches and zip fasteners'.[91] As Genet's readers, we discover how from the fissures of being there emerges a new kind of image set free from the oppressive weight of imperial history as well as the contentious symbolisms of rival religious faiths.

Genet's prose explicitly conjoins his experience of post-melancholic jouissance with insight into the illusory quality of unicity. Finally recuperating from his depression, Genet gains the capacity to look retrospectively at the previous five years in their paralysing non-differentiation. Safely returned to a normative reality in which distinct objects can be recognized and alterity, however precariously, distinguished from an image of the self, Genet can now enjoy the incompletion of being rather than seek the means of resolving it. The new outlook allows him to revel in the play of appearances in all their groundlessness and contingency as he is now emancipated from the insistent and paralysing demand for consistency and fullness. The Genet of *Prisoner of Love* has gained this decisive piece of knowledge: the signifier that grants the world its impression of reality, that organizes its systems of value, harbours an absence within it whose function is simply to prevent ontological disaster, to stave off depressive or even psychotic experiences of desireless non-differentiation. On the other side of feminine melancholia lies the lightness and laughter, the cheer and curiosity, of a world whose moorings to sense and meaning are recognized for their precarity, and whose incompletion makes possible the creation of poetic images that destroy the misleadingly ordered consistency of being.

What is perhaps the most quintessential poetic image in all of *Prisoner of Love* takes us back to the Palestinians. Genet is on the trail of Hamza, the fida'i friend he met on a previous trip to the Jordanian refugee camps years earlier. Knocking on the door of someone named Hamza, Genet is disappointed to discover that the young man who answers 'is not (his) friend of a day who had lived with his mother'.[92] At this precise moment, an arresting image of absence spontaneously appears in Genet's consciousness. As 'one or more fedayeen' are 'setting out on a mission in Israeli territory', 'a sudden hole that seemed to be of human dimensions' appears 'behind them, like a shadow ready to receive them'.[93] Lest the image seem too apt, too convincing, Genet places its description in quotation marks, framing it as one of many possible relevant figures, any of which would fail spectacularly properly to render the experience as lived. To be sure, the image is meant to stand for the graves lying in wait for the fighters, outmanned and outgunned by Israel's formidable US-backed security forces. 'I've only got to hear the word ("Palestinian") and the hole is there,' Genet attests.

The image that indexes the absence of that which it would normally figure is the Genetian poetic image par excellence. If Genet had wished to represent the fida'iyeen as martyrs to the Palestinian cause, a trope made globally familiar over the last half-century by endless media footage of funeral processions in Gaza and the Occupied Territories, he could have chosen to paint the portrait of a particular hero, like one of the faces figured on the posters and banners proudly held aloft by the throngs of justifiably angry mourners. In a more macabre vein, Genet might have evoked the dead body of a fida'i lying in a flag-draped coffin for instance, or else awaiting burial in a freshly dug grave. But the 'hole' Genet depicts in his image is empty and his fida'iyeen are still alive, captured and immortalized at the moment when their deathly destiny is fixed. Genet shows himself to be fully aware of the banality of the truth his image discloses. If 'all men are mortal', however, 'not many of them have the courage to know it, and those who flaunt their knowledge are even rarer',[94] he concludes.

In the original French the sentence reads as follows: If all men are mortal, 'peu osent le savoir et rares qui se font parure de ce savoir'.[95] Unfortunately, the classic and revelatory Genetian phrasing is lost in translation, which misses entirely the crucial connection between the knowledge, or rather the explicit marking, of the indwelling negativity of death and the central concept of *parure*. As I have argued throughout this book, this term, together with the similarly used and etymologically related substantive *paraître*, signal Genet's distinctive artistic confabulation of the world of appearances, which foregrounds their lack of a conventional ontological ground. As is made clear in the French, Genet's act of poetry turns the knowledge of death into an appearance, more precisely a modality of appearance that reflects and registers the properly feminine choice to dissimulate neither the inconsistency nor the incompletion of being.

Genet's role as an artist is to sublimate the historical existence of the Palestinian fighters as they appear to his faculty of perception into the form of an image that indexes the performative act of foregrounding absence, of framing the void. In his literary hands, the poetic image can take a form as subtle as the fida'iyeen's 'knack' for 'giving a crooked smile with a cigarette between their lips' or as direct as the 'sign like a knowing wink' lodged 'in the oblong shape that followed them like a shadow'.[96] Along with the creation of the poetic image comes a kind of transparency, an attribute that Genet decides to give the 'last page of (his) book'.[97] As *Prisoner of Love* has taught its transfixed and transformed reader, this transparency reveals only reality's difference from itself, the absolute difference that generates the subject in the gap of the unconscious.

In writing his memoir, Genet discovers a truth more precious than some putative objective knowledge of either the ultimate historical significance of the resistance or his personal encounter with Hamza and his mother, his elusive Palestinian friends. The only truth available to the subject is the truth of being's incompletion, the psychical manifestation of which is the enmeshment of enjoyment and the void. To be sure, Genet's poetic images of absence, brought to their maximum effect in his masterwork *Prisoner of Love*, figure this void. But they also mark the enjoyment that ordinarily remains repressed and therefore unacknowledged. Through this marking, Genet's literary practice of sublimation, the jouissance that binds us to an unjust status quo is brought out into the light, and newfound possibilities for transformation both psychical and political are brought enliveningly to the fore.

Notes

Introduction

1 Genet, *Prisoner of Love*, trans. Barbara Bray (New York: New York Review Books, 2003), 5 (translation modified); *Un captif amoureux* (Paris: Gallimard, 1986), 11.

2 Ibid.

3 The major contemporary propagandist for Genet's presumed antisemitism is Éric Marty, whose crypto-psychoanalytic and one-dimensional attack abstracts completely from the concrete political situation of historical Palestine as it makes a number of quite ridiculous claims. Not only does the word 'Hitler' become a master signifier in Genet that would stand as the emblem for his construction of 'a world of domination', but also Genet's work as a whole effects the death of meaning in language in a way that aims to rescue, rather than subvert, the tradition of Western metaphysics. This book argues strongly against both of these claims. I should add that Marty's voice has contributed significantly to a disturbing trend in recent French scholarship that aims to rescue and indemnify Europe, whiteness and Judeo-Christianity (not to mention the legitimacy of the Israeli state) from Genet's critique. Marty, *Jean Genet, post-scriptum* (Paris: Verdier, 2006), 69. For an illuminating perspective on the role 'Genet' has played in recent polemics around the Israel-Palestine situation in France, see Camille Toffoli, 'La question de l'antisémitisme chez Jean Genet: un débat sur le "sens du monde"', *Postures* 24 <revuepostures.com/fr/articles/toffoli-24>, accessed 17 April 2022.

4 Though Bersani takes care to distinguish Genet's engagement with what we might call the Nazi aesthetic from 'a plea for the specific goals pursued by Nazi Germany', he does however qualify Nazism's metaphorical role in Genet's text as 'hardly … untroubling'. 'The Gay Outlaw', *Diacritics* 24.3–4 (Summer–Autumn 1994): 13–14.

5 In addition to functioning as a kind of exorcism of the libidinal pull of the fascist aesthetic, *Funeral Rights* is also on the most manifest level an expression of grief around a homosexual attachment (to Jean Decarnin, a young Communist resistance fighter shot dead by the Nazis at a late stage of the occupation) for which no generally recognizable social institutions of mourning exist. The narrative persona's explicit eroticization of the Nazis is both a manifestation of his sense of alienation from

French society and a psychical strategy for mourning his lover's death by imaginatively inhabiting the subjectivity of the enemy. In this complex and ambivalent context, in which any one-dimensional condemnation is patently reductive, it is fair to claim that the view of the text as pro-Nazi (or antisemitic) does not go without an element of homophobia. See Genet, *Funeral Rites*, trans. Bernard Frechtman (New York: Grove Press, 1969); *Pompes funèbres* (Paris: Gallimard, 1978).

6 Bataille's chapter ostensibly on Genet in *Literature and Evil* is much more convincing as a reading of Sartre's *Saint Genet* than as a contribution to our understanding of the early work of Genet himself. In any case, much of this book will work towards the replacement of the Sartrean-Bataillean view of an oppositional negativity in Genet with an alternative variety of negativity that is both indeterminate and non-predicative. See Bataille, 'Genet', *La littérature et le mal* (Paris: Gallimard, 1967), 199–244.

7 Foucault, *The History of Sexuality, Volume 1: An Introduction*, trans. Robert Hurley (New York: Vintage, 1990), 33.

8 Plato, *The Symposium*, trans. Christopher Gill (London: Penguin, 2003), 49 (211d-e).

9 In Lacan's view, Plato's work reveals an 'incorruptible, material, super-essential, purely ideal, participatory, eternal and uncreated' order, 'ironically perhaps'. *Le Séminaire, livre VIII. Le transfert*, ed. Jacques-Alain Miller (Paris: Seuil, 2001), 97 (my translation).

10 Aristotle, *Poetics*, trans. Richard Janko (Indianapolis: Hackett, 1987), 18 (53b12).

11 I acknowledge here the eccentricity of writing a work 'on Genet' in which the material on the author does not appear until the second chapter. Though the book can be read without engaging with it, Chapter 1 does function structurally as a kind of second, more specific theoretical introduction, laying the groundwork for, among other things, the counter-intuitive argument concerning the importance of logic discourse, via Lacan's approach, for an exercise in what in many ways remains a work of (psychoanalytic and philosophical) literary criticism.

12 'At present, Genet is perhaps a thief because he is a homosexual,' writes Sartre in 1952. 'But he became a homosexual because he was a thief. A person is not born homosexual or normal. He becomes one or the other, according to the accidents of his history and to his own reaction to these accidentals.' *Saint Genet: Actor and Martyr*, trans. Bernard Frechtman (New York: George Braziller, 1964), 91.

13 The key texts on femininity and ontology that have informed this study are Copjec's *Imagine There's No Woman: Ethics and Sublimation* (London: MIT Press, 2000) and Zupančič, *What IS Sex?* (London: MIT Press, 2017).

14 See Kadji Amin, *Disturbing Attachments: Genet, Modern Pederasty, and Queer History* (Durham, NC: Duke University Press, 2017) for the most recent example of this approach.

15 Michael Lucey, *Someone: The Pragmatics of Misfit Sexualities, from Colette to Hervé Guibert* (London: University of Chicago Press, 2019), 85–108.

16 Meillassoux, *After Finitude: An Essay on the Necessity of Contingency*, trans. Ray Brassier (London: Continuum, 2008), 5.

17 Lacan, *Le Séminaire, livre XIV. Logique du fantasme (1966–67)*. For Lacan's unpublished seminars I have relied on <staferla.free.fr>.

18 Zupančič, *What Is Sex?* 73–84.

19 Worth singling out here is the work of Ivan Jablonka which, through a depoliticized application of Bourdieusian sociology, not only returns to the old theme of an assumed pro-Nazism and antisemitism in Genet, but also places itself in the decidedly awkward position of defending Europe against 'the implacable hatred (Genet) feels for the white and Judeo-Christian occident'. Further, Jablonka explicitly positions his research against what he calls 'Genet's literary ontology', which is of course the central agenda of this book. Jablonka, *Les vérités inavouables de Jean Genet* (Paris: Seuil, 2004), 16, 27.

20 Derrida, *Glas*, trans. John P. Leavey, Jr and Richard Rand (London: University of Nebraska Press, 1986), 93.

21 This is incidentally the aspect of Genet's textual praxis that Jérôme Neutres struggles to recognize in his valuable literary-historical work on what he calls the 'eroticism of the South' in Genet. Neutres's analysis brings forward in tremendous detail the seeming contradiction between, for example, Genet's hatred of the Lebanese Phalange, perpetrators with probable tacit Israeli support of the massacres in the Palestinian camps of Sabra and Shatila, and his frank admission of the soldiers' libidinal attractiveness, which hearkens back to the controversial theme of Nazi sex appeal in *Funeral Rites*. What Neutres and so many other critics fail to appreciate is the properly causal connection between the two affects: the literary evocation of 'Genet's desire for the Phalangists' is the condition of possibility for both the concrete analysis of their participation in the Palestinian tragedy and the textual self-exorcism that finally allows Genet to diminish the subjective effects of the seductive power exerted by the aesthetic qualities of reactionary political movements. Neutres, *Genet sur les routes du Sud* (Paris: Fayard, 2002), 112–13.

22 Though it cannot be denied that elements of Arab and Muslim opposition to Israeli policy slide into overt antisemitism, this opposition cannot be reduced entirely to prejudice or racism. If it too often fails to differentiate between the Israeli state and the Jewish people, then Israel itself, in not only the aggressive coupling of its idea of nationhood with Jewishness but also its massive efforts ideologically to annex the diaspora, must be held significantly, though of course not exclusively, responsible.

23 Indeed, Genet would surely have endorsed the refreshingly acerbic recent remarks of Elaine Brown, former (and sole woman) leader of the Black Panther Party and author of the recently republished (in the UK) memoir *A Taste of Power: A Black Woman's Story*. 'I find (the BLM movement) embarrassing,' she tells journalist Michael Segalov. 'I'm bored by most people who call themselves "activists". So you had a little parade, and you've started a hashtag in the ether world? You painted a pavement, went home for a vegan meal, and called it a day?' 'Activist Elaine Brown: "You must be willing to die for what you believe in"', *The Guardian*, 27 March 2022.

Chapter 1

1. Sigmund Freud, *Moses and Monotheism* (1939), *The Standard Edition of the Complete Psychological Works of Sigmund Freud* (*SE*), ed. James Strachey, vol. 23 (London: Hogarth Press and the Institute for Psycho-Analysis, 1953–74), 3–140.

2. Strachey attributes to Ernest Jones the suggestion that 'Freud may have been partly drawn into making this analysis of the feelings depicted in Michelangelo's statue by his own attitude towards the dissident movements of Adler and Jung, which had so much occupied his mind during the period immediately preceding' the writing of his paper. Freud, 'The Moses of Michelangelo' (1914), *SE* vol.13, 230n1.

3. Ibid., 212.

4. Ibid., 237.

5. Carlo Ginzburg and Anna Davin compare Freud's adoption of the Morelli method for psychoanalysis to the modus operandi of that quintessential detective of Anglophone modernity, Conan Doyle's Sherlock Holmes, in 'Morelli, Freud and Sherlock Holmes: Clues and Scientific Method', *History Workshop* 9 (Spring 1980): 5–36.

6. Freud, 'The Moses of Michelangelo', 222.

7. Ibid. German terms are taken from 'Der Moses des Michelangelo' (1914), *Sigmund Freud Studienausgabe. Bildene Kunst und Literatur* (Frankfurt: Fischer Taschenbuch Verlag, 2000), 195–222.

8. Freud, 'The Moses of Michelangelo', 222.

9. Ibid., 222–3.

10. Ibid.

11. Ibid. (my emphasis).

12. Ibid., 226.

13. For good examples of the existing commentary on Lacan's notion of the act (with which I do not have the space here to engage), see Ed Pluth, *Signifiers and Acts: Freedom in Lacan's Theory of the Subject* (Albany: State University of New York Press, 2007); Adrian Johnston, *Badiou, Žižek, and Political Transformations: The Cadence of Change* (Evanston, IL: Northwestern University Press, 2009); and Slavoj Žižek, 'The Act and Its Vicissitudes', *Lacan.com* <zizek.uk/the-act-and-its-vicissitudes>, accessed 4 January 2022.

14. Freud, *The Interpretation of Dreams* (1900), *SE* vol. 4, 382. Lacan uses the term in reference to Ella Sharpe's work on sublimation, which alludes to the famous cave paintings of Altamira. Jacques Lacan, *The Seminar of Jacques Lacan, Book VII: The Ethics of Psychoanalysis, 1959–1960* (New York: Norton, 1992), 139.

15 Jacques-Alain Miller influentially develops the theme in his essay 'Extimité', *Lacanian Theory of Discourse: Subject, Structure and Society*, ed. Mark Bracher (New York: New York University Press, 1994), 74–87.

16 Lacan speaks of the 'function of truth' inherent in any signifying system in the domain of mathematics or mathematical logic, which he distinguishes from a signification that would purport to refer to the truth value of something outside that signifying system. 'This logical usage of truth is encountered only in mathematics', Lacan says, 'where in no case is it known what is being talked about'. See Lacan, *Le Séminaire, livre XIV. Logique du fantasme (1966–67)*, lesson of 21 June 1967 (my translation). For Lacan's unpublished seminars I have relied on <staferla.free.fr>.

17 Lacan develops the former point in 'Science and Truth', *Écrits*, trans. Bruck Fink (London: Norton, 2006), 726–7; and the latter in various lessons of *Logique du fantasme*, ibid.

18 'To be a subject is to have one's place in the big Other, in the locus of speech (*le lieu de la parole*)'. Lacan, *Le Séminaire, livre VIII. Le transfert*, ed. Jacques-Alain Miller (Paris: Seuil, 2001), 303 (my translation).

19 Lacan, *Logique du fantasme*, lesson of 28 February 1967 (my translation).

20 Ibid.

21 The complicated (for non-specialists at least) story begins with Russell's famous question, Does the set of all sets that contain themselves contain itself? For a detailed summary of how various logicians attempt to resolve the paradoxes of so-called naive set theory through, among other techniques, axiomatization, see 'The Philosophy of Mathematics after Frege', William Kneale and Martha Kneale, *The Development of Logic* (Oxford: The Clarendon Press, 1962), 652–88. Lacan's intervention implies for me that so-called naive set theory may not in fact be so naive.

22 See, for example, Graham Priest, Richard Routley, and Jean Norman, eds, *Paraconsistent Logic: Essays on the Inconsistent* (Munich: Philosophia Verlag, 1990). There is illuminating prose on the significance of paraconsistent logic for the reading of Lacan in Molly Anne Rothenberg, *The Excessive Subject: A New Theory of Social Change* (Cambridge: Polity Press, 2010), 30–45.

23 'No subject emerges without a passionate attachment to those on whom he or she is fundamentally dependent', Butler writes, though her enlistment of Foucault's late formulation of power muddies the waters of her psychoanalytic insight. *The Psychic Life of Power: Theories in Subjection* (Stanford, CA: Stanford University Press, 1997), 7.

Chapter 2

1 David Cooper sets the general tone of future reproaches in a 1964 review. Sartre 'demystifies the social world, but may there not be mystery which is not mystification?'

he asks. By positioning Genet as the very emblem of the existentialist concept of freedom, Sartre not only overlooks the specificity of his subject's situation, but also overstates the overlap of selfhood and choice. Cooper's valorization of the 'not-self' in his consideration of agency is laudable, as is his identification of a 'fissuring of the plenitude of being'. He does however fail to acknowledge the full consequences of this fissuring by assuming a Sartre-sanctioned 'ontological continuum' that spans and conjoins being and the void. Cooper, 'Sartre on Genet', *New Left Review* 1.25 (May–June 1964): 72.

2 Jean-Paul Sartre, 'Introduction', in Jean Genet, *Our Lady of the Flowers*, trans. Bernard Frechtman (New York: Grove Press, 1991), 4.

3 Jean Genet, *Our Lady*, 6.

4 For example: 'Hope can cling only to free and active characters', Sartre writes. 'Genet, however, is concerned only with satisfying his cruelty … The author is a barbaric god who revels in human sacrifice'. 'Introduction', 11.

5 Ibid., 32.

6 Ibid., 33.

7 Ibid.

8 Ibid.

9 Several manuscript versions of *Our Lady of the Flowers* were in circulation in Parisian literary circles before its first publication. Sartre had access to prose that did not make it into what became the canonical version of the novel.

10 Genet, *Our Lady*, 136.

11 Ibid.

12 Henceforward in this chapter the name Genet will refer to the problematic conjunction of the writing persona fictionalized in the novel and the author of the work.

13 Ibid., 138.

14 Ibid., 137.

15 Genet, *Our Lady*, 292.

16 Ibid.

17 Ibid., 293.

18 Ibid.

19 Freud, *The Interpretation of Dreams*, *The Standard Edition of the Complete Psychological Works of Sigmund Freud* (*SE*), vol. 5, ed. James Strachey (London: Hogarth Press and the Institute for Psycho-Analysis, 1953–74), 535–6.

20 Indeed, Genet's work is quite radically opposed to Éribon's project to define the poetic act along the lines of the discourse of pride in gay liberation culture. For Genet, though

poetry does provide a place in discourse for the marginal and oppressed, its work rejects the gesture of idealization that obfuscates ontological incompletion. Further, Genet's thinking is anathema to Éribon's desire to predicate sexual politics on the model of a minority community. I would also add that Éribon's book, ostensibly a reading of Genet's oeuvre, leads up to a not entirely unfounded but extremely reductive (and passionately *ad hominem*) attack on Lacan's alleged homophobia and misogyny. Didier Éribon, *Une morale du minoritaire. Variations sur un thème de Jean Genet* (Paris: Fayard, 2001), 22.

21 Genet, *Our Lady*, 296.

22 Ibid.

23 Ibid.

24 Ibid., 297.

25 Ibid., 296.

26 Ibid., 296–7.

27 Ibid., 142.

28 Ibid., 297.

29 Ibid.

30 Ibid., 298.

31 Ibid., 297.

32 Here an opportunity presents itself to stress the connection between sublimation and literary, as opposed to directly sexual, practice in Genet and psychoanalysis. In an important reading of *Funeral Rites*, Leo Bersani writes about sublimation as 'an activity of consciousness coterminous with a particular sexual activity, indeed lasting no longer than that activity', one that manages to 'bypass the social as a field of symbolic mediations of and substitutions for the sexual'. My suggestion is that this contention unhelpfully idealizes sexual practice. For psychoanalysis, on the contrary, even the most 'animalistic' of human sexual practices have always-already taken a detour through symbolic mediation, and the link between sex and (the internal limit of) language is properly transcendental. Bersani, 'The Gay Outlaw', *Diacritics* 24.2–3 (Summer-Autumn 1994): 17.

33 Ibid., 299.

34 Ibid., 300.

35 Ibid.

36 Ibid., 301.

37 Ibid.

38 Ibid. (italics in original).

39 Ibid. (my italics).

40 Ibid.

41 Ibid.

42 Ibid., 301–2.

43 Lacan, *Encore: On Feminine Sexuality: The Limits of Love and Knowledge*, trans. Bruce Fink (New York: Norton, 1999), 78.

44 See, for example, Luce Irigaray, *An Ethics of Sexual Difference*, trans. Carolyn Burke (Ithaca, NY: Cornell University Press, 1993).

45 Freud, 'Some Psychical Consequences of the Anatomical Distinction between the Sexes' (1925), *SE* vol. 19 (London: Vintage, 2001), 252.

46 See for example Martin Heidegger, 'Letter on Humanism', *Basic Writings*, trans. David Farrell Krell (London: Routledge, 1978).

47 Lacan, *Encore*, 73.

48 Though critics of Lacan on femininity routinely cite his contention that 'a woman can but be excluded by the nature of things, which is the nature of words', a few paragraphs later in the transcript we find a less misleading pronouncement: 'It's not because she is not-wholly in the phallic function that she is not there at all. She is *not* not at all there. She is there in full (*à plein*)'. The paradox is that the feminine subject is at once unlocatable as a consistent being within language and knowable as feminine nowhere else. In other words, a woman psychoanalytically defined is the subject who is fully inscribed in the symbolic order in its incompletion. Lacan, *Encore*, 73, 74.

49 See, for example, Butler, *Undoing Gender* (New York: Routledge, 2004).

50 See Riviere, 'Womanliness as a Masquerade' (1929), *Female Sexuality: Contemporary Engagements*, ed. Donna Bassin (London: Jason Aronson, 1999).

51 Genet, *Our Lady*, 224.

52 Ibid., 225.

53 Ibid., 225; *Notre-Dame-des-Fleurs* (Paris: Gallimard Folio, 1996), 258.

54 Ibid., 225–6.

55 Ibid., 226.

56 Ibid., 227.

57 Ibid., 227–8.

58 Ibid., 228.

59 Ibid., 229.

60 Ibid., 228.

61 Ibid., 230.

62 Ibid., 302; Genet, *Notre-Dame*, 370 (translation modified). In a fascinating article about the priority of the image over theoretical reflection in Genet, Mairéad Hanrahan reminds us that *théorie* can refer to a religious procession. Though Hanrahan interprets the abundance of recursive images of cortèges in Genet's work as a sign of his theoretical ambivalence, her keen observation that the image of Nasser's coffin in *Prisoner of Love* frees it 'from the forces of gravity' could also be taken to support my own claim about the role religious imagery plays in Genet to strip the image of both its power of reference as well as its ontological ground. Hanrahan, 'Genet and Theory: An Introduction', *Paragraph: A Journal of Modern Critical Theory* 27.2 (July 2004): 4.

63 Ibid., 302–3.

64 Ibid., 303.

65 Ibid.

66 Ibid.

67 Ibid., 303–4.

68 Ibid., 304.

69 Ibid.

70 Ibid., 306.

71 Ibid.

72 Ibid., 307.

Chapter 3

1 Jean Genet, *The Balcony*, trans. Bernard Frechtman (New York: Grove Press, 1966), 78.

2 Jacques Lacan, 'The Signification of the Phallus', *Écrits*, trans. Bruce Fink (London: Norton, 2006), 582.

3 The association of comedy with movement and change has a long history, as explored exhaustively by George McFadden in *Discovering the Comic* (Princeton, NJ: Princeton University Press, 1982), for example. Whereas McFadden sees comic dynamism as consistent with the self-perpetuating and self-sustaining nature of being, I will argue that comedy momentarily uncovers being's inconsistency, and therefore its inherent, however rare or even miraculous, susceptibility to change.

4 My view of *The Balcony* as a political study of the workings of ideology finds an exceptional forerunner in an article by David H. Walker, who argues that the play stages a Gramscian 'crisis of hegemony'. See 'Revolution and Revisions in Genet's *Le Balcon*', *The Modern Language Review* 79.4 (1984): 819.

5 This should not be taken to imply that all such agents are men; this is clearly not the case. Women politicians who engage with this dynamic tend to do so, however, in the name of a male figure who embodies this exception. The classic example here would be France's Marine Le Pen, daughter of nationalist far-right *Front national* icon, Jean-Marie. The point here is not to diminish the accomplishments of the women concerned, such as they are, but rather to underline how these accomplishments are presented as instantiations of a properly masculine symbolic authority. Though the woman's agency is sovereign, it assigns itself a place, here quite literally, under (a perversion of) the Name-of-the-Father.

6 Genet, 'Comment jouer *Le balcon*,' in *Le balcon* (Paris: Gallimard, 2009), 12.

7 Genet, 'Avertissement', in *Le balcon*, 16.

8 Genet, 'Comment jouer', 8 (my translation).

9 Genet, 'Avertissement', 9 (my translation).

10 Even Sartre's famous analysis of *The Maids* finally falls into this trap. In Sartre's view, though Genet's stagecraft seeks 'to radicalize appearances', these appearances only render being (viewed as an 'absolute reality') diabolically 'evanescent'. The classical reality-appearance binarism is preserved in the distinction being-artifice, which survives the Sartrean analysis in however complex a form. Jean-Paul Sartre, *Saint Genet: Actor and Martyr*, trans. Bernard Frechtman (New York: Pantheon Books, 1963), 611, 625 (translation modified).

11 This is the memorable phrase coined by Todd McGowan to summarize 'the structure of the concept' according to Hegel in his illuminating book *Emancipation After Hegel: Achieving a Contradictory Revolution* (New York: Columbia University Press, 2019), 3.

12 Lacan, *Le Séminaire, livre V: les formations de l'inconscient*, ed. Jacques-Alain Miller (Paris: Seuil, 1998), 262 (my translation).

13 Alain Badiou, *Le Séminaire: images du temps présent 2001–2004*, ed. Isabelle Vodoz (Paris: Fayard, 2014), 19 (my translation).

14 Freud, 'From the History of an Infantile Neurosis' (1918), *The Standard Edition of the Complete Psychological Works of Sigmund Freud*, vol. 17, ed. James Strachey (London: The Hogarth Press and the Institute for Psycho-Analysis, 1953–74), 23.

15 Badiou, *Images*, 27 (my translation).

16 Ibid. (my translation).

17 Ibid. (my translation).

18 Friedrich Nietzsche, *The Gay Science*, trans. Walter Kaufmann (New York: Vintage, 1974), 373–74.

19 Badiou's view of *The Balcony*'s political conservatism finds notable precedents in Coe's characterization of Genet as a right-wing anarchist and Thody's sense of the play as the product of 'an essentially reactionary view of mankind'. See Richard N. Coe, *The Vision*

of Jean Genet (London: Peter Owen, 1968), 254–60; and Philip Thody, *Jean Genet: A Study of His Novels and Plays* (London: Hamish Hamilton, 1968), 185, 194.

20 Lacan, *Formations*, 268 (my translation).

21 Genet, *Balcony*, 88.

22 In a fascinating article, Jean-Joseph Goux traces the evidence for phallic rites in (Egyptian) Antiquity through Voltaire, Plutarch and Herodotus back to the myth of Osiris. God of fertility and a significant source for the Greek cult of Dionysus, Osiris was killed and dismembered by the giant Typhon. Reassembling the pieces of his body, his companion Isis discovers that his virile member is missing. She goes on to erect a 'simulacrum which she orders everyone to honor'. Goux, 'The Phallus: Masculine Identity and the "Exchange of Women"', *Differences: A Journal of Feminist Cultural Studies* 4.14 (1992): 41.

23 Lacan, 'Signification', *Écrits*, 581.

24 Ibid.

25 Lacan, *Télévision* (Paris: Seuil, 1974).

26 Lacan, 'Signification', *Écrits*, 581. Aidos is the Greek god of shame and modesty. Lacan adds the German *Scham* ('shame', but also roughly 'private parts') to his text to reinforce the connection to Freud's theory of sexuality.

27 Genet, *Balcony*, 78.

28 Ibid., 94.

29 Ibid., 95.

30 Ibid., 95–6 (translation modified); *Le balcon*, 153.

31 Lacan, 'Overture', *Écrits*, 4.

32 Genet, *The Balcony*, 94.

33 With great insight, Alenka Zupančič expounds on this theme of the coincidence of the sublime and the ridiculous in the phallic object in *The Odd One In: On Comedy* (Cambridge: MIT Press, 2008), 213–18. Zupančič has also published a remarkable reading of *The Balcony*. Though our analyses accord in many respects, in my view the police chief's consecration in the mausoleum is meant to rescue, rather than replace, the classical figures of authority by buttressing their democratization. Also, my reading places greater emphasis on the subversiveness of Genet's play as against Badiou's and Lacan's views of its political conservatism or ambiguity. Zupančič's piece is particularly strong on what she calls the 'imaginary display of castration' inherent in our late capitalism; it fleshes out my own interpretation of Roger's final sacrifice. See 'Power in the Closet (and Its Coming Out)', in *Lacan, Psychoanalysis, and Comedy*, ed. Patricia Gherovici and Manya Steinkoler (New York: Cambridge, University Press, 2016), 231.

34 Genet, *Le Balcon* (Paris: L'Arbalète, 1960), 210 (my translation).

Chapter 4

1. Genet, 'What Remains of a Rembrandt Torn into Little Squares All the Same Size and Shot Down the Toilet', *Fragments of the Artwork*, trans. Charlotte Mandel (Stanford: Stanford University Press, 2003), 98.

2. Theodor Adorno and Max Horkheimer, *Dialectic of Enlightenment*, trans. John Cumming (London: Verso, 1997).

3. See Taylor, 'Two Theories of Modernity', *The Hastings Center Report* 25.2 (March–April 1995): 24–33.

4. See for example Bill Ashcroft, 'Alternative Modernities: Globalization and the Post-Colonial', *Ariel: A Review of International English Literature* 40.1 (2009): 81–105.

5. Mladen Dolar offers a more complete reading of Lacan's engagement with Descartes in 'Cogito as the Subject of the Unconscious', *Cogito and the Unconscious*, ed. Slavoj Žižek (Durham, NC: Duke University Press, 1998), 11–40.

6. Lacan, 'Réponse au commentaire de Jean Hyppolite sur la Verneinung de Freud', *Écrits* (Paris: Seuil, 1966), 388.

7. Lacan, *Le Séminaire, livre XIV. Logique du fantasme (1966–67)*, lesson of 12 April 1967 (my translation). For Lacan's unpublished seminars I have relied on <staferla.free.fr>.

8. John Lloyd Ackrill, ed., *Aristotle's Categories and De interpretatione* (Oxford: Clarendon Press, 1963), Chapter 5, 2a11, 5.

9. Lacan, *SXIV*, lesson of 31 May 1967 (my translation).

10. Ibid.

11. See Metzinger, *The Ego Tunnel: The Science of the Mind and the Myth of the Self* (New York: Basic Books, 2009).

12. Hadrien Laroche provides excellent context on the important shift in Genet's view during this period of the relation between literature and the political in *The Last Genet: A Writer in Revolt*, trans. David Homel (Vancouver: Arsenal Pulp Press, 2010).

13. Genet, 'What Remains', 98.

14. Ibid., 92.

15. Ibid., 91 (translation modified); Genet, 'Ce qui est resté d'un Rembrandt déchiré en petits carrés bien réguliers, et foutu aux chiottes', *Œuvres complètes*, vol. 4 (Paris: Gallimard, 1995), 21.

16. I am trying to make precisely such a link, of course. But despite the rare statement of respect for Freud's work to be found in Genet's interviews, the psychoanalytic influence is not manifestly traceable in his discourse on the strict level of the signifier (idiom, vocabulary, terminology).

17 Genet, 'The Studio of Alberto Giacometti', *Fragments*, 49 (translation modified); 'L'atelier d'Alberto Giacometti', *Œuvres complètes*, vol. 5 (Paris: Gallimard, 1979), 50–1.

18 Genet, 'Studio', *Fragments*, 49.

19 Ibid.

20 Ibid.

21 See Nancy Fraser and Axel Honneth, *Redistribution or Recognition: A Political-Philosophical Exchange* (London: Verso, 2003) for the development of this debate.

22 Genet, 'Studio', 49.

23 Ibid.; 'L'atelier', 51.

24 Genet, 'Studio', 41.

25 Ibid.

26 Ibid.

27 Ibid., 45–6.

28 Ibid., 55.

29 Rolland wrote to Freud after receiving from him a copy of *The Future of an Illusion*, as Freud recounts in *Civilization and Its Discontents*. In the latter essay Freud describes the oceanic affect as 'a feeling of an indissoluble bond, of being one with the external world as a whole'. In the context of my own discussion, this notion of 'the world as a whole' is what is most objectionable. Freud, *Civilization and Its Discontents, The Standard Edition of the Complete Psychological Works of Sigmund Freud (SE)*, ed. James Strachey, vol. 21 (London: Hogarth Press and the Institute for Psychoanalysis, 1953–74), 64.

30 Genet, 'Studio', 55.

31 Ibid.

32 'Je m'étais écoulé', Genet writes, evoking the feeling of melting or streaming into the ugly stranger's body. Genet, 'Ce qui est resté', 28.

33 Genet, 'Studio', 55 (translation modified); 'L'Atelier', 58.

34 Ibid. (translation modified); 'L'Atelier', 59.

35 Ibid., 42.

36 Haver, 'The Art of Dirty Old Men: Rembrandt, Giacometti, Genet', *Parallax* 11.2 (2005): 27.

37 Ibid., 28.

38 Ibid.

39 Ibid., 29.

40 The signal text here is Leo Bersani and Adam Phillips, *Intimacies* (Chicago: University of Chicago Press, 2008), but the thematic also variously develops in work by Tim Dean, Lauren Berlant, Heather Love and Lee Edelman, for example.

41 Haver, 'Dirty', 29.

42 Ibid., 30.

43 Lacan, *Seminar VII: The Ethics of Psychoanalysis*, trans. Dennis Porter (London: Norton, 1997), 133.

44 Haver, 'Dirty', 34.

45 Ibid.

46 Bersani, *Is the Rectum a Grave?* (London: University of Chicago Press, 2010), 100.

47 I expand upon this summary critique of Bersani's reading of psychoanalysis in 'Reading Freud: Bersani and Lacan', *Leo Bersani: Queer Theory and Beyond*, ed. Mikko Tuhkanen (Albany, NY: SUNY Press, 2014), 105–122.

48 Genet, 'Remains', 97; 'Ce qui est resté', 26-7.

Chapter 5

1 Jean Genet, *The Screens*, trans. Bernard Frechtman (New York: Grove Press, 1962), 170 (translation modified); *Les paravents* (Paris: Gallimard, 2001), 238.

2 Ibid.

3 Ibid.

4 Ibid.

5 Ibid.

6 Ibid. (translation modified); ibid.

7 Though *paravent* translates univocally into 'screen', the reverse does not hold. The French term suggests a panelled room divider, whereas the more generic translation of 'screen' is *écran*. These details are tangential, however. Genet wants his *paravents* to suggest a framed, neutral void on which appear images that at once reveal and (ambiguously) conceal. Both movie screen (including all its technological descendants) and Freudian screen memory, as well as Lacan's well-commented idea of the *écran* in the context of his theory of the gaze, are well within the connotative orbit of Genet's linguistic and theatrical usage, not to mention the general and now, in the digital age, ubiquitous concept of 'media'. For an insightful analysis of the play's eponymous screens as prescient commentary on the media landscape, see David Fieni, 'Genet's *The Screens*

as Media Allegory', in *Jean Genet: Performance and Politics*, ed. Clare Finburgh, Carl Lavery and Maria Shevtsova (New York: Palgrave Macmillan, 2007), 57–67.

8   Genet's remarks on the play's relation to geopolitics are contradictory, at least on the surface. In a 1964 interview with Madeleine Gobeil, Genet opines that if the play 'is never produced in France, it's because the French will think they've discovered something in it that isn't there: the problem of the Algerian war'. Two years later, in a letter to Roger Blin, director of the infamous 1966 production at the Théâtre de l'Odéon whose performances were repeatedly and violently disrupted by right-wing and veterans' groups, he wants the mise en scène to 'evoke the Algerian war in a few details'. In my view, the seeming inconsistency merely signals Genet's desire to place a limit on the play's contextual circumscription. In other words, though the reader or spectator is clearly meant to be aware of the Algerian or North African historical reference, the drama and its poetry must also be understood to gesture towards a universal significance. *La Bataille des Paravents. Théâtre de l'Odéon 1966*, ed. Lynda Bellity Peskine and Albert Dichy (Paris: Éditions IMEC, 1991), 59 (my translation).

9   Genet, *Screens*, 10.

10 In a famous article, Jacques-Alain Miller provides a helpful gloss on Lacan's development of his concept with reference to philosopher and mathematician Gottlob Frege's construction of zero as a number in his *Foundations of Arithmetic*. For Miller, Frege grounds numeration in what amounts to the counting of zero as one, in so doing excluding the 'prior', absolute zero from the chain of numbers in the same way that the subject of the unconscious is excluded from the system of signifiers. In other words, the void or 'zero' of the subject is already a derivation from a preceding 'pre-subjective' negativity, and the *trait unaire* is effectively the signifier that stands for the marking of this primordial non-being in its absolute difference. See Miller, 'Suture (Elements of the Logic of the Signifier)', *Screen* 18.4 (Winter 1977), 24–34.

11 Deleuze and Guattari distinguish between 'an exclusive, restrictive and negative use of the disjunctive synthesis' and an alternative version they qualify as 'fully affirmative, nonrestrictive, inclusive'. The idea is to conceive of disjunction as the difference between its constitutive terms, but also at once to affirm and possibly also multiply these terms. The ultimate aim is to produce the possibility of a co-presence of disjunctive elements without abolishing their immanent difference, such that the 'Oedipal' choice of 'child *or* parent', for example, opens into what they call the 'trans-parentchild'. By contrast, the Lacanian negativity resulting from the *trait unaire* already divides from itself the field of affirmative differences available to the Deleuzo-Guattarian operation. In other words, the Lacan-inspired ontological disjunction I am evoking in this book rests on a difference that logically precedes, and thereby divides from themselves, the terms of the disjunctions that the philosophers wish affirmatively to synthesize. In sum, whereas Deleuze and Guattari aim to conceive of a series of differences amenable nonetheless to a variety of non-homogenizing synthesis, Lacan wants instead to posit the non-synthesis that divides each term of a difference from itself. Gilles Deleuze and Félix Guattari, *Anti-Oedipus: Capitalism and Schizophrenia*,

trans. Robert Hurley, Mark Seem and Helen R. Lane (Minneapolis: University of Minnesota Press, 1992), 76–7.

12 Genet, 'L'Étrange mot d'...', *Œuvres complètes*, vol. 4 (Paris: Gallimard, 1968), 13 (my translation).

13 Genet, *Screens*, 10.

14 Ibid., 21 (translation modified); *Paravents*, 33.

15 Ibid., 20.

16 Ibid., 21 (my translation). To compare, Frechtman renders 'Elles reniflent, mes robes, la viande qui bande' as 'They sniff the hot meat'; *Paravents*, 32 (my translation).

17 Lacan, *Le Séminaire, livre XX. Encore* (Paris: Seuil, 1975), 75 (my translation).

18 It should be noted that Lacan's use of the term 'beyond the phallus' in the seminar is already aporetic. Indeed, he comments ironically that it will become the title of 'the next book in the Galilée collection', Galilée being at the time a new Parisian publishing venture close to such figures as Jacques Derrida, Jean-Luc Nancy and Sarah Kofman, viewed to be working outside the Lacanian orbit. Lacan, *On Feminine Sexuality: The Limits of Love and Knowledge (The Seminar of Jacques Lacan, Book XX)*, trans. Bruce Fink (London: Norton, 1998), 74.

19 Lacan in fact makes this abundantly clear: 'It's not because she is not-wholly in the phallic function that she is not there at all. She is *not* not at all there. She is there in full (*à plein*).' Ibid.

20 Lacan, *Encore*, 75 (my translation).

21 Ibid.

22 This is Genet's stage direction, not included in the English version: 'The dead will look above, while the scene they are watching is played out below.' *Les paravents*, 215 (my translation). For an illuminating study of Genet's use of scenography to evoke the strange positivity of absence, see Clare Finburgh, 'Unveiling the Void: The Presence of Absence in the Scenography of Jean Genet's *The Screens*', *Theatre Journal* 56.2 (May 2004): 205–24.

23 Lacan, *Encore*, 75 (my translation).

24 Genet, *Screens*, 19 (translation modified); *Paravents*, 30. Perhaps because of their importance as ports in the Second World War, or alternatively because of their greater familiarity to English sex tourists, Frechtman renders Genet's 'de Toul ou de Nancy' as 'from Cherbourg or Le Havre'.

25 Ibid., 22 (translation modified); ibid., 33.

26 Ibid., 20–1.

27 Ibid., 20 (translation modified); ibid., 31.

28 Ibid., 22 (translation modified); ibid., 33–4.

29 Ibid., 168.

30 Ibid., 129 (translation modified); ibid., 197.

31 Ibid., 131.

32 Ibid., 129.

33 Ibid.

34 Ibid., 181 (translation modified); ibid., 252.

35 Ibid., 130 (translation modified); ibid., 198.

36 Though strategic discipline grants the soldiers a more directly sexual relation to Warda, it would be a mistake to qualify the change as an instance of desublimation (as might seem the more intuitively convincing interpretation), with its attendant problematic political implications as famously developed in Herbert Marcuse's notion of repressive desublimation, for instance. The key factor is the attenuation of the fantasy of the (phallic) woman engendered by the sublimatory activity of anti-colonial organizing.

37 Genet, *Screens*, 130–1.

38 Ibid., 139 (translation modified); *Paravents*, 206.

39 Ibid. (translation modified); ibid., 206.

40 Ibid., 140 (translation modified); ibid., 207.

41 Ibid., 183.

42 Ibid., 181 (translation modified); ibid., 252.

43 *Paravents*, 252 (my translation); not included in English version.

44 *Screens*, 182.

45 Ibid., 183–4.

46 Ibid., 116.

47 Ibid. (translation modified); *Paravents*, 178.

48 Ibid., 117.

49 Ibid., 117–18 (translation modified); ibid., 180.

50 Ibid., 118.

51 Ibid., 97.

52 Ibid., 97, 98, 99.

53 Karl Ågerup provides a thorough overview of the reception of the discourse on violence in the later works in 'La Réception critique de l'écriture engagée de Jean

Genet: les exemples de "Violence et brutalité" et d'*Un captif amoureux*', *Notthingham French Studies* 60.1 (March 2021): 50–63.

54 Ibid., 104 (translation modified); ibid., 160.

55 Ibid.

56 Julia Kristeva, *Pouvoirs de l'horreur. Essai sur l'abjection* (Paris: Seuil, 1980), 9 (my translation).

57 Ibid., 10 (my translation).

58 *Screens*, 108.

59 *Paravents*, 169 (my translation); not included in English version.

60 *Screens*, 108.

61 Ibid.

62 Ibid., 109 (translation modified); *Paravents*, 170.

63 *Paravents*, 170 (my translation); not included in English version.

64 Ibid. (my translation); not included in English version.

65 *Screens*, 177.

66 Unlike the protectorates of Morocco and Tunisia, colonial Algeria had been fully annexed by France, its *départements* having the same legal status as their counterparts across the Mediterranean.

67 Ibid., 201.

68 Not all non-Europeans in North Africa at the time were Arabs, of course; among others, there were Jews, Berbers and Tuareg. Arabs were and are the majority in the region, however, and this is the term Genet uses to refer in a generic way to the non-European population present before the French conquest in the mid-nineteenth century. In any case, as should be clear, for Genet the parties engaged in the debate are not primarily defined by categories of race or ethnicity. Nor is a thinker like Genet invested in any direct valorization of indigeneity. The two communities at odds in the play, European and Arab, represent more fundamentally two contrasting notions of the image.

69 *Screens*, 178.

70 Ibid., 179.

71 Ibid., 194.

72 Ibid., 195; *Paravents*, 270.

73 Ibid.

74 Ibid., 197; ibid., 272.

75 Ibid., 198.

76 Ibid., 199 (translation modified); ibid., 274.

77 Ibid., 199–200.

78 Ibid., 201; ibid., 275.

79 Ibid.

Chapter 6

1 Félix Guattari, 'Genet retrouvé', *Revue d'études palestiniennes* 21 (Fall 1986): 27–42, 34 (my translation). Though the work of this chapter is very much in keeping with Guattari's view of the generative aspect of Genet's poetic praxis and its subversion of dominant meaning systems, my own argument foregrounds the agency of a particular brand of negativity in a manner that departs from the logic of Guattari's nonetheless invaluable reading of *Prisoner of Love*. In short, while for Guattari the term signals a reality that synthesizes subjectivity and objectivity, language and nature, 'the real' in my usage here is simply another term for what I have been calling the ontology of incompletion.

2 Jean Genet, *Prisoner of Love*, trans. Barbara Bray (New York: New York Review Books, 2003), 30.

3 Ibid., 29 (translation modified); Genet, *Un captif amoureux* (Paris: Gallimard, 1986), 45.

4 Ibid., 28–9.

5 Ibid., 29.

6 Ibid.

7 Ibid., 30.

8 Ibid., 34.

9 Ibid., 124.

10 Ibid., 287.

11 Ibid.

12 Ibid.

13 Ibid., 30.

14 Ibid., 349.

15 Ibid.

16 Ibid., 364.

17 Ibid.

18 Ibid.

19 Ibid., 365.

20 Ibid., 364 (translation modified); *Captif*, 518.

21 Ibid., 365.

22 *Captif*, 519.

23 *Prisoner*, 365.

24 Ibid.

25 Ibid., 365–6.

26 Ibid., 104.

27 Ibid., 105.

28 Ibid., 366 (translation modified); *Captif*, 521.

29 Ibid.

30 Ibid.

31 Ibid., 368.

32 Ibid., 425.

33 Ibid. (translation modified); ibid., 604.

34 Ibid.

35 Ibid., 368.

36 Ibid., 37.

37 Ibid., 38 (translation modified); ibid., 58.

38 Ibid., 39.

39 Ibid.

40 Ibid.

41 Ibid., 43.

42 Ibid., 228.

43 Ibid., 271. Hitler's German Shepherd Blondi was a fixture of Nazi propaganda, serving as a symbol for both the Führer's supposed love of animals and, hilariously, German canine racial purity. Hitler may not have loved his dog as he wished others to believe, however. On the day before his death, he tested the cyanide capsules the SS gave him

on poor Blondi, who died as a result. See <en.wikipedia.org/wiki/Blondi>, accessed 4 January 2022.

44 Ibid., 8 (translation modified); ibid., 15.

45 Ibid., 350.

46 Ibid., 351.

47 Ibid.

48 Ibid.

49 Ibid., 353.

50 Ibid., 351 (translation modified); ibid., 498.

51 Ibid., 353.

52 Ibid., 376 (translation modified); ibid., 535.

53 Ibid.

54 Ibid.

55 *Captif*, 535; not included in English version.

56 *Prisoner*, 376.

57 Ibid. (translation modified); *Captif*, 536.

58 Ibid. The imam's anecdote has exactly the same logical structure as the famous one Freud relates in *Jokes and Their Relation to the Unconscious* (1905). 'Two Jews met in a railway carriage at a station in Galicia. "Where are you going?" asked one. "To Cracow", was the answer. "What a liar you are!" broke out the other. "If you say you're going to Cracow, you want me to believe you're going to Lemberg. But I know that in fact you're going to Cracow. So why are you lying to me?"' The stories have in common the assumption that the Other will assume I am attempting to deceive it. In consequence, the best way for me to fake the Other out is to tell the truth. *The Standard Edition of the Complete Psychological Works of Sigmund Freud*, vol. 8, trans. James Strachey (London: Hogarth Press and Institute of Psycho-Analysis, 1953–74), 115.

59 Ibid., 189 (translation modified); ibid., 272.

60 Ibid., 190 (translation modified); ibid., 273.

61 Ibid.

62 Ibid.

63 Ibid., 191.

64 I consider this element of the text in detail in previous work on *Prisoner of Love*. See my 'Loving the Terrorist', *The Structures of Love: Art and Politics beyond the Transference* (Albany: SUNY Press, 2012), 127–58.

65 Ibid.

66 Ibid., 327 (translation modified); ibid., 466.

67 Ibid., 326.

68 Ibid., 326–7.

69 Ibid., 327.

70 Ibid., 328.

71 Adopted unanimously by the United Nations Security Council on 22 November 1967 at the conclusion of the Six-Day War, Resolution 242 called for the withdrawal of Israeli armed forces from the territories it occupied at the war's conclusion: the West Bank, Gaza, East Jerusalem and the Golan Heights.

72 Ibid., 327.

73 Ibid., 329.

74 Ibid., 328.

75 Genet fell into his depression following the suicide of his Moroccan acrobat lover Abdallah Bentaga. He vowed never to write again and destroyed many manuscripts. According to biographer Edmund White, one day during this period Spanish novelist and close friend Juan Goytisolo thrust a pen into Genet's hand in a desperate attempt to get him to resume writing. Instead, Genet 'hurled it to the other side of the room' and refused to speak to Goytisolo or his partner Monique Lange 'for the next two years'. White, *Genet: A Biography* (New York: Vintage, 1994), 474.

76 Colette Soler broaches the controversy around femininity and depressive affect in 'A Feminine Affliction', *What Lacan Said about Women*, trans. John Holland (New York: Other Press, 2006), 87–107.

77 *Prisoner*, 361.

78 Ibid. (translation modified); *Captif*, 514.

79 Ibid., 361–2.

80 Ibid., 362 (translation modified); ibid., 514.

81 Ibid. (translation modified); ibid.

82 Ibid.

83 Ibid.

84 Ibid., 363.

85 This variety of solitude is radically opposed to the solitude in abject self-difference valorized by Genet and examined in detail in Chapter 4.

86 Ibid., 367.

87 Ibid.

88 Ibid., 368.

89 Ibid.

90 Ibid., 364.

91 Ibid.

92 Ibid., 398.

93 Ibid.

94 Ibid., 399.

95 *Captif*, 568.

96 *Prisoner*, 399.

97 Ibid., 430.

Bibliography

Theodor Adorno and Max Horkheimer, *Dialectic of Enlightenment*, trans. John Cumming (London: Verso, 1997).
Karl Ågerup, 'La Réception critique de l'écriture engagée de Jean Genet: les exemples de "Violence et brutalité" et d'*Un captif amoureux*', *Notthingham French Studies* 60.1 (March 2021): 50–63.
Kadji Amin, *Disturbing Attachments: Genet, Modern Pederasty, and Queer History* (Durham, NC: Duke University Press, 2017).
Aristotle, *Categories* and *De interpretatione*, trans. John Lloyd Ackrill (Oxford: Clarendon Press, 1963).
Aristotle, *Poetics*, trans. Richard Janko (Indianapolis: Hackett, 1987).
Bill Ashcroft, 'Alternative Modernities: Globalization and the Post-Colonial', *Ariel: A Review of International English Literature* 40.1 (2009): 81–105.
Alain Badiou, *Le Séminaire. Images du temps présent 2001–2004*, ed. Isabelle Vodoz (Paris: Fayard, 2014).
Georges Bataille, *La littérature et le mal* (Paris: Gallimard, 1967).
Leo Bersani, 'The Gay Outlaw', *Diacritics* 24.2–3 (Summer–Autumn 1994): 4–18.
Leo Bersani, *Is the Rectum a Grave?* (London: University of Chicago Press, 2010).
Leo Bersani and Adam Phillips, *Intimacies* (Chicago: University of Chicago Press, 2008).
Elaine Brown. *A Taste of Power: A Black Woman's Story* (London: Penguin, 2022).
Judith Butler, *The Psychic Life of Power: Theories in Subjection* (Stanford, CA: Stanford University Press, 1997).
Judith Butler, *Undoing Gender* (New York: Routledge, 2004).
Richard N. Coe, *The Vision of Jean Genet* (London: Peter Owen, 1968).
David Cooper, 'Sartre on Genet', *New Left Review* 1.25 (May–June 1964).
Joan Copjec, *Imagine There's No Woman: Ethics and Sublimation* (London: MIT Press, 2000).
Gilles Deleuze and Félix Guattari, *Anti-Oedipus: Capitalism and Schizophrenia*, trans. Robert Hurley, Mark Seem and Helen R. Lane (Minneapolis: University of Minnesota Press, 1992).
Jacques Derrida, *Glas*, trans. John P. Leavey, Jr and Richard Rand (London: University of Nebraska Press, 1986).
Mladen Dolar, 'Cogito as the Subject of the Unconscious', *Cogito and the Unconscious*, ed. Slavoj Žižek (Durham, NC: Duke University Press, 1998), 11–40.
Didier Éribon, *Une morale du minoritaire. Variations sur un thème de Jean Genet* (Paris: Fayard, 2001).

David Fieni, 'Genet's *The Screens* as Media Allegory', in *Jean Genet: Performance and Politics*, ed. Clare Finburgh, Carl Lavery and Maria Shevtsova (New York: Palgrave Macmillan, 2007), 57–67.
Clare Finburgh, 'Unveiling the Void: The Presence of Absence in the Scenography of Jean Genet's *The Screens*', *Theatre Journal* 56.2 (May 2004): 205–24.
Michel Foucault, *The History of Sexuality, Volume 1: An Introduction*, trans. Robert Hurley (New York: Vintage, 1990).
Nancy Fraser and Axel Honneth, *Redistribution or Recognition: A Political-Philosophical Exchange* (London: Verso, 2003).
Sigmund Freud, *Civilization and Its Discontents* (1930), *SE* vol 21, 59–145.
Sigmund Freud, 'Der Moses des Michelangelo' (1914), *Sigmund Freud Studienausgabe. Bildene Kunst und Literatur* (Frankfurt: Fischer Taschenbuch Verlag, 2000), 195–222.
Sigmund Freud, *The Interpretation of Dreams* (1900), *SE* vol. 5.
Sigmund Freud, *Jokes and Their Relation to the Unconscious* (1905), *SE* vol. 8.
Sigmund Freud, 'The Moses of Michelangelo' (1914), *SE* vol. 13, 211–40.
Sigmund Freud, *Moses and Monotheism* (1939), *SE* vol. 23, 3–140.
Sigmund Freud, 'Some Psychical Consequences of the Anatomical Distinction between the Sexes' (1925), *SE* vol. 19, 243–60.
Sigmund Freud, *The Standard Edition of the Complete Psychological Works of Sigmund Freud (SE)*, ed. James Strachey, 24 vols (London: Hogarth Press and the Institute for Psycho-Analysis, 1953–74).
Jean Genet, 'L'atelier d'Alberto Giacometti', *Œuvres complètes* vol. 5 (Paris: Gallimard, 1979), 40–73.
Jean Genet, *Le balcon* (Paris: L'Arbalète, 1960).
Jean Genet, *Le balcon* (Paris: Gallimard, 2009).
Jean Genet, *The Balcony*, trans. Bernard Frechtman (New York: Grove Press, 1966).
Jean Genet, *Un captif amoureux* (Paris: Gallimard Folio, 1986).
Jean Genet, 'Ce qui est resté d'un Rembrandt déchiré en petits carrés bien réguliers, et foutu aux chiottes', *Œuvres complètes* vol. 4 (Paris: Gallimard, 1995), 19–31.
Jean Genet, 'L'Étrange mot d'...', *Œuvres complètes* vol. 4 (Paris: Gallimard, 1968), 7–18.
Jean Genet, *Fragments of the Artwork*, trans. Charlotte Mandel (Stanford, CA: Stanford University Press, 2003).
Jean Genet, *Funeral Rites*, trans. Bernard Frechtman (New York: Grove Press, 1969).
Jean Genet, *Notre-Dame-des-Fleurs* (Paris: Gallimard, 1996).
Jean Genet, *Our Lady of the Flowers*, trans. Bernard Frechtman (New York: Grove Press, 1991).
Jean Genet, *Les paravents* (Paris: Gallimard, 2001).
Jean Genet, *Pompes funèbres* (Paris: Gallimard, 1978).
Jean Genet, *Prisoner of Love*, trans. Barbara Bray (New York: New York Review Books, 2003).
Jean Genet, *The Screens*, trans. Bernard Frechtman (New York: Grove Press, 1962).
Carlo Ginzburg and Anna Davin, 'Morellli, Freud and Sherlock Holmes: Clues and Scientific Method', *History Workshop* 9 (Spring 1980): 5–36.
Jean-Joseph Goux, 'The Phallus: Masculine Identity and the "Exchange of Women"', *Differences: A Journal of Feminist Cultural Studies* 4.1 (1992): 40–75.

Félix Guattari, 'Genet retrouvé', *Revue d'études palestiniennes* 21 (Fall 1986): 27–42.
Mairéad Hanrahan, 'Introduction: Genet and Theory', *Paragraph: A Journal of Modern Critical Theory* 27.2 (July 2004): 1–6.
William Haver, 'The Art of Dirty Old Men: Rembrandt, Giacometti, Genet', *Parallax* 11.2 (2005): 25–35.
Martin Heidegger, 'Letter on Humanism', *Basic Writings*, trans. David Farrell Krell (London: Routledge, 1978), 213–66.
Luce Irigaray, *An Ethics of Sexual Difference*, trans. Carolyn Burke (Ithaca, NY: Cornell University Press, 1993).
Ivan Jablonka, *Les vérités inavouables de Jean Genet* (Paris: Seuil, 2004).
Adrian Johnston, *Badiou, Žižek, and Political Transformations: The Cadence of Change* (Evanston, IL: Northwestern University Press, 2009).
William Kneale and Martha Kneale, *The Development of Logic* (Oxford: The Clarendon Press, 1962).
Julia Kristeva, *Pouvoirs de l'horreur. Essai sur l'abjection* (Paris: Seuil, 1980).
Jacques Lacan, *Encore: On Feminine Sexuality, The Limits of Love and Knowledge (Seminar XX)*, trans. Bruce Fink (New York: Norton, 1999).
Jacques Lacan, *Le Séminaire, livre V: les formations de l'inconscient*, ed. Jacques-Alain Miller (Paris: Seuil, 1998).
Jacques Lacan, *Le Séminaire, livre VIII. Le transfert*, ed. Jacques-Alain Miller (Paris: Seuil, 2001).
Jacques Lacan, *Le Séminaire, livre XIV. Logique du fantasme* (unpublished), <staferla.free.fr>.
Jacques Lacan, *Le Séminaire, livre XX. Encore*, ed. Jacques-Alain Miller (Paris: Seuil, 1975).
Jacques Lacan, *The Seminar of Jacques Lacan, Book VII: The Ethics of Psychoanalysis, 1959–1960*, trans. Dennis Porter (New York: Norton, 1992).
Jacques Lacan, 'The Signification of the Phallus', *Écrits*. Bruce Fink (London: Norton, 2006), 575–84.
Jacques Lacan, *Télévision* (Paris: Seuil, 1974).
Hadrien Laroche, *The Last Genet: A Writer in Revolt*, trans. David Homel (Vancouver: Arsenal Pulp Press, 2010).
Éric Marty, *Jean Genet: post-scrtiptum* (Paris: Verdier, 2006).
George McFadden, *Discovering the Comic* (Princeton, NJ: Princeton University Press, 1982).
Todd McGowan, *Emancipation after Hegel: Achieving a Contradictory Revolution* (New York: Columbia University Press, 2019).
Quentin Meillassoux, *After Finitude: An Essay on the Necessity of Contingency*, trans. Ray Brassier (London: Continuum, 2008).
Thomas Metzinger, *The Ego Tunnel: The Science of the Mind and the Myth of the Self* (New York: Basic Books, 2009).
Jacques-Alain Miller. 'Extimité', *Lacanian Theory of Discourse: Subject, Structure and Society*, ed. Mark Bracher (New York: New York University Press, 1994), 74–87.
Jacques-Alain Miller, 'Suture (Elements of the Logic of the Signifier)', *Screen* 18.4 (Winter 1977), 24–34.
Jérôme Neutres, *Genet sur les routes du Sud* (Paris: Fayard, 2002).

Friedrich Nietzsche, *The Gay Science*, trans. Walter Kaufmann (New York: Vintage, 1974).
James Penney, 'Reading Freud: Bersani and Lacan', *Leo Bersani: Queer Theory and Beyond*, ed. Mikko Tuhkanen (Albany: State University of New York Press, 2014), 105–22.
James Penney, *The Structures of Love: Art and Politics beyond the Transference* (Albany: State University of New York Press, 2012).
Lynda Bellity Peskine and Albert Dichy, eds, *La Bataille des Paravents. Théâtre de l'Odéon, 1966* (Paris: Éditions IMEC, 1991).
Plato, *The Symposium*, trans. Christopher Gill (London: Penguin, 2003).
Ed Pluth, *Signifiers and Acts: Freedom in Lacan's Theory of the Subject* (Albany: State University of New York Press, 2007).
Graham Priest, Richard Routley, and Jean Norman, eds, *Paraconsistent Logic: Essays on the Inconsistent* (Munich: Philosophia Verlag, 1990).
Joan Riviere, 'Womanliness as a Masquerade' (1929), *Female Sexuality: Contemporary Engagements*, ed. Donna Bassin (London: Jason Aronson, 1999).
Molly Anne Rothenberg, *The Excessive Subject: A New Theory of Social Change* (Cambridge: Polity Press, 2010).
Jean-Paul Sartre, 'Introduction', in Jean Genet, *Our Lady of the Flowers*, trans. Bernard Frechtman (New York: Grove Press, 1991), 1–49.
Jean-Paul Sartre, *Saint Genet: Actor and Martyr*, trans. Bernard Frechtman (New York: Pantheon Books, 1963).
Colette Soler, *What Lacan Said about Women*, trans. John Holland (New York: Other Press, 2006).
Charles Taylor, 'Two Theories of Modernity', *The Hastings Center Report* 25.2 (March–April 1995): 24–33.
Philip Thody, *Jean Genet: A Study of His Novels and Plays* (London: Hamish Hamilton, 1968).
Camille Toffoli, 'La question de l'antisémitisme chez Jean Genet: un débat sur le "sens du monde"', *Postures* 24 <revuepostures.com/fr/articles/toffoli-24>.
David H. Walker, 'Revolution and Revisions in Genet's *Le Balcon*', *The Modern Language Review* 79.4 (1984): 817–30.
Edmond White, *Genet: A Biography* (New York: Vintage, 1994).
Slavoj Žižek, 'The Act and Its Vicissitudes', *Lacan.com* <zizek.uk/the-act-and-its-vicissitudes>.
Alenka Zupančič, *The Odd One In: On Comedy* (Cambridge: MIT Press, 2008).
Alenka Zupančič, 'Power in the Closet (and Its Coming Out)', *Lacan, Psychoanalysis, and Comedy*, ed. Patricia Gherovici and Manya Steinkoler (New York: Cambridge, University Press, 2016).
Alenka Zupančič, *What IS Sex?* (London: MIT Press, 2017).

Index

abjection, the abject 120, 129, 144–5, 147, 149–50, 152–4
Abou Omar. *See* Mikhail, Hanna
act (poetic, of interpretation. *See also* poetic image) 7–10, 19, 30–7, 40–2, 123–4, 129, 173–4
Adorno, Theodor 199 n.2
Ågerup, Karl 204–5 n.53
Algeria, Algerian war 78, 127, 131, 202 n.8, 205 n.66
Amin, Kadji 189 n.14
antisemitism 5, 190 n.22
Arafat, Yasser 165
Aristotle, 8, 31, 115, 134
Ashcroft, Bill 199 n.4
Ataturk, Kemal 184

Badiou, Alain 78–83, 91
Bataille, Georges 5
Beauvoir, Simone de 46, 65, 138
Bentaga, Abdallah 111, 114, 209 n.75
Bergson, Henri 118
Berlant, Lauren 201 n.40
Bersani, Leo 5, 124–5, 188 n.4, 194 n.32, 201 n.40, n.46 and n.47
Bistami, Bayazid 164
Black Lives Matter 19
Black Panthers, Black Panther Party 4, 18, 157, 169, 175
Blin, Roger 202 n.8
Brown, Elaine 190 n.23
Butler, Judith 64, 192 n.23, 195 n.49

Cantor, Georg 35
capitalism 99–100, 119, 162

causality 158, 175
Coe, Richard N. 197–8 n.19
colonialism 130, 151–3
comedy 73–4, 77–8
Cooper, David 192–3 n.1
Copjec, Joan 11, 189 n.13

Dean, Tim 201 n.40
Deleuze, Gilles 132, 202–3 n.11
Derrida, Jacques 15–17, 107, 111
Descartes, René 32–3, 97, 99–102
Dolar, Mladen 199 n.5

Edelman, Lee 201 n.40
enjoyment. *See* jouissance
Enlightenment 113
epistemology 33–4, 102
Éribon, Didier, 50, 193–4 n.20
ethics 110, 173–4
Exodus 22, 40

Fatah 158, 170, 180
femininity. *See also* hysteria *and* sex 58, 67–8, 129–30, 142, 150–1, 195 n.48
in Freud and Lacan 59–64, 136–7
and hysteria 134–40
and ontology 10–12, 176–81
Fieni, David 201–2 n.7
Finburgh, Clare 203 n.22
Foucault, Michel 6
Franco, Francisco 86, 153
Fraser, Nancy 200 n.21
Frechtman, Bernard 58
Frege, Gottlob 202 n.10

Freud, Sigmund 103, 118, 124, 208 n.58
  'The Moses of Michelangelo' 21-9, 39-40, 42
  'oceanic feeling' 118, 200 n.29
  and sexual difference 59-62, 80, 177
  and sexuality 6
  Studies on Hysteria 99

Gemayel, Pierre 168
gender theory 11, 59-64
Genet, Jean 19, 132
  on art (Giacometti and Rembrandt) 110-19
  and ascesis 121-2
  The Balcony 73-96, 133-4, 142, 153, 157
  The Declared Enemy 157
  Funeral Rites 5, 188-9 n.4, 194 n.32
  The Maids 197 n.10
  and ontology 77, 129-30, 131-4
  Our Lady of the Flowers 7, 11, 45-59, 64-71
  paraître, parure 77, 84, 90, 92, 135, 186
  Prisoner of Love 1, 3, 157-87
  Querelle 12
  saintliness 50-5
  The Screens 127-36, 138-56, 157, 170
  solitude 114-19, 122
  wound 120-5
Giacometti, Alberto 95, 112, 114, 116-18, 119, 120
Goux, Jean-Joseph 198 n.22
Guattari, Félix 132, 158, 202-3 n.11, 206 n.1

Hanrahan, Mairéad 196 n.62
Haver, William 119-25
Hegel, G. W. F. 114
Heidegger, Martin 32, 63
homosexuality 10, 18
Honneth, Axel 200 n.21
Horkheimer, Max 199 n.2
Hussein bin Talal, King of Jordan 179, 180
Husserl, Edmund 32
hysteria. *See also* femininity 52-3, 66, 99, 134-40

ideology 74, 79
image. *See* poetic image
Irigaray, Luce 61
Islam 160
Israel 19, 161, 171, 185, 190 n.22

Jablonka, Ivan 190 n.19
Johnston, Adrian 191 n.13
jouissance 17, 109-10, 134, 164-7, 168-9, 185-7

Kataeb Party (Lebanese) 168-9, 190 n.21
Kristeva, Julia 149

Lacan, Jacques 2, 7-8, 14, 103, 120-2, 134, 138, 157, 165
  on Aristotle's ontology 107-11
  on *The Balcony* 83-7
  écriture 32, 36, 42
  fundamental fantasy 37, 70, 109-10
  on logic 9, 29-37
  objet petit a 97, 108-10
  the Other, barred Other 32-3, 38, 57, 92, 101, 132, 192 n.18
  phallus 88-92
  on (modern) science 99-105
  on sexual difference 59-64, 136-8, 195 n.48
  subjective destitution 70
  sublimation 122-5
  transference 35
  on truth, 33-4
Laplanche, Jean 124
Laroche, Hadrien 199 n.12
liberalism 114-15
libido. *See* jouissance
linguistics 103-4
logic 9, 29-37
Love, Heather 201 n.40
Lucey, Michael 12

Marcuse, Herbert 204 n.36
Maronite Christianity 168-9
Marty, Éric 188 n.3

Marx, Marxism 84, 160, 165
masculinity. *See also* sex 11, 59, 60–4, 75, 136, 176, 178
mathematics 13–14, 35, 103, 108, 192 n.16, 202 n.10
McFadden, George 196 n.3
McGowan, Todd 197 n.11
Meillassoux, Quentin 12–14
#MeToo 105
Metzinger, Thomas 110
Michelangelo 12–28, 39–40
Mikhail, Hanna 170–4
Miller, Jacques-Alain 192 n.15, 202 n.10
modernism 98
modernity, the modern 77, 98–101

Nasser, Gamal Abdel 171
negativity, negation, the negative 19, 132, 151, 154–6, 172–3, 180–1
Neutres, Jérôme 190 n.21
Nietzsche, Friedrich 83

ontology 12–14, 32, 162
　in Aristotle 106–9
　and art 117–18, 123–5
　and defecation 127–9
　and Descartes 100–2
　extensible 124–5
　and femininity 66–71, 138–40, 142, 150–1, 176–81
　Genet's 77, 124–5, 131–4, 174
　and history 118–19
　and negativity 120–1, 202 n.11
　and politics 123–5
　social 120–5
　as wound 120–5

Palestine, Palestinians 4, 18, 157–87
perversion 68
Phalange (Lebanese; *See* Kataeb Party)
phallus, phallic signifier 10, 28, 60, 79–82, 88–92, 144
Phillips, Adam 201 n.40
Picasso, Pablo 111

Plato 7–8, 33–4
PLO (Palestine Liberation Organization) 170
Pluth, Ed 191 n.13
poetic image, poetry 5, 50, 71, 151, 162–3
　and absence 185–7
　and commemoration 154–6, 170–4
　difference from antiquity 7–10
　and gay politics 193–4 n.20
　and negativity 13–31
power 75, 77, 79–80, 85, 131
Priest, Graham 36

queer theory 122

recognition 114–15
Rembrandt van Rijn 95, 112, 117, 119
repression 41, 89, 144, 169, 184
Riviere, Joan 64
Rothenberg, Molly Ann 192 n.22
Russell, Bertrand 31, 35, 192 n.21

Sabra and Chatila massacre 169, 190 n.21
Said, Edward 170
Sartre, Jean-Paul 5, 7, 10, 15, 40, 54, 197 n.10
　on *Our Lady of the Flowers* 45–50
Saussure, Ferdinand de 16–17, 80, 103–4
science 13, 33–4, 100–5
sex, sexual difference, sexuation. *See also* femininity *and* masculinity 6, 10–12, 59–64, 104–5, 136–8, 168, 176, 180
Shahid, Leila 161
Sharon, Ariel 170
Soler, Colette 209 n.76
subject (of the unconscious), the 101, 108, 173
sublimation 55, 129, 142, 149–50, 153–4, 167, 186
substance 106–10, 115
Sufism 164, 183

Taylor, Charles 99
Thody, Philip 197–8 n.19
Toffoli, Camille 188 n.3
Trump, Donald 18

violence 146, 204–5 n.53

Walker, David H. 196 n.4
White, Edmund 209 n.75

Zionism 161, 172, 179
Žižek, Slavoj 191 n.13
Zupančič, Alenka 11, 14, 189 n.4, 198 n.33

www.ingramcontent.com/pod-product-compliance
Lightning Source LLC
Chambersburg PA
CBHW062222300426
44115CB00012BA/2187